AILA TITLES OF INTEREST

AILA'S OCCUPATIONAL GUIDEBOOKS
Immigration Options for Artists and Entertainers
Immigration Options for Academics and Researchers
Immigration Options for Investors and Entrepreneurs

STATUTES, REGULATIONS, AGENCY MATERIALS & CASE LAW
Immigration & Nationality Act (INA)
Immigration Regulations (CFR)

CORE CURRICULUM
Navigating the Fundamentals of Immigration Law
AILA's Toolbox for Immigration Paralegals

TOOLBOX SERIES
AILA's Immigration Practice Toolbox
AILA's Immigration Litigation Toolbox
AILA's Immigration Practice and Professionalism Toolbox

AILA'S FOCUS SERIES
EB-2 & EB-3 Degree Equivalency
by Ronald Wada
The Child Status Protection Act
by Charles Wheeler

TREATISES & PRIMERS
Kurzban's Immigration Law Sourcebook
by Ira J. Kurzban
AILA's Asylum Primer
by Dree K. Collopy
Immigration Consequences of Criminal Activity
by Mary E. Kramer
Representing Clients in Immigration Court
by CLINIC
Essentials of Immigration Law
by Richard A. Boswell
Litigating Immigration Cases in Federal Court
by Robert Pauw
Immigration Law & the Family
edited and written by Charles Wheeler
Immigration Law & the Military
by Margaret D. Stock
Build and Manage Your Successful Immigration Law Practice (Without Losing Your Mind)
by Ruby Powers
Provisional Waivers: A Practitioner's Guide
by CLINIC
Business Immigration: Law & Practice
by Daryl Buffenstein, Bo Cooper, Kevin Miner, and Crystal Williams

OTHER TITLES
AILA's Guide to PERM Labor Certification
The I-9 and E-Verify Handbook
The Physician Immigration Handbook
The Waivers Book: Advanced Issues in Immigration Practice
AILA's Guide to U.S. Citizenship & Naturalization Law
Immigration Practice Pointers
The Diplomatic Visas Handbook
The Consular Practice Handbook

ONLINE RESEARCH TOOLS
AILALink

PROVISIONAL WAIVERS
A Practitioner's Guide
THIRD EDITION

Charles Wheeler
with Ilissa Mira and Deborah Smith
Catholic Legal Immigration Network, Inc.

Managing Editor
Sarah K. Redzic

AMERICAN IMMIGRATION LAWYERS ASSOCIATION

> **Website for Corrections and Updates**
>
> Corrections and other updates to AILA publications
> can be found online at: www.aila.org/errata
>
> If you have any corrections or updates to the information in this book,
> please let us know by sending a note to the address below, or e-mail us at
> *books@aila.org*.

This publication is designed to provide accurate and authoritative information in regard to the subject matter covered. It is distributed with the understanding that the publisher is not engaged in rendering legal, accounting, or other professional service. If legal advice or other expert assistance is required, the services of a competent professional should be sought.

—from a Declaration of Principles jointly adopted by a Committee of the American Bar Association and a Committee of Publishers

Proceeds from the sales of AILA publications are reinvested in the association to help support member programs and services in the areas of federal and state advocacy, government liaison, practice assistance, ethics education, media outreach, and timely dissemination of members-only information via *www.aila.org*. In addition, contributions are made to the American Immigration Council (AIC).

Copyright © 2014, 2017, 2020 by the American Immigration Lawyers Association

All rights reserved. No part of this publication may be reproduced or transmitted in any form or by any means, electronic or mechanical, including photocopy, recording, or any information storage retrieval system, without written permission from the publisher. No copyright claimed on U.S. government material or material owned and copyrighted by other entities.

Requests for permission to make electronic or print copies of any part of this work should be mailed to Director of Publications, American Immigration Lawyers Association, 1331 G Street NW, Ste. 300, Washington, DC 20005, or e-mailed to *books@aila.org*.

Printed in the United States of America

ISBN 978-1-57370-469-4
Stock No. 54-69

SUMMARY TABLE OF CONTENTS

Preface vii
Acknowledgments viii
About the Authors ix

Detailed Table of Contents 1
Chapter 1: Overview of Provisional Waiver Eligibility 7
Chapter 2: Unlawful Presence 21
Chapter 3: Other Grounds of Inadmissibility 29
Chapter 4: Extreme Hardship 49
Chapter 5: Working with the Client 65
Chapter 6: Documenting the Case 75
Chapter 7: Putting the Case Together 85
Chapter 8: Filing Procedures 91
Chapter 9: Requests for Evidence and Denials 103
Chapter 10: Approvals and What Comes Next 109

Appendices 115
Appendix 1: Provisional Waiver Regulations 117
Appendix 2: I-601A Comparison Chart 121
Appendix 3: General Immigration Law Intake Form 123
Appendix 4: Extreme Hardship Intake Sheet – Questions for Practitioners ... 127
Appendix 5A: Extreme Hardship Intake Sheet – Questions for Clients 137
Appendix 5B: Extreme Hardship Intake Sheet – Questions for Qualifying Relative ... 139
Appendix 6: Sample List of Documents 149
Appendix 7: Expert Reports and Other Resources 153
Appendix 8: Guidelines for Writing Declarations 157
Appendix 9: Sample Letters for Doctors, Employers, Teachers, and Others in Preparing Declarations 159
Appendix 10A: Sample Declaration of Qualifying Relative 163
Appendix 10B: Sample Declaration of Qualifying Relative 167
Appendix 10C: Sample Declaration of Waiver Applicant 169
Appendix 11: Sample Financial Statement 171
Appendix 12A: Sample Cover Letters and Index of Exhibits 173
Appendix 12B: Sample Cover Letter and Index of Exhibits 177
Appendix 13: Sample Legal Brief 181
Appendix 14A: Sample IV Fee Receipt 191

Appendix 14B: Sample NVC Instruction Packet 193
Appendix 14C: Sample NVC Interview Appointment Packet 195
Appendix 14D: Sample NVC Medical Exam Letter 197
Appendix 15: Sample Advisal 201

PREFACE

The unlawful presence ground of inadmissibility has separated families and hampered the immigration of vast numbers of noncitizens who were otherwise eligible for legal permanent residency. This ground of inadmissibility, commonly understood as the three- and ten-year bars, has severely affected intending immigrants who entered the United States without authorization or overstayed their nonimmigrant status. Faced with the Hobbesian choice of attending a consular interview abroad and triggering the three- or ten-year bar, or remaining in the United States without status, many noncitizens chose to remain in the United States with their families rather than face lengthy separations.

For nearly two decades, until January 2013, no remedial legislation, regulation, or policy had tempered the devastating consequences of these bars. With the implementation of this program and its expansion in 2016 to include all family-based applicants as well as others, the provisional waiver program has become an essential remedy for many vulnerable populations. The 2016 guidance on how the agency should apply the extreme hardship standard has encouraged even more people to apply. Somehow, in this era of heightened enforcement, the provisional waiver program has managed to survive unscathed. Family-based immigration remains one of the major paths for obtaining legal status, and it appears that provisional waivers will continue to be an important way of achieving that.

Charles Wheeler
CLINIC
March 2020

ACKNOWLEDGMENTS

We want to acknowledge and thank the many people who worked on and assisted in making this book a reality. These included Jennie Guilfoyle, Susan Schreiber, Sarah Bronstein, Kristina Karpinski and Ilissa Mira. Their writing and editing contributions were invaluable.

CLINIC is grateful for the comments, peer review, and sample documents submitted by the following persons: Jan Austerlitz, attorney in private practice, Berkeley, CA; Rebecca Bogyo, BIA representative, International Institute of the Bay Area, Redwood City, CA; Sarah Flagel, BIA representative, Immigrant Legal Services, World Relief, Wheaton, IL; Juan Gil Garcia, BIA representative, Catholic Charities of Santa Clara County, San Jose, CA; Veronica Garza, attorney, Immigration Consultation Services, Catholic Charities of Fort Worth, TX; Juan and Jane Laguna, Santa Ana, CA; Richard Gorman, BIA representative, UFW Foundation, Bakersfield, CA; Nancy Hormachea, attorney in private practice, Berkeley, CA; Kirsten (Kish) Inquilla, attorney, Immigration Legal Services, Catholic Diocese of Grand Rapids, MI; and Ruby Lieberman, attorney in private practice, San Francisco, CA. Others in the CLINIC network have been helpful. Thanks to all of you—your work guides and inspires us.

Portions of Chapters 2, 3, and 10 were previously published in *Immigration Law & the Family*, copyright ©2016 American Immigration Lawyers Association. Reprinted with permission.

Debbie Smith and Charles Wheeler

ABOUT THE AUTHORS

Debbie Smith is Associate General Counsel/Immigration Law at the Service Employees International Union (SEIU). Prior to that she was a senior attorney at CLINIC. Ms. Smith has worked as a staff attorney at the U.S. Court of Appeals for the Ninth Circuit in San Francisco, a partner at the immigration law firm Simmons & Ungar, the national coordinator of the American Baptist Churches (ABC) class action settlement, and a staff attorney at the International Institute of the East Bay.

Charles Wheeler directs CLINIC's Training & Legal Support division. Prior to that he directed the National Immigration Law Center in Los Angeles and the Colorado Rural Legal Services Farmworker Program. He has been involved in immigration law and immigrants' rights efforts for 40 years.

Ilissa Mira is a staff attorney in CLINIC's Training and Legal Support division and is based in Oakland. She was previously an attorney fellow at California Rural Legal Assistance Foundation.

ABOUT AILA

The American Immigration Lawyers Association (AILA) is a national bar association of more than 14,000 attorneys who practice immigration law and/or work as teaching professionals. AILA member attorneys represent tens of thousands of U.S. families who have applied for permanent residence for their spouses, children, and other close relatives for lawful entry and residence in the United States. AILA members also represent thousands of U.S. businesses and industries that sponsor highly skilled foreign workers seeking to enter the United States on a temporary or permanent basis. In addition, AILA members represent foreign students, entertainers, athletes, and asylum-seekers, often on a pro bono basis. Founded in 1946, AILA is a nonpartisan, not-for-profit organization that provides its members with continuing legal education, publications, information, professional services, and expertise through its 39 chapters and over 50 national committees. AILA is an affiliated organization of the American Bar Association and is represented in the ABA House of Delegates.

American Immigration Lawyers Association
www.aila.org

TABLE OF CONTENTS

TABLE OF CONTENTS 1

CHAPTER 1 7

OVERVIEW OF PROVISIONAL WAIVER ELIGIBILITY 7
    Scope of This Book 7
    Purpose of the Provisional Waiver 8
    Eligibility for Provisional Waiver 8
        Immigrant Visa Applicants 9
            Family-Based Applicants–Immediate Relatives 9
            Family-Based Applicants–Preference Categories 11
            Other Immigrant Visa Applicants 12
        Inadmissible Based Only on Unlawful Presence Followed by Leaving United States 13
        Hardship to U.S. Citizen or LPR Spouse or Parent 14
        Present in the United States 14
        Approved I-130, I-140, or I-360 and Receipt of Immigrant Visa Processing Fee 15
    Provisional Waiver Disqualifications 15
        Applicant Under Age 17 15
        Removal Proceedings and Reinstatement of Removal 15
        Pending Application for Adjustment of Status 17
    Filing the Provisional Waiver 17
    Notifying the NVC or Consulate 17
    Filing Fees 18
    Circumstances in Which USCIS Rejects Provisional Waiver Applications 18
    Adjudication of Provisional Waiver 18
        By USCIS in the United States 18
        Burden and Standard of Proof 19
        Request for Evidence 19
        Decisions 19
    Revocation 19
    Interim Benefits 20

CHAPTER 2 21

UNLAWFUL PRESENCE 21
    What Is Unlawful Presence? 21
        Definition of Unlawful Presence 21
        Statutory Exceptions to Unlawful Presence 22
        Further Agency Exceptions to Unlawful Presence 25
    Triggering Unlawful Presence 26
        Basic Principles: Three– and Ten-year Bars 26
        Effect of Leaving on Advance Parole 27

How to Advise Clients Who May Have Unlawful Presence 27

CHAPTER 3 29

OTHER GROUNDS OF INADMISSIBILITY 29
Review of Selected Grounds of Inadmissibility 30
    Health-Related Grounds 30
        Communicable Diseases 30
        Lack of Vaccination 30
        Physical or Mental Disorders 30
        Drug Abusers or Addicts 31
    Criminal Grounds 32
        Introduction 32
        Crimes of Moral Turpitude 35
            What Is a Crime of Moral Turpitude? 35
            Exceptions 36
        Multiple Criminal Convictions 36
        Controlled Substance Violations 37
        Traffickers in Controlled Substances 37
        Prostitution and Commercialized Vice 37
        Significant Traffickers in Persons 38
        Crimes and Provisional Waiver Eligibility 38
    Illegal Entrants and Previous Immigration Violations 39
        Aliens Present Without Permission or Parole 39
        Failure to Attend Removal Proceedings 39
        Fraud or Willful Misrepresentation 40
        False Claim of U.S. Citizenship 41
        Stowaways 43
        Smugglers and Encouragers of Unlawful Entry 43
    Aliens Previously Removed 44
        Prior Removals 44
        Reentering the United States Without Authorization 44
Reinstatement of Removal 45
Public Charge 46
        Posting of Public Charge Bonds 48
Conclusion 48

CHAPTER 4 49

EXTREME HARDSHIP 49
Extreme Hardship in Unlawful Presence Waivers 49
    Qualifying Relatives in General 49

    Qualifying Relatives for Provisional Waiver 50
What Is Extreme Hardship? 50
    Possible Extreme Hardship Factors—A Review of Case Law 50
    Extreme Hardship and Regulations 53
    USCIS Final Guidance on Extreme Hardship 54
        Should I Stay or Should I Go? 54
        In the Aggregate 55
        "Ordinary" Hardship Insufficient 56
        Hardship to a Non-Qualifying Relative 56
        The Five Factors 56
        No Presumption but "Likely to Support" Finding of Extreme Hardship 57
    Employing the Five Factors 58
        Family Ties and Impact 58
        Social and Cultural Impact 59
        Economic Impact 59
        Health Conditions and Care 60
        Country Conditions 61
    Discretionary Factors 62
    Conclusion 63

CHAPTER 5 65

WORKING WITH THE CLIENT 65
Developing the Facts of the Case 65
Interviewing the Client 65
    Building Trust with Your Client 65
    Explain Confidentiality 65
    Explain the Process 66
    Describe What You Are Looking for 66
    Listen Carefully to Your Client's Story and Ask Questions 66
    Retain the Information 67
    Team Review of Case 67
    Interviews—How Much Is Enough? 67
Inadmissibility Issues 68
    Accessing Records Regarding Criminal History 68
        FBI Record Check 68
        State Record Check 68
    Accessing Information Through FOIA 68
        Form to Use for a FOIA Request 69
        Filing the FOIA Request 69
Building a Strong Theory of the Case 71

Copyright © 2020. American Immigration Lawyers Association.

How and When to Create a Theory of the Case	71
Preparing Effective Declarations	71
What Is a Declaration?	71
Whose Declaration?	72
What Makes Declarations Effective	72
How to Prepare Declarations	73
Incorporating Non-Qualifying Relatives	73
Qualifying Relative Can't Leave and Can't Live Without Applicant	74
Establish a Nexus Between Hardship and Absence or Residence Abroad	74
Be Consistent	74

CHAPTER 6 75

DOCUMENTING THE CASE 75

The Importance of Personal Documents	75
Declarations from the Applicant and the Qualifying Relative	75
Objective Evidence Regarding Hardship Conditions	77
Personal Documents	77
Personalized Expert Evidence	78
Working Directly with an Expert	78
Expert Evidence on Living Conditions	78
Documenting Hardship Claims	79
Family Ties and Impact	79
Social and Cultural Impact	79
Financial and Economic Hardship	80
Health Conditions and Care	80
Country Conditions	81
Documenting Discretionary Factors	81
Documentation in Action	82
Health-Related Hardship	82
Financial-Related Hardship	82
Education-Related Hardship	83
Family Ties and Impact	83
Country Conditions	83

CHAPTER 7 85

PUTTING THE CASE TOGETHER 85

Exhibits Basics	85
Reviewing Exhibits	85
An Organized Approach	85
Using Placement of Documents to Reflect Importance of Evidence	86
Readability and Legibility Matters	87
Cover Letter	87
Format of Cover Letter	87

Copyright © 2020. American Immigration Lawyers Association.

Length of Cover Letter	88
Legal Arguments	88
Index of Exhibits	88
Contents of Index of Exhibits	89
Preparing the Index of Exhibits	89

CHAPTER 8 91

FILING PROCEDURES 91

Completing the Form I-601A	91
Part 1—Information About the Applicant	92
Part 2—Information About the Applicant	98
Part 3—Information About the Immigrant Visa Case	99
Part 4—Information About the Qualifying Relative	99
Part 5—Statement from the Applicant	99
Part 6—Applicant's Statement, Contact Information, Certification, and Signature	100
Part 7—Interpreter's Contact Information, Certification, and Signature	100
Part 8—Preparer's Contact Information, Certification, and Signature	100
Part 9—Additional Information	100
Filing Requirements	100
The Application and Biometrics Fee	100
USCIS Address for Filing Waiver Packet	100
Copy of the Immigrant Visa Application Fee Bill Receipt	101
Name of Applicant and USCIS Receipt Number on Supporting Documents	101
Copy of the I-797 Approval Notice	101
Copy of Administrative Closure Order	101
Biometrics Appointment	101
Applicant and Qualifying Relative Declarations	101
Documents Proving Extreme Hardship and Supporting Favorable Exercise of Discretion	102

CHAPTER 9 103

REQUESTS FOR EVIDENCE AND DENIALS 103

RFEs	103
RFE: Reason to Issue and Form of Request	103
Time Frame to Respond to RFE	104
Notice of Intent to Deny (NOID)	104
Application Rejected and Returned	105
Failure to Attend Biometrics Appointment	105
Denials	105
Appeals	105
Motion to Reopen or Reconsider	106
Removal Proceedings Following Denial	106

CHAPTER 10 ....**109**

APPROVALS AND WHAT COMES NEXT..**109**
    Approval Notices... 109
    Significance of an Approved I-601A... 109
    Advising the Client... 110
    Preparing the Client for Consular Processing... 111
        Immigrant Visa Application and Document Submission... 111
        Appointment Letter for Immigrant Visa Applicants 112
        The Medical Examination 113
        Consular Interview 113
        USCIS Immigrant Fee 114
        Termination of Registration 114

Chapter 1
Overview of Provisional Waiver Eligibility

The provisional waiver program provides a process by which the U.S. Citizenship and Immigration Services (USCIS) will adjudicate waivers of unlawful presence before applicants depart the United States for their immigrant visa interview. On January 3, 2013, USCIS finalized its regulations regarding the provisional adjudication of waivers for those who will be attending a consular appointment at a U.S. embassy or consulate and would be triggering the unlawful presence ground of inadmissibility.[1] The rule became effective on March 4, 2013. On July 29, 2016, the agency amended its regulations and expanded the program in significant ways.[2] Those changes took effect on August 29, 2016. Although this provisional waiver process is limited to the unlawful presence ground of inadmissibility, this ground is currently the most common reason for refusing the applicant an immigrant visa.[3] In fiscal year 2018, a total of 53,676 immigrant visa applicants were refused based on the unlawful presence ground of inadmissibility, which is 45 percent of the total 119,712 applicants who were refused visas that year.[4]

After the provisional waiver is approved and the consular interview is scheduled, an applicant who is eligible for an immigrant visa can travel abroad for the interview with the knowledge that there will likely be no delay in the issuance of the immigrant visa. The reason that the waiver is approved on a "provisional" basis is because the U.S. Department of State (DOS) will still conduct its own investigation as to potential inadmissibility based on other grounds, as well as verify eligibility for the underlying visa. If the applicant is determined to be inadmissible based on another ground, the provisional waiver will automatically be revoked.

This procedure for allowing intending immigrants to apply for waivers of unlawful presence before they leave the United States for their consular interviews has encouraged many family members of U.S. citizens and lawful permanent residents (LPRs) to initiate or continue with family-based immigrant visa processing.

Scope of This Book

The purpose of this book is to guide the practitioner along the path from initial intake to evaluating potential inadmissibility, determining eligibility to file for the provisional waiver, preparing declarations, gathering other supporting documentation, filing the waiver packet, responding to requests for evidence (RFEs) or denials, and preparing the approved waiver applicant for the consular interview. Consider this a step-by-step guide to effective representation in these cases.

The book will focus on representing clients from Mexico and Central America, because the unlawful presence ground of inadmissibility disproportionately affects citizens from those countries. In addition, Mexico has more immigrant visas processed abroad than any other country. The DOS table on immigrant visas issued abroad in fiscal year 2018 indicates that 74,901 immigrant visas were processed for Mexicans.[5] In comparison, 49,942 immigrant visas were processed for citizens from the Dominican Republic, the country in second place.[6] As a result, the chapter on gathering documentation to support the hardship claims will be geared toward evidence related to financial, health, and personal safety conditions in Mexico and Central America.

In this book we will explore the legal theory and practical requirements for successfully obtaining a provisional waiver of the unlawful presence ground of inadmissibility. The book is designed to cover the following topics:

---

[1] 78 *Federal Register* (Fed. Reg.) 536 (Jan. 3, 2013).

[2] 81 Fed. Reg. 50243 (July 29, 2016). A copy of the regulations is included as Appendix 1.

[3] U.S. Department of State, Immigrant and Nonimmigrant Visa Ineligibilities (by Ground for Refusal Under the Immigration and Nationality Act) Fiscal Year 2018.

[4] *Id.* The 119,712 does not include those who were refused temporarily based on Immigration and Nationality Act (INA) §221(g) for failure to submit enough documentary evidence.

[5] U.S. Department of State, Immigrant Visas Issued (by Foreign State of Chargeability or Place of Birth): Fiscal Year 2018.

[6] *Id.*

- Chapter 1 will introduce the concept of, and eligibility criteria for, provisional waiver adjudication.
- Chapter 2 will discuss the unlawful presence ground of inadmissibility, including the definition of unlawful presence, exceptions to it, and eligibility for a waiver.
- Chapter 3 will examine the other grounds of inadmissibility to enable the practitioner to determine if the client is eligible for the provisional waiver.
- Chapter 4 will cover the agency's guidance on the definition of "extreme hardship," which is a requirement for the provisional waiver and is essential to case preparation.
- Chapter 5 will discuss developing the theory of the case, building trust with the client, using materials to identify issues and obtain information, and preparing effective declarations.
- Chapter 6 will suggest other ways to document the case (in addition to declarations), including use of experts and availability of evidence on conditions in Mexico.
- Chapter 7 will address the best way to package the waiver case, including using cover letters and developing an index of the exhibits.
- Chapter 8 will look at provisional waiver filing procedures, including tips on completing the Form I-601A, Application for Provisional Unlawful Waiver.
- Chapter 9 will cover responding to RFEs, denials, and possible re-filing.
- Chapter 10 will discuss preparing the approved waiver applicant for consular processing.

Purpose of the Provisional Waiver

If a family member does not qualify to apply for permanent residency in the United States through adjustment of status, he or she must be processed for an immigrant visa at a U.S. embassy or consulate abroad. This procedure, known as consular processing, includes the taking of biometrics from the applicant, as well as the applicant's undergoing a medical examination and being interviewed by a U.S. consular officer. Normally, it takes only a few days for these procedures to be completed and the immigrant visa to be issued, after which the applicant may enter the United States as an LPR. However, if the consular officer conducting the interview determines that the applicant is inadmissible, the applicant will be refused the visa. If the ground is waivable, the applicant must remain abroad until a Form I-601, Application for Waiver of Grounds of Inadmissibility, is filed, adjudicated, and granted, and the approval is forwarded to the consulate. Processing time for adjudication of the I-601 is currently over 12 months, though that time period is quite variable.[7] While the waiver adjudication is pending, the applicant is typically unemployed and separated from family members in the United States. If the waiver is denied, the applicant will be refused entry as an immigrant, either permanently or for a designated period of time. For those found inadmissible based on unlawful presence and denied a waiver, that period is either three or ten years from the date of departure, depending on how much unlawful presence was accrued before the applicant departed the United States.

The purpose of the provisional waiver process is to reduce the period of time that immigrant visa applicants subject to the unlawful presence ground are separated from family members after traveling overseas for consular appointments. In addition, the provisional waiver adjudication is intended to limit the uncertainty of the waiver process by providing either a provisional approval or a denial before the applicant leaves for the consular interview. USCIS anticipates that this process will encourage those who qualify for permanent residency and who otherwise would be reluctant to leave their family—due to the long wait abroad or uncertainty—to proceed with family-based immigration.

Eligibility for Provisional Waiver

The provisional waiver adjudication procedure is available to all immigrant visa applicants who will be found inadmissible based on unlawful presence–and no other ground–and who can establish extreme hardship

---

[7] Nebraska Service Center Processing Time Report (Mar. 19, 2018), AILA Doc. No. 18032034.

CHAPTER 1: OVERVIEW OF PROVISIONAL WAIVER ELIGIBILITY

to a U.S. citizen or LPR spouse or parent. To be eligible, the provisional waiver applicant must also meet the following requirements:

- Have an approved immigrant visa petition (Form I-130, Petition for Alien Relative; Form I-360, Petition for Amerasian, Widow(er), or Special Immigrant; or Form I-140, Immigrant Petition for Alien Worker) or be selected to participate in the Diversity Visa Program under Immigration and Nationality Act (INA) §203(c);
- Have a pending case with DOS and have paid the immigrant visa fee bill with the National Visa Center (NVC);
- Not be an applicant for adjustment of status;
- Not be inadmissible under any other ground of inadmissibility;
- Not be in removal proceedings (where no final order has been entered) unless those proceedings have been administratively closed and not been re-calendared at the time of filing the provisional waiver;
- Not be subject to a final order of removal, deportation, or exclusion unless USCIS has already granted the applicant's Form I-212, Application for Permission to Reapply for Admission into the United States After Deportation or Removal;
- Not be subject to a prior order of removal that has been reinstated by Customs and Border Protection (CBP) or Immigration and Customs Enforcement (ICE);
- Be at least 17 years old; and
- Be present in the United States at the time of filing the waiver application and biometrics collection.[8]

Immigrant Visa Applicants

Family-Based Applicants–Immediate Relatives

Family-based immigration allows certain family members of U.S. citizens and LPRs to become lawful permanent residents. These family members immigrate either as immediate relatives or in one of the preference categories.

Family members included in the immediate relative category are: (1) spouses of U.S. citizens; (2) unmarried minor (under 21) children of U.S. citizens; and (3) parents of U.S. citizens age 21 or older.[9] Of these immediate relatives, the most common relationship for purposes of the provisional waiver will be the spouses of U.S. citizens or LPRs.

Example: Peter, a U.S. citizen, is married to Andrea, from Mexico. Andrea entered the United States without inspection (EWI) and is ineligible to adjust status. When she departs the country for her immigrant visa interview at the consulate, she will trigger the ten-year unlawful presence bar. She qualifies to apply for the provisional waiver by demonstrating extreme hardship to her U.S. citizen husband.

Other immediate relatives might also benefit from the expanded provisional waiver. For example, the unmarried children under 21 could also be eligible to apply. Unlawful presence does not begin until the child turns 18 and does not become a ground of inadmissibility until the applicant departs after accruing more than 180 days of it. Therefore, the child would have to be 18½ or older at the time of departure for the provisional waiver to be necessary and be under 21 when the parent files the petition. The Child Status Protection Act allows unmarried children of U.S. citizens who were under 21 when the U.S. citizen parent filed the petition to remain immediate relatives even if they subsequently turn 21.[10]

Example: Beatrice, a naturalized U.S. citizen, filed an I-130 petition for her son, Arturo, when he was 18 and she was an LPR. She naturalized last month before Arturo turned 21, thus converting the peti-

---

[8] 8 Code of Federal Regulations (CFR) §§212.7(e)(3) and (e)(4); USCIS, Instructions for Application for Provisional Unlawful Presence Waiver, p. 5 (Feb. 13, 2019), http://www.uscis.gov/i-601a.
[9] INA §201(b)(2)(A)(i).
[10] INA §201(f).

tion to immediate relative. He is eligible to file a provisional waiver and demonstrate extreme hardship to his mother.

Parents of U.S. citizen children over the age of 21 are unlikely to be eligible for the provisional waiver, unless they in turn have a U.S. citizen or LPR spouse or parent. Those who do qualify would likely be basing the extreme hardship to a parent.

Example: Carla, a 21-year-old U.S. citizen, petitioned for her mother, Ana, six months ago. The petition has been approved and forwarded to the NVC. Ana's father (Carla's grandfather) is an LPR, so Ana can file a provisional waiver and base extreme hardship to him. Ana's father could have petitioned for Ana, assuming she was unmarried, but the F-2B category is backlogged 20 years. Without her LPR father, Ana would not have a qualifying relative and could not file a provisional waiver because Carla is not a qualifying relative.

The immediate relative classification also includes certain widows and widowers of U.S. citizens and their minor children. Death of the petitioner automatically revokes the I-130 petition, but there is relief for widows and widowers of U.S. citizens who have not remarried or who were not legally separated from the U.S. citizen on the date of his or her death.[11] The pending or approved I-130 petition automatically converts to a pending or approved Form I-360.[12] The widow/widower who is ineligible to adjust status may use consular processing and immigrate as an immediate relative; any unmarried children under 21 are classified as derivatives and may immigrate as immediate relatives, too. Widows and widowers who were the beneficiaries of an I-130 petition that was pending on October 28, 2009 will not be deemed to have accrued any unlawful presence.[13] But if the widow or widower has accrued unlawful presence, departing the country may trigger the three- or ten-year bar. Because the qualifying relative spouse has died, this would seem to create a legal roadblock. However, USCIS has provided a remedy through an instructional memorandum.[14]

Those widows or widowers who were residing in the United States on the date that the U.S. citizen spouse died, who have continued to reside in the United States, and whose spouse had filed an I-130 petition before his or her death qualify to file a provisional waiver, assuming they satisfy the other eligibility requirements. USCIS will consider the deceased U.S. citizen spouse to be the qualifying relative. It will also presume extreme hardship, so no evidence of hardship need be alleged or included in the provisional waiver application.[15] The only supporting documentation that needs to be included in the application should address the applicant's relationship to the decedent, the applicant's residence in the United States on the date of the decedent's death, and the applicant's continued residence in the United States since that date.

Example: Maria entered the United States without inspection (EWI) in 2009. She married Frank, a U.S. citizen, in 2017, and he filed an I-130 petition for her in 2018. While the petition was pending, however, Frank died. The I-130 automatically converted to an I-360. Since Maria was residing in the United States when Frank died, she qualifies to file a provisional waiver and does not need to establish any extreme hardship.

This special rule applies only to cases in which the U.S. citizen spouse died while the I-130 petition was pending or after it was approved. If the citizen spouse died before filing an I-130, and the widow or widower has an approved I-360 self-petition, he or she may still qualify to file a provisional waiver. But, in that case, the widow or widower would need to establish extreme hardship to a U.S. citizen or LPR parent.

---

[11] INA §204.2(b)(2)(A)(i), as amended by FY2010 Department of Homeland Security Appropriations Act, Pub. L. No. 111-83, 123 Stat. 2142, §568(c)(1), Oct. 28, 2009.

[12] 8 CFR §204.2(i)(1)(iv).

[13] U.S. Citizenship and Immigration Services (USCIS) Interoffice Memorandum, D. Neufeld, L. Scialabba & P. Chang, "Additional Guidance Regarding Surviving Spouses of Deceased U.S. Citizens and Their Children (REVISED)" (Dec. 2, 2009), American Immigration Lawyers Association (AILA) Doc. No. 09121430.

[14] USCIS Memorandum, "Approval of Petitions and Applications after the Death of the Qualifying Relative Under New Section 204(*l*) of the Immigration and Nationality Act" (Dec. 16, 2010), AILA Doc. No. 11011061.

[15] *Id.*

Example: In the above example, assume that Frank had not filed an I-130 for Maria before he died. Maria filed an I-360 petition within two years of his death, and it has been approved. Maria may be eligible to file a provisional waiver, but she must establish extreme hardship to a qualifying relative. To qualify to file an I-360, Maria must not have re-married. Therefore, unless Maria has an LPR or U.S. citizen parent, she would not be eligible to file a provisional waiver.

In situations in which the petitioning parent or spouse died after filing an I-130 petition—whether in the immediate relative category or one of the preference categories—the surviving beneficiary may also qualify for relief under INA §204(*l*). This section of the law allows the agency to reinstate the petition, either pending or approved, that was automatically denied or revoked upon the death of the petitioner. These beneficiaries would need to establish that they were residing in the United States at the time the petitioner died, that they continue to reside here, and that they have an LPR or U.S. citizen substitute sponsor. Another regulation allows for those who do not meet the residency requirements to request that USCIS reinstate a revoked petition based on humanitarian factors.[16] In both cases, if the agency reinstates the petition, the beneficiary may apply for the provisional waiver. USCIS will consider the deceased U.S. citizen or LPR spouse or parent to be the qualifying relative and his or her death to be the functional equivalent of extreme hardship.[17] The applicant would still need to demonstrate why he or she merits a favorable exercise of discretion.

Family-Based Applicants–Preference Categories

Family members in the four family-based preference categories include the following:

- Unmarried adult children of U.S. citizens [first preference or F-1];
- Spouses and unmarried minor (under 21) children of LPRs [second preference F-2A];
- Unmarried adult children of LPRs [second preference F-2B];
- Married children of U.S. citizens [third preference or F-3]; and
- Brothers and sisters of U.S. citizens who are age 21 or older [fourth preference or F-4].[18]

The original provisional waiver program–which benefited only immediate relatives–was expanded on August 29, 2016 to include all family-based immigrant visa applicants. The major group that is now eligible to apply for the provisional waiver is the spouses of LPRs.

Example: Arturo, an LPR, petitioned for his wife, who entered illegally from Mexico five years ago. The I-130 was approved and the priority date is current. Arturo's wife will need to consular process and will trigger the unlawful presence bar when she departs the United States. She qualifies to file a provisional waiver and base extreme hardship to her LPR husband.

The married or unmarried sons and daughters of U.S. citizens and the unmarried sons and daughters of LPRs may also benefit from this expansion of the provisional waiver. By definition, those beneficiaries have qualifying relatives: a U.S. citizen or LPR parent.

Example: Kathy, a naturalized U.S. citizen, petitioned for her 31-year-old daughter, Margaret, who has been living in the United States for the past five years. Even though Margaret entered with a nonimmigrant visa, she has failed to maintain lawful immigration status and must consular process. The priority date in the F-1 category is now current. Margaret qualifies to file a provisional waiver and base extreme hardship to her mother.

The siblings of U.S. citizens are also eligible to apply for the provisional waiver, assuming they have a qualifying relative. (Their petitioner is not a qualifying relative.) For practical purposes, this would usually require the siblings to have an LPR parent. If they had an LPR spouse, they would be immigrating based on that relationship, since the F-4 category is backlogged much farther than the F-2A category. Similarly, if they

---

[16] 8 CFR §205.1(a)(3)(i)(C).

[17] USCIS, Instructions for Application for Provisional Unlawful Presence Waiver, p. 7 (Feb. 13, 2019), http://www.uscis.gov/i-601a.

[18] INA §203(a).

had a U.S. citizen parent, they would be immigrating based on that relationship, since the F-4 category is backlogged farther than the F-1 or F-3 category.

Example: Florence filed a petition for her married brother, Frank, and the priority date in the F-4 category is now current. Florence and Frank have an LPR mother, who was not able to petition for Frank because he is married. But Frank can file a provisional waiver and base the extreme hardship to his mother.

The spouses and unmarried children of the principal beneficiary in the preference categories—called derivatives—are also eligible to apply for the provisional waiver. This will typically require them to apply for the waiver after the principal beneficiary has immigrated and established LPR status, which allows them to be a qualifying relative.

Example: David, a naturalized U.S. citizen, petitioned for his married daughter, Eugenia, and the priority date in the F-3 category is now current. Eugenia and her 19-year-old son, Patrick, overstayed their nonimmigrant visa five years ago and will have to consular process. Eugenia qualifies to file a provisional waiver and base it on extreme hardship to her U.S. citizen father. Patrick, however, does not have a qualifying relative. He must wait for Eugenia to immigrate and re-enter the United States as an LPR. He could then file a provisional waiver based on extreme hardship to his LPR mother.

Derivative children in the F-2A category may be eligible to immigrate and apply for the provisional waiver together with the principal beneficiary, since the LPR petitioner can be a qualifying relative for both the principal (the spouse) and the derivative (the child).

Example: Roberta, an LPR, petitioned for her husband, and the priority date is now current in the F-2A category. Her husband, Jorge, entered without inspection and must consular process. Jorge is eligible to file for a provisional waiver and demonstrate extreme hardship to his wife. Roberta also named their son, Carlos, as a derivative on the I-130. He is now 20 years old and also entered EWI. Carlos qualifies to file a provisional waiver based on extreme hardship to his mother. Both Jorge and Carlos intend to consular process together. Care should be taken to make sure that Jorge did not smuggle Carlos into the United States.

Other Immigrant Visa Applicants

The immediate relative classification also includes certain battered spouses and children of U.S. citizens who can gain relief pursuant to the Violence Against Women Act (VAWA). In addition, the F-2A category includes those spouses and children who have been abused by an LPR spouse or parent. They qualify to self-petition by filing an I-360. If their petition is approved, the vast majority will qualify to adjust status, regardless of how they entered the United States.[19] Therefore, they will not need to file a provisional waiver.

Battered spouses who entered as fiancé(e)s in the K-1 category, as well as their children who entered as derivatives in the K-2 category, are prohibited from adjusting status unless the adjustment is based on "the marriage of the nonimmigrant (or in the case of a minor child, the parent) to the citizen who filed the petition to accord that alien's nonimmigrant status under section 101(a)(15)(K)."[20] That means that they will be required to consular process, and will probably trigger the unlawful presence bar. They would be eligible to file a provisional waiver, assuming they have a U.S. citizen or LPR spouse or parent to act as the qualifying relative.

Example: Magdalena is the beneficiary of an F-2A self-petition based on abuse by her LPR spouse. Magdalena entered the United States with a K-1 visa in 2012, but then decided not to marry the U.S. citizen petitioner. In 2014, she married Miguel, an LPR, and when she suffered physical abuse, she filed a self-petition. Her F-2A priority date is now current, but under INA §245(d), she is ineligible to adjust status. Since Magdalena has an LPR father, she can apply for the provisional waiver and base the extreme hardship to him.

---

[19] INA §245(a).

[20] INA §245(d).

Both principal beneficiaries and derivatives in the employment-based categories are eligible for the provisional waiver, assuming they have an LPR or U.S. citizen parent or spouse. The employer is the petitioner on the I-140. Most beneficiaries in the employment-based categories qualify to adjust status, since they have typically entered the United States legally and have been working in the country with employment authorization. But those who entered EWI or who overstayed their lawful nonimmigrant status by more than 180 days are required to consular process.

Example: Pierre, a 25-year-old from France, entered the United States under the Visa Waiver program to visit his father and then stayed beyond the authorized 90 days. His father, who recently became an LPR, could file an I-130 for Pierre, but the DOS Visa Bulletin indicates it could take more than five years for a priority date in the F-2B category to become current. Pierre is now out of status, but given his engineering degree from a prestigious French university, he was recently offered a job by a U.S. software company. However, even if Pierre's prospective employer can get a labor certification approved by the Department of Labor and an I-140 approved by USCIS, he will not be eligible to adjust status because he entered under Visa Waiver program. He will have to consular process and will trigger the unlawful presence bar. He would, however, qualify to apply for a provisional waiver by showing extreme hardship to his LPR father.

In addition, those who qualify to adjust on an approved employment-based petition may have a derivative spouse or child who has failed to maintain lawful immigration status and who will have to consular process. Therefore, only those derivatives who have a qualifying relative are likely to pursue this immigration benefit, which may entail waiting for the principal beneficiary to obtain LPR status.

Example: Raj initially came to the United States as an F-1 student. Upon graduating, he got a job with a design firm that sponsored him for an H-1B visa. His employer later agreed to sponsor him for an immigrant visa, and Raj now has an approved I-140 petition in the EB-2 category. His priority date just became current, so he is eligible to file for adjustment. However, he recently married Roberta, who entered the United States from Mexico EWI three years ago. Roberta cannot qualify to adjust status as a derivative of Raj's employment-based adjustment application under §245(k) since she has failed to continuously maintain lawful status. If Roberta waits until Raj adjusts status, she can base extreme hardship to her LPR husband and can apply for a provisional waiver.

Persons who have been selected for the Diversity Visa (DV) program, as well as their derivative spouse and children, are also eligible to file for the provisional waiver, assuming they have a qualifying relative. They must be in the process of obtaining an immigrant visa, which means that the DOS Kentucky Consular Center has assigned them a DV case number and they are awaiting an immigrant visa interview while in the United States.[21] Most DV lottery winners who are in the United States and who must consular process will not have an LPR or U.S. citizen spouse or parent. But those who do will be able to file for the provisional waiver. Note that they must have the waiver approved and must consular process within the strict fiscal year limitations.

Example: Amadou, from Senegal, entered the United States seven years ago on a tourist visa and chose to overstay. He has just received word that he was selected for the FY2020 Diversity Visa program. He is not eligible to apply for adjustment because he has failed to maintain continuous lawful immigration status. Fortunately, he has an LPR mother who would be the qualifying relative. He is eligible to file for a provisional waiver, but he must make sure that he immigrates within the required period of time under the DV program.

Inadmissible Based Only on Unlawful Presence Followed by Leaving United States

The most common ground of inadmissibility stems from having accrued a certain amount of unlawful presence in the United States and then departing the country. A noncitizen usually begins to accrue unlawful presence when he or she enters the United States without inspection or stays in the United States beyond an

---

[21] USCIS, Instructions for Application for Provisional Unlawful Presence Waiver, p. 1 (Feb. 13, 2019), http://www.uscis.gov/i-601a.

authorized period. Note that there are a number of exceptions to the accrual of unlawful presence in these situations, and a noncitizen who is out of lawful status is not necessarily accruing unlawful presence. Chapter 2 will cover in detail the unlawful presence ground of inadmissibility, including the exceptions to unlawful presence accrual.

Persons who have accrued more than 180 days, but less than one year, of unlawful presence and then depart the country trigger a three-year bar to readmission. Persons who have accrued one year or more of unlawful presence and then depart the country trigger a ten-year bar to readmission.[22] The provisional waiver process is available only to applicants seeking a waiver based on the unlawful presence ground of inadmissibility.[23] Persons who have accumulated more than one year of unlawful presence in the aggregate, depart the United States, and then reenter illegally or attempt to reenter illegally trigger a separate ground of inadmissibility called the "permanent" bar.[24] Other common grounds of inadmissibility that could be uncovered during the consular interview, and thus result in revocation of an approved provisional waiver, include smuggling,[25] health-related grounds (*e.g.*, prior DUIs or use of marijuana),[26] criminal conduct,[27] public charge,[28] fraud,[29] and false claims of U.S. citizenship.[30]

Hardship to U.S. Citizen or LPR Spouse or Parent

Applicants for the provisional waiver for unlawful presence must demonstrate extreme hardship to a U.S. citizen or LPR spouse or parent, who are considered "qualifying relatives."[31] Bear in mind that a U.S. citizen or LPR child is never considered a qualifying relative. For this reason, it will be rare for the parents of U.S. citizens to be eligible for the provisional waiver, since the parent would need to have a U.S. citizen or LPR spouse or parent as his or her qualifying relative.

> ***Example:*** Phillip, a U.S. citizen, is petitioning for his mother and father. His father entered the United States without inspection and has been residing in the country for the past two years. His mother still resides in Guatemala. Both will be using consular processing. His father is ineligible for the provisional waiver because he does not have a qualifying relative. He will not have one until his wife (Phillip's mother) immigrates as an LPR.

The provisional waiver program does not change the existing standard governing an extreme hardship determination. Chapter 4 will discuss extreme hardship in detail. The instructions to Form I-601A provide examples of extreme hardship factors that adjudicators will consider.

Present in the United States

In order to be eligible for the provisional waiver, an applicant must be present in the United States from the time of filing the waiver application through the time that the applicant attends the biometrics appointment.[32] After the taking of the biometrics, the provisional waiver applicant may depart the United States. USCIS may still approve the provisional waiver application even though the applicant is no longer present in the United States.[33] Persons who are outside the United States and did not file the I-601A and submit to bio-

---

[22] INA §§212(a)(9)(B)(i)(I) and (II).

[23] 8 CFR §212.7(e)(3)(iii).

[24] INA §212(a)(9)(C)(i)(I).

[25] INA §212(a)(6)(E).

[26] INA §212(a)(1).

[27] INA §212(a)(2).

[28] INA §212(a)(4).

[29] INA §212(a)(6)(C)(i).

[30] INA §212(a)(6)(C)(ii).

[31] INA §212(a)(9)(B)(v).

[32] 8 CFR §212.7(e)(3)(i).

[33] USCIS, "Questions and Answers, USCIS—American Immigration Lawyers Association (AILA) Meeting" (Apr. 11, 2013), AILA Doc. No. 13041143.

CHAPTER 1: OVERVIEW OF PROVISIONAL WAIVER ELIGIBILITY

metrics while they were in this country cannot take advantage of the provisional waiver process. They will instead have to file their waiver application after being found inadmissible by the consulate using the centralized processing system established in 2012.

Approved I-130, I-140, or I-360 and Receipt of Immigrant Visa Processing Fee

To qualify for provisional waiver processing, an applicant must be the beneficiary of an approved I-130, I-140, or I-360 petition,[34] or be selected for the Diversity Visa program (or be a derivative family member),[35] and have paid the immigrant visa processing fee.[36] For family-based petitions, the U.S. citizen or LPR petitioner indicates on the Form I-130 that the beneficiary will be consular processing and files the petition with USCIS, which in turn approves it and forwards the file to the NVC. The NVC then sends a request to the immigrant visa applicant for payment of the immigrant visa processing fee. Once the applicant pays the fee, it can take up to a week for NVC to process the payment.

The provisional waiver applicant must include a fee receipt with the Form I-601A as evidence of eligibility. USCIS will accept only an official receipt from the NVC containing the NVC case number with the fee status "paid" or, if the fee was paid online, a printed receipt from the online payment.[37] For a sample copy of a fee receipt, see Appendix 14A. The USCIS I-601A instructions state that the waiver applicant must place the fee receipt on top of the Form I-601A when submitting the waiver packet.[38]

Provisional Waiver Disqualifications

Provisional waiver applicants are disqualified if they fall into several categories, which include age restrictions, currently being in removal proceedings, having been ordered removed, or having filed for adjustment of status.[39]

Applicant Under Age 17

Children under the age of 18 do not accrue unlawful presence for purposes of the three– or ten-year bars due to a specific statutory exception.[40] Because children cannot begin to accrue unlawful presence until the day after their 18th birthday,[41] those who depart the United States before they are 18½ do not require a waiver for unlawful presence. USCIS chose age 17 as the cut-off for filing for the provisional waiver; children under that age are not eligible to file.[42]

Removal Proceedings and Reinstatement of Removal

Eligibility for the provisional waiver for those in removal proceedings, and the procedures that must be followed, depend on whether the individual has received a final order of removal, deportation, or exclusion, and if so, whether the order was issued in absentia.

The final regulations broadened eligibility to include some persons who have received a final order. When the person departs the United States while a final order is outstanding, he or she effects or executes that order.[43] And execution of the order would then make the person inadmissible for a period of five or 10 years (or

---

[34] 8 CFR §212.7(e)(3)(iv)(A).

[35] 8 CFR §212.7(e)(3)(iv)(B).

[36] 8 CFR §212.7(e)(3)(iv)(A).

[37] USCIS, Invitation to Stakeholders Teleconference on Provisional Waivers (May 10, 2013), AILA Doc. No. 13050641.

[38] USCIS, Instructions for Application for Provisional Unlawful Presence Waiver, p. 14 (Oct. 20, 2019), http://www.uscis.gov/i-601a.

[39] 8 CFR §212.7(e)(4).

[40] INA §212(a)(9)(B)(iii)(I).

[41] *Adjudicator's Field Manual* (AFM) §40.9(b)(2)(A).

[42] 8 CFR §212.7(e)(4)(i).

[43] INA §101(g); 8 CFR §241.7.

20 years, in some situations).[44] Persons who execute the order (*e.g.*, self-deport) may apply for a "waiver" of this ground of inadmissibility on Form I-212, Application for Permission to Reapply for Admission into the United States After Deportation or Removal. They would apply for that waiver while outside the United States. The standard is simply a balancing of the equities, which is much lower than the extreme hardship standard. If the person has not executed the order by departing the country, he or she could move to reopen the case, vacate the order, and have it administratively closed. Persons in removal proceedings in which no final order has been entered are ineligible to file the provisional waiver unless the proceedings have been administratively closed.[45] The ability to move for administrative closure was curtailed, however, with the Attorney General's decision in *Matter of Castro-Tum,* which held that immigration judges and the BIA lacked the authority to administratively close cases, with some exceptions.[46] These exceptions include situations where administrative closure is specifically authorized by regulations promulgated by the Department of Justice or judicial settlement agreements. Practitioners should argue that the regulation's express reference to administrative closure for provisional unlawful presence waiver applicants is tantamount to regulatory authority to administratively close the case for purposes of pursuing this remedy. In addition, practitioners should continue to challenge the legality of the *Matter of Castro-Tum* decision. One court of appeals has already held that it violated established regulatory authority.[47] That court held that 8 CFR §§1003.10(b) and 1003.1(d)(1)(ii) unambiguously conferred upon immigration judges and the BIA the authority to administratively close cases.

Prior to the decision in *Matter of Castro-Tum*, if the immigration judge or BIA had administratively closed the case, it must not have re-calendared the proceeding at the time of the filing of the waiver application.[48]

Should the waiver be granted, the person is then advised to move to terminate the proceedings before departing the country. Individuals who have been granted voluntary departure by an immigration judge are still considered to be in removal proceedings.[49]

The final regulation also allows persons who have been ordered removed and who have not executed the order to apply for a waiver of this ground of inadmissibility before they leave. This is done by filing the Form I-212 with USCIS in the jurisdiction in which the person was ordered removed.[50] If the I-212 is approved, the individual's order of removal, deportation, or exclusion would no longer bar him or her from obtaining an immigrant visa abroad. After obtaining such consent, the person would then be eligible to apply for the provisional waiver. Otherwise, persons subject to a final order of deportation or removal who have not been granted a Form I-212 would be ineligible to file for the provisional waiver.[51]

Persons who without "reasonable cause" fail or refuse to attend or remain in attendance at an immigration hearing commenced on or after April 1, 1997, will be issued a final order of removal in absentia. When that order is executed by departing the United States, the person will trigger a separate ground of inadmissibility that renders him or her inadmissible for a mandatory five-year period.[52] There is no waiver for this ground of inadmissibility. The five-year period begins upon departure from the United States, though the five years does not have to be spent outside the United States. The granting of a Form I-601A would waive the three– or ten-year bar under INA §212(a)(9), but would not cure the separate ground of inadmissibility under INA §212(a)(6)(B). For that reason, persons subject to an in absentia removal order would not be eligible for the provisional waiver; if granted, it would be revoked by the consulate at the immigrant visa interview. These

---

[44] INA §212(a)(9)(A).

[45] *Id.*

[46] *Matter of Castro-Tum*, 27 I&N Dec. 271 (A.G. 2018).

[47] *Jesus Romero v. Barr*, No. 18-1850 (4th Cir. 2019).

[48] 8 CFR §212.7(e)(4)(iii).

[49] USCIS, "Questions and Answers, USCIS—American Immigration Lawyers Association (AILA) Meeting" (Apr. 11, 2013), AILA Doc. No. 13041143.

[50] 8 CFR §212.2(j).

[51] 8 CFR §212.7(e)(4)(iv).

[52] INA §212(a)(6)(B).

persons would need to reopen their case and have the order vacated. This five-year bar does not apply to those who are subject to an in absentia deportation order; proceedings in those cases were commenced prior to April 1, 1997.

Persons who have executed the deportation or removal order by departing the United States and then reentering without inspection on or after April 1, 1997 have triggered a separate ground of inadmissibility called the "permanent bar."[53] This ground may not be cured through the provisional waiver process. Instead, the person must reside abroad for 10 years and then obtain a waiver (consent to reapply) by filing a Form I-212.

Finally, illegal reentry to the United States after a deportation, removal, or exclusion order renders the person subject to reinstatement of removal.[54] But in the final regulation, the Department of Homeland Security (DHS) clarified that ICE or CBP must have formally reinstated such an order for the person to be ineligible for a provisional waiver.[55] Evidence of the agency's formal reinstatement is service of a Form I-871, Notice of Intent/Decision to Reinstate Prior Order.

Pending Application for Adjustment of Status

The provisional waiver process is not available to those applying to immigrate through adjustment of status.[56] Persons who entered the United States illegally and accrued more than 180 days of unlawful presence will not trigger that ground of inadmissibility unless and until they depart the country. So only those who departed and reentered would even need a waiver. Also, because the processing of the adjustment of status and waiver applications occurs while the applicant is in the United States, he or she is not separated from U.S. citizen family members during the processing of the applications. The stated rationale for the provisional waiver—preventing lengthy family separation—would not be applicable for adjustment applicants.

Filing the Provisional Waiver

The waiver application packet must contain a copy of the I-130, I-140, or I-360 petition approval notice, Form I-797, Notice of Action, and a copy of the fee receipt showing payment of the DOS immigrant visa processing fee.[57] Those who have been selected for the DV Program, either as a principal or derivative, do not need to include the DOS immigrant visa processing fee receipt. In addition, if hardship is based on a qualifying relative who is not the I-130 petitioner, the applicant must submit evidence showing the qualifying relationship.[58] This includes those who are seeking to immigrate on an employment-based petition or through selection in the DV program.

Notifying the NVC or Consulate

When implementation of the program began, DOS advised provisional waiver applicants to notify the NVC of their intention to apply for the provisional waiver after paying the immigrant visa fee bill but before filing the Form I-601A. Such notification would stop the processing of the immigrant visa application and the scheduling of the consular interview. DOS subsequently changed its advisal and indicated that the NVC will only accept notification of the Form I-601A filing from USCIS.[59] If the applicant or the practitioner does notify the NVC of an intention to file a provisional waiver but fails to file a Form I-601A within six months, the NVC will proceed to scheduling the consular interview. In that case, the applicant or practitioner would need

---

[53] INA §212(a)(9)(C).

[54] INA §241(a)(5).

[55] 8 CFR §212.7(e)(4)(v).

[56] 8 CFR §212.7(e)(4)(vi).

[57] USCIS, Instructions for Application for Provisional Unlawful Presence Waiver, pp. 13–14 (Feb. 13, 2019), http://www.uscis.gov/i-601a.

[58] *Id.* at p. 14.

[59] AILA DOS Liaison Committee, "Practice Alert: Change in NVC Procedures Regarding I-601A Provisional Waivers AILA Doc. No. 13122604 and DOS instructions at http://travel.state.gov/content/dam/visas/I-601AProvisionalWaiver/Provisional%20Waiver%20English.pdf.

to contact the consulate or embassy directly, inform them of an intention to file a Form I-601A, and request that the interview be continued until after the waiver is adjudicated.

Filing Fees

At the time of this writing, the provisional waiver filing fees are $630, plus an additional $85 for biometrics.[60] Fee waivers will not be granted for the provisional waiver application or for biometrics. Filing fee refunds will also not be granted if the waiver application is withdrawn before the waiver adjudication. The failure to pay the correct filing fee will cause the application to be automatically rejected.[61] If the applicant pays the correct filing fee but does not include the correct biometrics fee, the applicant will be notified of the mistake and given an opportunity to pay the correct fee.[62]

Circumstances in Which USCIS Rejects Provisional Waiver Applications

In certain instances, USCIS will automatically reject a provisional waiver application and return the application packet and filing fee to the applicant.[63] These circumstances will occur if the applicant fails to do the following: (1) pay the correct filing fee; (2) sign the Form I-601A waiver application; (3) include his or her family name, address in the United States, date of birth, country of birth, alien registration number (A-number) (if any), basis on which immigrating to the United States, DOS Diversity Visa case number (if applicable); (4) include evidence of an approved I-130 visa petition along with USCIS receipt number; or (5) include the DOS Consular Case Number (NVC Case Number) and a copy of the fee receipt indicating that the NVC immigrant visa processing fee has been paid. In addition, if the applicant is under the age of 17, the provisional waiver application packet and filing fee will be returned to the applicant. USCIS will also reject the I-601A if it is filed together with a Form I-485, Form I-130, Form I-212, Form I-131, or Form I-765.[64]

The agency has also listed the following as required evidence that must be submitted with the I-601A:

- A copy of the Department of Justice EOIR Administrative Closure Order (if applicable);
- A copy of the Form I-797, Notice of Action, showing approved Form I-212, Application for Permission to Reapply for Admission into the United States After Deportation or Removal (if applicable);
- Evidence of relationship to qualifying relative (if applicable);
- Evidence of U.S. citizenship or lawful permanent resident status of qualifying relative (if applicable);
- Evidence of admission or parole; or
- Evidence of extreme hardship.

Adjudication of Provisional Waiver

By USCIS in the United States

Applications are currently being adjudicated at the USCIS Nebraska Service Center (NSC) and the Potomac Service Center (YSC) based on the information provided on the waiver application form and the supporting documentation. USCIS reserves the right to schedule an interview of the parties,[65] but experience has shown that to be rare.

---

[60] 8 CFR §103.7(b)(1)(i)(AA).

[61] 8 CFR §212.7(e)(5)(ii)(A).

[62] 8 CFR §103.17(b).

[63] 8 CFR §212.7(e)(5)(ii).

[64] USCIS, Instructions for Application for Provisional Unlawful Presence Waiver, pp. 2–3 (Feb. 13, 2019), http://www.uscis.gov/i-601a.

[65] *Id.* at p. 5.

Burden and Standard of Proof

The applicant has the burden of proving eligibility for the provisional waiver, extreme hardship to the qualifying relative, and a favorable exercise of discretion. The standard of proof is a preponderance of the evidence.

Request for Evidence

USCIS may issue a request for evidence (RFE) when the waiver application is missing critical information concerning extreme hardship or information related to the exercise of discretion. In the past, practitioners have complained of receiving boilerplate RFEs that did not contain specific information regarding the reason for the request. But the agency has worked to correct that problem. USCIS may also deny an application without prior issuance of an RFE or a notice of intent to deny.[66] For more information on RFEs and the current policy, see Chapter 9.

Decisions

USCIS will send the applicant and the applicant's representative a notice of the decision on the provisional waiver.[67]

If USCIS denies the waiver, it may notify the NVC of the decision.[68] There is no process for filing an appeal or motion to reopen or reconsider by the applicant after the denial of a provisional waiver application.[69] However, USCIS may reopen and reconsider its decision at any time. An applicant may choose to reapply for a provisional waiver following a denial with additional evidence if the immigrant visa application is still pending with DOS.[70] The applicant may also file a Form I-601 waiver application under the normal waiver process after an interview at the consulate or embassy and a finding of inadmissibility.

If the provisional waiver is denied by USCIS, the agency will not automatically institute removal proceedings.[71] However, the applicant will be subject to the current USCIS policy on the commencement of removal proceedings in certain circumstances. Chapter 8 will discuss denials in greater detail.

After the provisional waiver is approved and the applicant has submitted all necessary documents, including the Form I-864, Affidavit of Support, the NVC will schedule an immigrant visa interview at the consulate or embassy. The immigrant visa interview will be scheduled after the applicant has submitted the required documents to the NVC; scheduling is dependent on backlogs at the designated consulate or embassy. Once the provisional waiver is approved and the consulate approves the immigrant visa application, the waiver is valid indefinitely.[72] However, an approved provisional waiver will be automatically revoked if the consulate determines that the applicant is inadmissible for grounds other than unlawful presence, the immigrant visa petition underlying the waiver is revoked or withdrawn, the immigrant visa registration is terminated, or the applicant attempts to reenter or reenters the United States without inspection before the immigrant visa is issued.[73] The approval of a provisional waiver does not provide permission to remain in the United States or grant legal status; prevent the accrual of unlawful presence; or provide eligibility for employment authorization, advance parole, a driver's license, or a Social Security card.

Revocation

Any of the following actions will automatically revoke an approved petition:

---

[66] 8 CFR §212.7(e)(8).
[67] 8 CFR §212.7(e)(9)(i).
[68] *Id.*
[69] 8 CFR §212.7(e)(11).
[70] 8 CFR §212.7(e)(9)(i).
[71] USCIS, Instructions for Application for Provisional Unlawful Presence Waiver, p. 4 (Oct. 20, 2019), http://www.uscis.gov/i-601a.
[72] 8 CFR §212.7(e)(13).
[73] 8 CFR §212.7(e)(14).

- The applicant enters or attempts to enter the United States illegally;
- DOS determines that the applicant is inadmissible based on a ground other than unlawful presence;
- The underlying immigrant visa petition was revoked, withdrawn, or rendered invalid;
- DOS terminates the immigrant visa registration pursuant to INA §203(g); or
- DOS determines that the immigrant is ineligible for an immigrant visa.[74]

Interim Benefits

The filing for or approval of a provisional waiver provides no interim benefits. For example, it does not allow eligibility for employment authorization, advance parole, adjustment of status, or a tolling of unlawful presence.[75]

---

[74] USCIS, Instructions for Application for Provisional Unlawful Presence Waiver, pp. 3–4 (Oct. 20, 2019).
[75] *Id.* at pp. 4–5.

CHAPTER 2
UNLAWFUL PRESENCE

Only applicants who will trigger the unlawful presence bars upon leaving the United States to attend the consular interview are eligible to apply for the provisional waiver. This chapter will define this inadmissibility ground, found in Immigration and Nationality Act (INA) §212(a)(9)(B). It covers noncitizens who were unlawfully present in the United States for specified periods of time, departed the United States, and now seek readmission. The provisional waiver process anticipates their departure, their being found inadmissible by the consulate, and their need for a waiver under INA §212(a)(9)(B)(v). This chapter will therefore define what is and is not considered unlawful presence and explain how it has been interpreted by U.S. Citizenship and Immigration Services (USCIS).

The three– and ten-year bars for unlawful presence are different from the "permanent" bar under INA §212(a)(9)(C)(i)(I). The latter ground is triggered when an applicant has accumulated more than one year of unlawful presence in the United States (measured in the aggregate), followed by a departure, and then followed by an attempted or successful illegal reentry. That ground of inadmissibility can be waived only after the person remains outside of the United States for 10 years and then applies for a "waiver" on Form I-212, Application for Permission to Reapply for Admission into the United States After Deportation or Removal. That ground of inadmissibility will be covered in Chapter 3. Persons subject to the "permanent" bar are ineligible for the provisional waiver process.

What Is Unlawful Presence?

Definition of Unlawful Presence

No regulation defines or interprets unlawful presence. The statute lists certain categories of individuals who are not subject to accruing unlawful presence,[1] and all other guidance on this topic comes from the Adjudicator's Field Manual (AFM), Section 40.9. Under the statute, an individual accrues unlawful presence when he or she is "present in the United States after the expiration of the period of stay authorized by the Attorney General or is present in the United States without being admitted or paroled."[2] For someone who enters on a nonimmigrant visa but subsequently violates the terms of the visa—such as by working without authorization—unlawful presence begins only after a determination by USCIS or an immigration judge that the person violated status.[3] This is a rarity. Therefore, unlawful presence for the overwhelming majority of cases starts when the person does one of two things: (1) enters without inspection; or (2) overstays a designated period of time. Most nonimmigrants are given a Form I-94, Admission/Departure Record, or an equivalent stamp in their passport upon admission to the United States.

For example, tourists who enter on B-1/B-2 visas are typically authorized to stay for 90 days or six months. Their unlawful presence would begin to run starting on the day after their I-94 or authorization expires. But some nonimmigrants are not issued I-94 cards. The two most common categories are Canadian tourists and Mexicans entering on border crossing cards (laser visas). Canadian citizens are not issued tourist visas and may enter the United States by presenting a passport; they are currently not issued an I-94 document. Therefore, the USCIS position is that they do not accrue unlawful presence.[4] They are treated as if they entered for "duration of

---

[1] Immigration and Nationality Act (INA) §212(a)(9)(B)(iii).

[2] INA §212(a)(9)(B)(ii).

[3] *Adjudicator's Field Manual* (AFM) §40.9.2(b)(1)(E)(i); *see also* 9 *Foreign Affairs Manual* (FAM) §302.9-14(B)(1)(d).

[4] "Nonimmigrants, who are not issued a Form I-94, Arrival/Departure Record, are treated as nonimmigrants admitted for D/S for purposes of determining unlawful presence." AFM §40.9.2(b)(1)(E)(iii). In liaison meetings and correspondence between AILA and U.S. Customs and Border Protection (CBP), CBP has expressed the view that a noncitizen may overstay and begin accruing unlawful presence, even when admitted without an I-94 document. *See* AILA Doc. Nos. 13022251, 13022252, 13041059, and 14031947. CBP has not released any official memo interpreting this area of the law, however, and USCIS has not changed its interpretation.

status" (D/S), which is discussed below.[5]

Similarly, most Mexicans who enter with border crossing cards do not receive I-94 cards unless they request one. The USCIS position, at least as stated in the *Adjudicator's Field Manual* (AFM), is that these nonimmigrants do not accrue unlawful presence, since they are not issued a document delineating how long they can stay.[6]

Students who enter the United States on F or J nonimmigrant visas are often issued an I-94 that is stamped "duration of status" or "D/S." Those students do not accrue unlawful presence until the day after the USCIS makes a formal finding that they have violated their status. Alternatively, unlawful presence would begin on the day after an immigration judge has ordered the student excluded, deported, or removed.[7]

On August 9, 2018, the USCIS issued a new interpretation that applied to those students who were admitted on D/S, as well as M nonimmigrants admitted for a specific period of time.[8] According to that interpretation, those students who failed to maintain their nonimmigrant status before August 9, 2018 started accruing unlawful presence based on that failure on that date, regardless of whether the USCIS had made a formal finding or an immigration judge had ordered them removed. After August 9, 2018, those F or J nonimmigrants admitted on D/S who fail to maintain their status would begin accruing unlawful presence on the day after: (1) they are no longer pursuing their course of study or the authorized activity; (2) they engage in an unauthorized activity; or (3) they complete the course of study or program, including any practical training. However, on May 3, 2019, a U.S. district court enjoined implementation of that interpretation and memo.[9] Due to the nationwide preliminary injunction, USCIS is preliminarily enjoined from applying the policies in that memoranda to F, J, and M nonimmigrants, and the agency will continue applying the prior policy guidance in AFM Chapter 40.9.2 issued on May 6, 2009.

Unlawful presence and unlawful status, or being out of status, are related but distinct concepts.[10] In many instances, an individual may be present in the United States without lawful status but is nevertheless protected from accruing unlawful presence based on statutory or policy-based exceptions, as summarized below.

Example: Michelle entered the United States on a B-1/B-2 nonimmigrant visa on September 1, 2015, and was issued an I-94 card authorizing her to stay in the United States for 90 days, or until December 1, 2015. She overstayed and started accruing unlawful presence. She filed for adjustment of status on February 1, 2016, based on marriage to a U.S. citizen, which stopped the running of her unlawful presence. Nevertheless, she was not in a lawful immigration status at the time she filed for adjustment.

Statutory Exceptions to Unlawful Presence

The statute recognizes six categories of individuals who do not accrue unlawful presence.[11] They are:

- Those under 18 years of age;

---

[5] AFM §40.9.2(b)(1)(E)(iii) ("Nonimmigrants, who are not issued a Form I-94, Arrival/Departure Record, are treated as nonimmigrants admitted for D/S for purposes of determining unlawful presence."); 9 FAM 302.9-10(B)(1)(b)(6).

[6] The Administrative Appeals Office (AAO) issued an unreported opinion, dated May 19, 2010, differentiating between the earlier versions of the border crossing cards (Form I-186 and Form I-586) and the current ones (B-1/B-2 NIV/BCC). DOS stopped issuing the earlier versions of the border crossing cards on March 31, 1998. Those who entered with the earlier versions are considered to have entered for "duration of status." According to this AAO decision, those Mexicans who enter with the more recent cards and are not issued an I-94 would be presumed to have overstayed their period of authorized stay after 30 days and would start accruing unlawful presence after that date. We are not aware of field offices implementing this practice, which would conflict with USCIS's stated policy.

[7] AFM §40.9.2.

[8] USCIS Policy Memorandum, "Accrual of Unlawful Presence and F, J, and M Nonimmigrants," PM-602-1060.1 (Aug. 9, 2018); AFM §40.9.2(b)(1)(E)(iii).

[9] *Guilford College v. McAleenan*, Case 1:18-cv-00891-LCB-JEP (M.D.N.C. 2019).

[10] AFM §40.9.2(a)(2).

[11] INA §§212(a)(9)(B)(iii), (iv).

Chapter 2: Unlawful Presence

- Applicants for asylum during the pendency of the application, provided the applicant did not work without employment authorization;
- Those who have been granted Family Unity during the authorized period;
- Battered spouses and children, provided there is a substantial connection between the abuse and the unlawful presence;
- Victims of a severe form of trafficking in persons if the trafficking was at least one central reason for the unlawful presence; and
- Nonimmigrants who have made a timely, non-frivolous application for an extension of stay or change of status during the 120-day period after filing the application.[12]

The most important exception is for children under 18 years of age. For purposes of the three- and ten-year bars, unlawful presence begins accruing the day after the child turns 18.

Example: Laura entered the United States in 2000 when she was three years old. She turned 18 on November 15, 2015, and started accruing unlawful presence the next day. As of May 15, 2016, she had accrued more than 180 days of unlawful presence. When Laura departed the United States for her consular interview on June 20, 2016, she triggered the three-year bar, and she needs a waiver of inadmissibility to return before that three-year period expires. If Laura had departed the United States before May 15, 2016, to await her consular interview abroad, she would not have been inadmissible for unlawful presence.

Persons who file a bona fide application for asylum do not accrue any unlawful presence beginning on the date of filing, so long as they have not worked without authorization at any time after entering the United States. This protection from accrual of unlawful presence continues after the application is denied by USCIS and through the removal proceeding, any appeal to the Board of Immigration Appeals (BIA), and any further appeal to federal court. Unlawful presence would start on the day after a denial became final. If the asylum application were granted at any point, then the applicant would not have accrued any unlawful presence beginning on the date of filing. A grant of asylum does not eliminate any prior periods of unlawful presence.[13] Since asylees are eligible to file for adjustment of status one year after obtaining asylum, however, any prior period of unlawful presence would be irrelevant.

Example: Winnie fled Uganda in 2005 and flew to Canada on a tourist visa. She entered the United States without inspection in early 2006 and applied for asylum five months later. Her application was pending before USCIS until 2009, when it was denied. She was placed in removal proceedings, and her case was set for a final hearing in 2013. The immigration judge denied her application but granted her voluntary departure, and she appealed to the BIA, where the case is still pending. Last month, she married a U.S. citizen and he has filed an I-130 petition on her behalf. To immigrate through her spouse, Winnie will need to use consular processing and withdraw her appeal. Because she has accrued only five months of unlawful presence, she will not trigger the three-year bar when she leaves the United States.

Family Unity is a program that allows the spouses and children of lawful permanent residents (LPRs) who legalized under one of the "amnesty" provisions of the 1986 law to stay and work in the United States in two-year increments.[14] In order to qualify, the family relationship must have been in existence as of May 5, 1988, or December 1, 1988, depending on which program the LPR legalized under. The spouse or child must have entered the United States before that date. The child must have been under the age of 21 on that date, though subsequently turning 21 will not be a basis for termination. Continued eligibility for spouses requires that the marriage not have been terminated. The benefits of Family Unity can continue until the family members obtain LPR status based on a petition filed by the legalized parent or spouse, assuming no disqualifying factors

---

[12] This period may extend to include all the time such an application is pending beyond the 120-day period stated in the statute. *See* AFM, §40.9.2(a)(2)(G); 9 FAM 302.9-14(B)(1)(b)(4).

[13] AFM §40.9.2(b)(1)(F)(ii).

[14] 8 Code of Federal Regulations (CFR) §§236.10–236.18.

appear. Any period of unlawful presence would stop on the date of applying for Family Unity benefits and would remain tolled until the application is denied or the benefits are terminated.[15]

Example: In 1987, when Lorena was 12, she entered the United States illegally with her mother. Her father obtained temporary resident status and then LPR status under the INA §245A amnesty program. He filed an I-130 petition for Lorena and her mother in 1992. When that priority date became current in 1997, Lorena had already aged out and converted to the F-2B category. She has continued to live in the United States and receive Family Unity benefits, renewing it every two years. She has never accrued any unlawful presence.

Battered spouses and children are eligible to self-petition and obtain LPR status based on the provisions of the Violence Against Women Act (VAWA).[16] They are not subject to the unlawful presence bars if they can show a substantial connection between the abuse suffered, the unlawful presence, and the departure from the United States.[17] It is also possible to argue that VAWA self-petitioners who arrived in the United States before April 1, 1997, are completely exempt from this ground of inadmissibility, although USCIS has not expressly recognized this interpretation of the law.[18] Most noncitizens granted VAWA relief are eligible to adjust status in the United States, regardless of the manner of their last entry. For this reason, their accrual of unlawful presence is usually irrelevant.

Example: Guadalupe entered the United States on a student visa on June 1, 2010, and was authorized to stay for one year. Guadalupe married Paul, a U.S. citizen, in May 2011. He refused to file a petition on her behalf and abused her both physically and verbally. At one point, she obtained a restraining order. Her VAWA self-petition was approved, and she concurrently applied for adjustment of status. Because Guadalupe is applying for adjustment as a VAWA self-petitioner, she does not need to be concerned with having accrued any unlawful presence.

Victims of a certain type of trafficking are also exempted from accruing unlawful presence.[19] This "severe form of trafficking" has been defined to include the use of force, fraud, coercion for sex, involuntary servitude, peonage, or slavery.[20]

Example: Adrijana left Croatia in 2012 and entered the United States on a false passport supplied by an international smuggling ring. She was told that she would be provided a job in a garment factory in New York City, but instead she was forced into prostitution. She was finally able to escape in 2015, and she applied for T visa status; her application is still pending. If she can demonstrate that a severe form of trafficking was at least one central reason for her unlawful presence, she will be deemed to have never accrued unlawful presence.

Nonimmigrants who apply for a change or an extension of their authorized stay will also not accrue unlawful presence for purposes of the three-year bar. In order to qualify for this exception, the nonimmigrant must file a non-frivolous application for a change or extension before the authorized stay expires. In addition, the nonimmigrant must not have been illegally employed. If the application is approved, then no period of unlawful presence accrues.[21] If a timely filed, non-frivolous application is denied, unlawful presence starts to run on the day after the denial date, not on the date the I-94 expired. However, where an extension request is found to be frivolous, untimely, or filed by an individual engaged in unauthorized employment, the application does not toll the accrual of unlawful presence; in such cases, the applicant's unlawful presence begins the

---

[15] AFM §40.9.2(b)(2)(D); *see* 9 FAM 302.9-14(B)(4)(b).

[16] Pub. L. No. 103-322, tit. IV, 108 Stat. 1796, 1902–55, codified in INA §§204(a)(1)(A)(ii–vii), (B)(ii–v).

[17] AFM §40.9.2(b)(2)(E); 9 FAM 302.9-14(B)(4)C).

[18] The unlawful presence exception for Violence Against Women Act (VAWA) self-petitioners at INA §212(a)(9)(B)(iii)(IV) is defined with reference to the VAWA exception to inadmissibility under INA §212(a)(6)(A) for being present without admission or parole. That section does not apply to battered spouses or children who first arrived in the United States before April 1, 1997.

[19] INA §212(a)(9)(B)(V).

[20] 22 USC §7102.

[21] AFM §40.9.2(b)(2)(G).

Chapter 2: Unlawful Presence

date after the expiration date noted on the I-94. If the applicant was admitted for D/S, unlawful presence begins the day after the request is denied.[22]

Example: Franc entered the United States on a B-1/B-2 visa. His I-94 card authorized him to stay until May 28, 2016. He has never worked in the United States. On May 15, 2016, he filed a non-frivolous application to extend his stay, which was approved on December 12, 2016. He was granted an additional six months, until June 12, 2017. If he leaves before that date, he will have accrued no unlawful presence.

Further Agency Exceptions to Unlawful Presence

Section 40.9 of the AFM lists additional classes of noncitizens whom USCIS regards as being present in the United States pursuant to a period of authorized stay:

- Persons with properly filed applications for adjustment of status under INA §§245(a) or 245(i), including persons in removal proceedings who renew adjustment applications that were denied by USCIS, but not including persons who first apply for adjustment when in removal proceedings[23];
- Persons admitted to the United States as refugees under INA §207 or granted asylum under INA §208[24];
- Persons granted withholding of removal under INA §241(b)(3)[25];
- Persons granted withholding or deferral of removal under the Convention Against Torture[26];
- Persons with legalization or special agricultural worker applications for lawful temporary residence pending through an administrative appeal[27];
- Persons granted deferred enforced departure[28];
- Applicants for adjustment of status under the Nicaraguan Adjustment and Central American Relief Act or the Haitian Refugee and Immigrant Fairness Act[29];
- Cuban/Haitian entrants, as defined under Pub. L. No. 99-603, §202(b)[30];
- Persons granted voluntary departure, during the period allowed[31];
- Persons granted suspension of deportation or cancellation of removal[32];
- Persons granted deferred action status[33];
- Persons under a current grant of temporary protected status (TPS), including applicants for TPS, provided the application was granted[34];
- Conditional residents who timely file a petition to remove the conditions on residence, or whose late filing is accepted by USCIS or an immigration judge[35];

---

[22] AFM §40.9.2(b)(3)(D); 9 FAM 302.9-14(B)(5).
[23] AFM §40.9.2(b)(2)(F); 9 FAM 302.9-14(B)(5).
[24] AFM §40.9.2(b)(1)(F)(i) and (ii); 9 FAM 302.9-14(B)(3). This group includes derivative asylees and refugees, from the date a bona fide I-730 Asylee/Refugee Relative Petition is filed with USCIS.
[25] AFM §40.9.2(b)(3)(K).
[26] AFM §40.9.2(b)(3)(L).
[27] AFM §40.9.2(b)(3)(E).
[28] AFM §40.9.2(b)(3)(M).
[29] AFM §40.9.2(b)(3)(A).
[30] *Id.*
[31] AFM §40.9.2(b)(3)(H).
[32] AFM §40.9.2(b)(1)(D).
[33] AFM §40.9.2(b)(3)(J).
[34] AFM §40.9.2(b)(1)(F)(iii).
[35] AFM §40.9.2(b)(1)(C).

- Parolees during the allowed parole period[36]; and
- Persons granted a stay of removal during the authorized stay period.[37]

Those *not* considered to be in a period of authorized stay under this ground include:

- Persons under an order of supervision (pending removal)[38];
- Persons with pending applications for cancellation of removal[39];
- Persons with pending applications for withholding of removal[40];
- Asylum applicants who have worked without employment authorization[41]; and
- Persons present pursuant to pending federal court litigation.[42]

Triggering Unlawful Presence

Basic Principles: Three– and Ten-Year Bars

The term "unlawful presence" was first introduced into the grounds of inadmissibility in 1996 by the Illegal Immigration Reform and Immigrant Responsibility Act of 1996 (IIRAIRA).[43] This ground of inadmissibility was implemented on April 1, 1997, and is applied prospectively. Therefore, time spent in the United States "unlawfully" prior to April 1, 1997, does not count toward this bar. Those who are unlawfully present in the United States for a period of more than 180 days (but less than one year) on or after April 1, 1997, who then voluntarily depart the United States prior to the commencement of removal proceedings, and who then seek admission to the United States are inadmissible for a period of three years from the time they departed.[44] Persons who are unlawfully present in the United States for one year or more after April 1, 1997, and who depart and then seek admission are inadmissible for a period of 10 years from the date they departed.[45]

> *Example*: Pedro entered the United States illegally on October 1, 2014. He returned to Mexico on March 5, 2015. He recently reentered the United States illegally and has applied for adjustment of status under INA §245(i) based on a petition his U.S. citizen brother filed for him in August 1996. Pedro has not triggered the three-year bar because he was not unlawfully present for more than 180 days. His unlawful presence began on October 1, 2014, and ended on March 5, 2015, for a total of 157 days.

The three-year bar applies only to noncitizens who voluntarily depart the United States before the commencement of removal proceedings.[46] If removal proceedings have commenced and the person has been unlawfully present for less than one year before departing, he or she will not be subject to the three-year bar. This means that those who leave the United States under an order of removal or voluntary departure granted by an immigration judge will not be subject to the three-year bar if they leave before accruing one year of unlawful presence. They will still be subject to the ten-year bar if they were placed in removal proceedings and then depart after accumulating a year or more of unlawful presence.[47]

> *Example*: Nilda entered the United States without inspection on December 6, 2012, and was arrested and placed in removal proceedings on June 10, 2013. On July 20, 2013, the immigration judge granted

---

[36] AFM §40.9.2(b)(1)(G).

[37] AFM §40.9.2(b)(3)(I).

[38] AFM §40.9.2(b)(6).

[39] *See* AFM §40.9.2(b)(1)(D).

[40] *See* AFM §40.9.2(b)(3)(K) and (L).

[41] *See* AFM §40.9.2(b)(2).

[42] *See* AFM §40.9.2(b)(5)(B).

[43] Illegal Immigration Reform and Immigrant Responsibility Act of 1996 (IIRAIRA), Pub. L. No. 104-208 (Sept. 30, 1996).

[44] INA §212(a)(9)(B)(i)(I).

[45] INA §212(a)(9)(B)(i)(II).

[46] INA §212(a)(9)(B)(ii).

[47] Note that AFM §40.9.2(a)(4)(D) wrongly states that the ten-year bar is triggered by *more* than one year of unlawful presence rather than a year or more, as written in the statute.

Nilda 60 days to depart the United States voluntarily, and she complied with this order. Nilda is now applying for an immigrant visa at the U.S. consulate in Nicaragua. Even though Nilda had accrued more than 180 days of unlawful presence before she departed the United States, she is not subject to the three-year bar because she left after the commencement of removal proceedings.

Under the three- and ten-year bars, periods of unlawful presence in the United States are not counted in the aggregate, but rather each period is counted separately. Thus, the three-year bar does not apply to a person with multiple periods of "unlawful presence" if no single period exceeded 180 days.[48]

Example: Maria entered the United States illegally on multiple occasions. She first entered illegally in 2014 and remained for four months before returning to Mexico. She reentered illegally in 2015 and stayed three months. She reentered illegally at the end of 2016 and has recently married a U.S. citizen. If she departs the United States before accruing more than 180 days of unlawful presence, measured from her most recent illegal reentry, she will not have triggered the three-year bar. She has not triggered the ten-year bar, either, since none of her periods of unlawful presence were one year or longer.

Effect of Leaving on Advance Parole

Prior to April 2012, noncitizens who had accrued more than 180 days of unlawful presence and then traveled abroad with a grant of advance parole would be found inadmissible under INA §212(a)(9)(B)(i)(I). Those who had accrued one year or more of unlawful presence before leaving with advance parole were subject to the ten-year bar under INA §212(a)(9)(B)(i)(II). This changed on April 17, 2012, when the BIA held that leaving the United States temporarily pursuant to a grant of advance parole does not constitute a "departure" for purposes of §212(a)(9)(B).[49] The case dealt with a noncitizen who obtained advance parole following his filing for adjustment of status. The doctrine has since been applied to advance parole granted in other contexts, such as pursuant to Temporary Protected Status (TPS) or Deferred Action for Childhood Arrivals (DACA). Note, however, that travel with advance parole does not cure inadmissibility that was previously triggered after prior departures.

The BIA's and USCIS's interpretation of "departure" may be of limited application to those who must use consular processing because they entered the United States without being "inspected and admitted or paroled" and are applying for a provisional waiver after having accrued more than 180 days of unlawful presence. In most instances, applicants for provisional waivers will not fall within the small category of individuals eligible for advance parole. However, for some immediate relatives who do qualify, travelling abroad with advance parole can create eligibility for adjustment of status upon returning and being "inspected and admitted or paroled into the United States."[50] Consider whether your client is eligible for advance parole and whether travel with advance parole could eliminate the need for your client to use consular processing.

How to Advise Clients Who May Have Unlawful Presence

Before advising any client to depart the United States for consular processing, it is critical that you first determine if your client has accrued any unlawful presence. If your client has accrued unlawful presence, you must accurately calculate how much has been accrued. If your client has not yet accrued 180 days of unlawful presence, advise him or her of the option of leaving the United States before triggering the three-year bar.

Finally, it is critical that you record all the times and dates on which your client has entered and departed the United States. This is important not only for determining if the three- or ten-year bars have been triggered, but also for determining if the "permanent" bar under INA §212(a)(9)(C)(i)(I) has been triggered. Remember that more than one year of unlawful presence in the aggregate, followed by a departure and then by

---

[48] AFM §40.9.2(a)(4)(A).

[49] *Matter of Arrabally and Yerrabelly*, 25 I&N Dec. 771 (BIA 2012).

[50] INA §245(a) requires that an applicant for adjustment of status has been inspected and admitted or paroled into the United States. The bars to eligibility for adjustment of status are found at INA §245(c). Two common bars include working without authorization and failing to maintain continuous lawful status since entry into the United States. Immediate relatives (the spouse and children of a U.S. citizen, and the parents of a U.S. citizen who is at least 21 years of age) are exempted from these bars and may qualify for adjustment of status if they are otherwise eligible.

either an attempted or successful entry without admission, will take your client out of eligibility for the provisional waiver. And the exceptions that apply to the three– and ten-year bars do not apply to the permanent bar. This is covered in greater detail in Chapter 3.

CHAPTER 3
OTHER GROUNDS OF INADMISSIBILITY

The provisional waiver process is available only to applicants who are inadmissible solely due to unlawful presence under Immigration and Nationality Act (INA) §212(a)(9)(B). Under prior regulations, USCIS would deny a provisional waiver application if it had "reason to believe" that the applicant *may* be subject to another ground of inadmissibility at the time of the immigrant visa interview with the Department of State (DOS). The rule resulted in confusion regarding the proper application of the standard and USCIS's role in assessing the admissibility of an applicant for an immigrant visa. With the implementation of regulations on August 29, 2016, DHS eliminated the "reason to believe" standard as a basis for denying provisional waivers.[1] While USCIS may consider inadmissibility under other grounds as a discretionary factor in determining whether to grant the waiver, the final assessment of inadmissibility is left to the consular official adjudicating the case. If the consular officer determines that the applicant is inadmissible for a ground other than unlawful presence, the provisional waiver is automatically revoked.[2] Assuming a waiver is available for the separate ground in addition to the unlawful presence, the applicant will need to file a Form I-601 waiver application with USCIS and have it approved before he or she is eligible for visa issuance.

How do you determine if your client is inadmissible on other grounds? This is a complicated task because the grounds of inadmissibility are extensive. In addition to unlawful presence under INA §212(a)(9)(B), the other inadmissibility categories include the following:

- §212(a)(1): Health-related grounds;
- §212(a)(2): Criminal-related grounds;
- §212(a)(3): National security grounds;
- §212(a)(4): Public charge;
- §212(a)(5): Labor protection grounds;
- §212(a)(6): Fraud or false claims of citizenship and smuggling;
- §212(a)(7): Documentation requirements;
- §212(a)(8): Grounds relating to military service in the United States;
- §212(a)(9)(A) and (C): Prior removals and the "permanent" bar; and
- §212(a)(10): Other miscellaneous grounds (including practicing polygamists and international child abductors).

In addition, each inadmissibility category comprises several subsections, so that these 10 separate categories of inadmissibility include 54 different ways that a person may be inadmissible, based on the conduct described in these subsections. As an immigration advocate, you must be aware of the scope of behavior described in each of these categories so that you can identify possible inadmissibility issues that may be triggered by your client's conduct or circumstances.

This chapter will not review all the inadmissibility categories listed above, but instead will focus on those grounds of inadmissibility that are either most commonly encountered (*e.g.*, crimes, smuggling, and misrepresentation) or not readily identified in the provisional waiver application process (*e.g.*, health-based inadmissibility, false claim to citizenship, public charge, and permanent bar). Note that while the I-601A provisional waiver form includes some questions that address the applicant's inadmissibility, the form is not an appropriate tool for screening your client for inadmissibility. The questions addressing inadmissibility concerns are insufficient to fully assess this issue; for example, the form does not include any questions on potential public charge. Consult Chapter 5 for additional information on client interviewing and inadmissibility assessment.

---

[1] 81 *Federal Register* (Fed. Reg.) 50243 (July 29, 2016). A copy of the regulations is included as Appendix 1.
[2] 8 Code of Federal Regulations (CFR) §212.7(e)(14)(i).

Review of Selected Grounds of Inadmissibility

Health-Related Grounds

There are four health-related grounds of inadmissibility. The first excludes aliens who have "a communicable disease of public health significance." The second excludes aliens who are seeking admission as permanent residents and who were not vaccinated against certain diseases. The third relates to physical or mental disorders with associated behavior that poses a threat to the property, safety, or welfare of the alien or others. The fourth ground excludes drug abusers and addicts.[3]

Communicable Diseases

The first health-related ground makes inadmissible any aliens who are found to have "a communicable disease of public health significance,"[4] as determined by the Centers for Disease Control and Prevention, Department of Health and Human Services (HHS/CDC). The HHS/CDC currently considers the following diseases to be communicable and of public health significance: active tuberculosis, infectious leprosy, and two venereal diseases (gonorrhea and the infectious stage of syphilis).[5] Several of these diseases may be treated, whereupon the individual may be admissible to the United States. A "communicable disease of public health significance" also includes any quarantinable, communicable disease specified by Presidential Executive Orders and any communicable disease that is a public health emergency of international concern reported to the World Health Organization.[6] Note that HIV infection is no longer one of the listed diseases, and therefore no longer leads to inadmissibility.[7]

Lack of Vaccination

Intending immigrants must present evidence that they were vaccinated against the following: mumps, measles, rubella, polio, tetanus and diphtheria toxoids, pertussis, influenza type B, hepatitis A, hepatitis B, rotavirus, meningococcal, varicella, pneumococcal, and any other vaccinations recommended by the Advisory Commission for Immunization Practices (ACIP) for which HHS/CDC determines there is a public health need.[8] Whenever the ACIP recommends new vaccinations for the general U.S. population, the CDC will determine which vaccinations are required for individuals immigrating to the United States.[9] The human papillomavirus and zoster vaccines, though recommended by the ACIP for the general U.S. population, are no longer required for intending immigrants.

Physical or Mental Disorders

Aliens are inadmissible under the physical or mental disorder ground if they have or had a condition that has an associated behavior that poses a threat to the property, safety, or welfare of themselves or others.[10] If the alien no longer has the condition, it does not constitute an inadmissibility ground unless the behavior is likely to recur or the condition is likely to lead to other harmful behavior.[11]

The current HHS/CDC regulations do not identify specific diseases that would immediately make an alien inadmissible under the physical or mental disorder inadmissibility ground. Physical or mental disorders are respectively defined by the most recent editions of the Manual of the International Classification of Diseases, Injuries, and Causes of Death (ICD), published by the World Health Organization; the Diagnostic and Statis-

---

[3] Immigration and Nationality Act (INA) §212(a)(1).

[4] INA §212(a)(1)(A)(i).

[5] 42 CFR §34.2.

[6] *Id.*

[7] 74 Fed. Reg. 56547 (Nov. 2, 2009).

[8] INA §212(a)(1)(A)(ii); 42 CFR §34.3.

[9] Centers for Disease Control and Prevention (CDC), Vaccination Requirements for Adjustment of Status for U.S. Permanent Residence: Technical Instructions for Panel Physicians and Civil Surgeons (Nov. 13, 2009*)*; Revised Vaccination Criteria for Immigration.

[10] INA §212(a)(1)(A)(iii)(I).

[11] INA §212(a)(1)(A)(iii)(II).

tical Manual (DSM), published by the American Psychiatric Association; or any another authoritative resource approved by the Director.[12] The CDC Technical Instructions for Panel Physicians and Civil Surgeons list the major diagnostic categories of mental disorders that are most frequently associated with harmful behavior. Note, however, that the disorders listed (such as mood disorders) do *not* always have associated harmful behavior; a doctor would have to make a specific finding of associated harmful behavior for an alien to be inadmissible because of some of these disorders. Alcohol dependence and abuse are disorders that trigger inadmissibility only where there is evidence of current or past harmful behavior as part of the diagnosis.[13]

If the doctor examining an alien uncovers a history of physical or mental disorder and an associated history of harmful behavior, the condition will be considered in remission—and, therefore, not likely to recur—if no pattern of the behavioral element has manifested in the previous 12 months. Panel physicians may use their clinical judgment to determine if 12 months is an acceptable period of time for the individual applicant to demonstrate full remission. This judgment is to be made based on an assessment of the history of associated harmful behavior and its likelihood of recurrence.[14]

Consular officers are required to refer visa applicants to a doctor if they have a single alcohol-related arrest or conviction within the past five years, two or more alcohol-related arrests or convictions within the past 10 years, or if there is any other evidence to suggest an alcohol problem.[15] The doctor will determine whether the applicant suffers from alcohol abuse or dependence.

Consider having an applicant with a DUI history attend the medical examination abroad with any records he or she may possess to defeat a finding of health-based inadmissibility. In this context, this may include records of participation in Alcoholics Anonymous meetings or counseling for alcohol abuse, evidence of a clean driving record, and treating-physician letters regarding the applicant's recovery from any prior alcohol abuse or dependence, as well as the absence of any associated harmful behavior.

Drug Abusers or Addicts

Aliens who are determined to be "drug abusers" or "addicts" are inadmissible.[16] The HHS/CDC regulations define "drug abuse" and "drug addiction" in accordance with the diagnostic criteria used in the most recent edition of the DSM. Drug abuse is referred to as mild "substance use disorder or substance-induced disorder ... of a substance listed in section 202 of the Controlled Substances Act,"[17] while drug addiction is referred to as moderate or severe substance use.[18] Section 202 of the Controlled Substances Act lists hundreds of controlled drugs arranged into five "schedules," which determine the degree of a criminal offense involving a particular drug.[19] For example, marijuana is included on the list in Schedule I, the most severely penalized category. Both drug abuse and drug addiction make an individual inadmissible, and there is no waiver for either category.

On June 1, 2010, the CDC issued Technical Instructions for Physical or Mental Disorders with Associated Harmful Behaviors and Substance-Related Disorders.[20] These instructions, modified in February 2015 to reflect the diagnostic standards of the fifth edition of DSM (DSM-5), appear to heighten the standard required to show substance abuse or addiction. In order to make a substance (either alcohol or drug)-related diagnosis,

---

[12] 42 CFR §34.2.

[13] CDC, Technical Instructions for Physical or Mental Disorders with Associated Harmful Behaviors and Substance Related Disorders (2015), http://www.cdc.gov/immigrantrefugeehealth/pdf/mental-health-pp-ti.pdf; 9 *Foreign Affairs Manual* (FAM) 302.2-7(B)(3)(a).

[14] 9 FAM 302.2-7(B)(2)(b).

[15] 9 FAM 302.2-7(B)(3)(b).

[16] INA §212(a)(1)(A)(iv).

[17] 42 CFR §34.2(h).

[18] 42 CFR §34.2(i).

[19] 21 USC §812.

[20] CDC, Technical Instructions for Physical or Mental Disorders with Associated Harmful Behaviors and Substance-Related Disorders (June 1, 2010).

the panel physician must document the pattern or use of the substance and behavioral, physical, and psychological effects associated with the use or cessation of use of that substance. Substance use disorder is characterized by various symptoms indicating that an individual continues to use a substance despite significant related problems. The presence of two to three symptoms suggests mild substance use disorder, while the presence of four or more symptoms indicates moderate to severe substance use disorder.[21] If an applicant's use of a controlled substance meets the criteria for either mild to severe substance use disorder, he or she will be found inadmissible for drug abuse or drug addiction. If the use does not involve a controlled substance, then a finding of harmful associated behavior is necessary to trigger inadmissibility.[22]

As is the case for general mental disorders, sustained, full remission of substance-related disorders is a period of 12 months during which no substance use has occurred. Panel physicians are instructed to use their discretion to determine whether 12 months is an acceptable period for an individual applicant to demonstrate full remission. Full remission can be shown through evidence such as completion of a drug treatment program.[23] Therefore, people who stopped using drugs more than 12 months before their medical examination may be able to show that they are not inadmissible.

Although the current CDC standard for a diagnosis for substance abuse would appear to exclude occasional use of marijuana, many immigrant visa applicants, particularly at the U.S. Consulate in Ciudad Juarez, have been found inadmissible on substance abuse grounds based on disclosure of casual and infrequent marijuana use. For an approved provisional waiver applicant, a finding of health-based inadmissibility due to substance abuse would trigger revocation of the approved waiver. The applicant would then need to remain outside the United States for at least a year to be eligible to meet the remission standard and apply for a Form I-601 waiver for unlawful presence with USCIS. Although drug use is not addressed in the provisional waiver application form, it is important to discuss this issue with your client so that she or he understands that the panel physician will be screening for drug abuse as part of the medical examination.

Criminal Grounds

Introduction

Aliens are inadmissible for having committed or engaged in the following:

- Controlled substance violations;
- Crimes involving moral turpitude;
- Multiple crimes;
- Controlled-substance trafficking;
- Prostitution and commercialized vice;
- Assertion of diplomatic immunity from prosecution for serious crimes;
- Being responsible for or carrying out particularly severe violations of religious freedom during the past 24 months while serving as a foreign government official, or being the spouse or child of such a person;[24]
- Money laundering; and
- Trafficking in persons.

A limited waiver is available for some of these "criminal" inadmissibility grounds,[25] and some forms of post-conviction relief also may cure inadmissibility.

Several of the criminal grounds of inadmissibility require that, to be inadmissible, the alien must have been convicted. The term "conviction" is defined in the statute.[26] A person is considered to have been con-

---

[21] *Id.*

[22] *Id.*

[23] 9 FAM 302.2-7(B)(2)(b).

[24] INA §212(a)(2).

[25] INA §212(h).

victed if a court has adjudicated him or her guilty or has entered a formal judgment of guilt against him or her.[27] In addition, even if the court has withheld such an adjudication, a person is considered to have been convicted for immigration purposes if: (1) the person was found guilty or entered a plea of guilty or nolo contendere, and (2) the judge ordered some form of punishment or restraint on the person's liberty.[28] The imposition of administrative costs alone may constitute punishment under the statute.[29]

Certain "pre-plea" or "diversionary" programs, which exist in many states and counties, are not convictions under state law but will be considered convictions under the INA definition. The exact descriptions differ, but generally, the accused agrees to participate in some sort of program or community service, without any admission or determination of guilt. If the program is successfully completed, the proceedings are dismissed. If the program is not successfully completed, the case is returned to court for a determination of guilt. You must be careful in these cases to make sure that the client has not pled guilty and has not admitted sufficient facts to establish guilt. If this has occurred, the client probably has a conviction under INA §101(a)(48)(A).

State offenses that do not require proof of guilt beyond a reasonable doubt or otherwise comport with standard criminal proceedings may also not be convictions for immigration purposes.[30] A nolle prosequi, or "nol pros" by the prosecutor, which means that the person was arrested and charged but that the prosecutor dismissed the charges before a determination, is also not a conviction for immigration purposes.

The authority to change or set aside a conviction belongs to the court in which the conviction occurred or to courts reviewing that conviction.[31] USCIS and the immigration court do not have that authority.

Prior to the 1996 amendments to the INA,[32] expungements and other means of vacating or ameliorating criminal convictions by criminal and reviewing courts were accepted as removals of convictions for immigration purposes. This rule was changed, however, with the Board of Immigration Appeals' (BIA) decision in *Matter of Roldan*.[33] In that case, Roldan's drug possession conviction had been expunged under a state counterpart of the Federal First Offender Act[34] (for first-time convictions for simple possession of drugs). The BIA held that, following the 1996 addition of a definition of "conviction" in the INA, any state action that purports to expunge, dismiss, cancel, vacate, discharge, or otherwise remove a guilty plea or other record of guilt or conviction by operation of a state rehabilitative statute, such as the one under which Roldan's conviction was expunged, will be given no effect for immigration purposes.

This does not mean, however, that persons with criminal convictions should not attempt to have the convictions vacated, set aside, or otherwise ameliorated, if there is a basis under federal or state law for making such a request. It is important to remember that the sort of expungement or vacating of conviction dealt with in *Matter of Roldan* occurred by operation of law, without regard to whether there were flaws in the underlying criminal procedure. In contrast, a vacating or setting aside of a conviction because of constitutional or other legal errors in the criminal proceeding, such as inaccurate translation or a failure to advise the accused of his or her rights, can serve to remove the conviction for immigration purposes.[35] The U.S. Court of Ap-

---

[26] INA §101(a)(48)(A).

[27] INA §101(a)(48)(A)(ii).

[28] INA §101(a)(48)(A)(i).

[29] *Matter of Cabrera*, 24 I&N Dec. 459 (BIA 2008).

[30] *Matter of Eslamizar*, 23 I&N Dec. 684 (BIA 2004); *but see Matter of Cuellar-Gomez*, 25 I&N Dec. 850 (BIA 2012) (municipal ordinance violation may constitute conviction where formal entry of guilty is entered and the proceedings are genuine criminal proceedings).

[31] *Rosendiz v. Kovensky*, 416 F.3d 952 (9th Cir. 2005).

[32] *See* Illegal Immigration Reform and Immigrant Responsibility Act of 1996 (IIRAIRA), Pub. L. No. 104-208, div. C, 110 Stat. 3009, 3009-546 to 3009-724.

[33] 22 I&N Dec. 512 (BIA 1999), *vacated by Lujan-Almendariz v. INS*, 222 F.3d 728 (9th Cir. 2000).

[34] 18 USC §3607.

[35] *Matter of Pickering*, 23 I&N Dec. 621 (BIA 2003).

peals for the Ninth Circuit reversed the BIA's decision in *Roldan,* in *Lujan-Armendariz v. INS.*[36] The Ninth Circuit held that the new definition of "conviction" did not repeal the Federal First Offender Act[37] or the rule that no alien may be deported based on an offense that could have been tried under the Act, but is instead prosecuted under state law, where the findings are expunged pursuant to a state rehabilitative statute. The Ninth Circuit subsequently reversed itself, however, and overturned *Lujan-Armendariz* prospectively in *Nunez-Reyez v. Holder.*[38] Because the decision is not retroactive, *Lujan-Armendariz* still controls in the Ninth Circuit for convictions that occurred prior to July 17, 2011.[39]

Lujan-Armendariz dealt specifically with expungements of first-time drug possession cases under the Federal First Offender Act or state law. The BIA's decision in *Roldan* is broader, however, and appears to apply to the expungement, vacating, or setting aside under a state rehabilitative statute of a conviction for any crime. Several circuit courts of appeals have upheld the BIA's *Roldan* decision.[40]

Some grounds of inadmissibility and deportability apply only to convictions for which there was a certain term of imprisonment. The INA contains a definition of "term of imprisonment" for this purpose.[41] Under this definition, a term of imprisonment includes the period of incarceration or confinement ordered by the court, regardless of any suspension of the imposition or execution of the sentence. Note that for offenses that have immigration consequences because of the length of the sentence imposed, a reduction of the sentence may serve to remove or lessen the immigration consequences of a conviction.[42]

Before the Illegal Immigration Reform and Immigrant Responsibility Act of 1996 (IIRAIRA), the rule was that a conviction should not be considered final until the direct appeal has been either waived or exhausted.[43] After IIRAIRA, many circuit courts have held that Congress eliminated the finality requirement when it added a definition of "conviction" to the INA.[44] Therefore, in these circuits, a conviction may be "final" even though the defendant has not exhausted or waived all appeals as of right—that is, even if the conviction is on direct appeal.

When a case is under collateral attack—*e.g.*, if a writ of coram nobis or a habeas corpus motion has been filed—the conviction is still final until the motion is decided. If the collateral attack is decided in the immigrant's favor, the disposition may cure the inadmissibility ground.

Unless Congress intended the inadmissibility ground to apply only to convictions in the United States, a conviction by a court in a foreign country may bring about the same immigration consequences as a conviction inside the United States.[45] To cause inadmissibility, the foreign conviction must be for conduct that also would be considered criminal in the United States.

The general rule is that findings of delinquency by a juvenile court are not convictions for immigration purposes.[46] However, if the minor is convicted by a court as if he or she were an adult, the conviction will

---

[36] *Lujan-Armendariz v. INS*, 222 F.3d 728 (9th Cir. 2000).

[37] 18 USC §3607(a).

[38] *Nunez-Reyes v. Holder*, 646 F.3d 684 (9th Cir. 2011) (en banc).

[39] *Id.*

[40] *See Ramos v. Gonzales,* 414 F.3d 800 (7th Cir. 2005); *Elkins v. Comfort,* 393 F.3d 1159 (10th Cir. 2004); *Resendiz-Alcaraz v. Att'y Gen.*, 383 F.3d 1262 (11th Cir. 2004); *Madiz v. Ashcroft,* 383 F.3d 321 (5th Cir. 2004); *Acosta v. Ashcroft,* 341 F.3d 218 (3d Cir. 2003); *Gill v. Ashcroft,* 335 F.3d 574 (7th Cir. 2003).

[41] INA §101(a)(48)(B).

[42] *Matter of Cota-Vargas,* 23 I&N Dec. 849 (BIA 2005); *Matter of Song,* 23 I&N Dec. 173 (BIA 2001).

[43] *Pino v. Landon,* 349 U.S. 901 (1955).

[44] *Planes v. Holder,* 652 F.3d 991 (9th Cir. 2011), pet.for reh'g den., 686 F.3d 1033(9th Cir. 2012); *U.S. v Saenz-Gomez,* 472 F.3d 791 (10th Cir. 2007); *Puello v. BCIS,* 511 F.3d 324 (2d Cir. 2007); *Abiodun v. Gonzales,* 461 F.3d 1210 (10th Cir. 2006); *Montenegro v. Ashcroft,* 355 F.3d 1035 (7th Cir. 2004); *Moosa v. INS,* 171 F.3d 994 (5th Cir. 1999); *see also Griffiths v. INS,* 243 F.3d 45 (1st Cir. 2001) (observing that finality is not required under the deferred-adjudication portion of §101(a)(48)(A)).

[45] *Lennon v. INS,* 527 F.2d 187 (2d Cir. 1975).

[46] INA §212(a)(2)(A)(ii)(I); *Matter of Devison,* 22 I&N Dec. 1362 (BIA 2000).

bring immigration consequences.[47] Within the United States, such a conviction may occur if a state court forgoes the option of treating the minor as a juvenile.

Two of the criminal inadmissibility grounds apply to an alien who admits either having committed a crime or having committed the essential elements of a crime, even though he or she was never convicted for that crime. For an admission to be valid, the consular officer or USCIS officer must establish all of the following:

- The act is considered criminal under the law in force where the act was alleged to have been committed;
- The alien was advised in a clear manner of the essential elements of the alleged crime;
- The alien has clearly admitted conduct constituting the essential elements of the crime; and
- The admission was made in a free and voluntary manner.[48]

Guilty pleas are considered admissions for immigration purposes.[49] However, the admission cannot have a greater effect than the criminal proceeding. Thus, if after the guilty plea the accused is not convicted, USCIS cannot use the plea as an admission for purposes of inadmissibility.[50]

Crimes of Moral Turpitude

Aliens are inadmissible if they are convicted of a crime of moral turpitude or if they admit having committed a crime of moral turpitude.[51]

What Is a Crime of Moral Turpitude?

No clearly delineated definition exists within the law for "crime of moral turpitude," though the term "moral turpitude" has been held to involve acts demonstrating "baseness, vileness, and depravity" on the part of the perpetrator.[52]

In evaluating whether a particular crime involves moral turpitude, USCIS does not look at the underlying conduct of the applicant, but rather at the language in the criminal statute.[53] If the statute is broad or multisectional (a "divisible statute," in the parlance of the law), the courts will look at the record of conviction—*i.e.*, the "charge (indictment), plea, verdict, and sentence"—to determine whether the crime for which the person was convicted involved moral turpitude.[54] In April 2015, in *Matter of Silva-Trevino*, the Attorney General resolved a split in the circuit courts of appeal and upheld this traditional framework for analyzing whether a conviction is for a crime involving moral turpitude. This decision vacated a prior holding which allowed for evidence outside of the record of conviction to be considered in circumstances in which the record of conviction is inconclusive on the issue of moral turpitude.[55]

Although you always must analyze the specific statute involved in your client's case, there are some basic concepts to apply to the analysis of whether a crime involves moral turpitude. Crimes that have fraud as an element are considered to involve moral turpitude.[56] Crimes of violence involving intent, such as murder, voluntary manslaughter, or rape, also involve moral turpitude.[57] On the other hand, involuntary manslaughter is not a crime of moral turpitude unless the statute requires reckless conduct involving the conscious disregard

---

[47] 22 CFR §40.21(a)(2)(ii).

[48] *Matter of K–*, 7 I&N Dec. 594 (BIA 1957).

[49] *Matter of Seda*, 17 I&N Dec. 550, 554 (BIA 1980).

[50] *Id.*

[51] INA §212(a)(2)(A).

[52] *Matter of Franklin*, 20 I&N Dec. 867 (BIA 1994), *aff'd*, 72 F.3d 571 (8th Cir. 1995).

[53] *Matter of L–V–C–*, 22 I&N Dec. 594 (BIA 1999).

[54] *Matter of Velasquez-Herrera*, 24 I&N Dec. 503 (BIA 2008).

[55] *Matter of Silva-Trevino*, 24 I&N Dec. 687 (A.G. 2008), *vacated* 26 I&N Dec. 550 (A.G. 2015).

[56] *Matter of Adetiba*, 20 I&N Dec. 506 (BIA 1992).

[57] *Matter of Awaijane*, 14 I&N Dec. 117 (BIA 1972) (attempted murder); *Carter v. INS*, 90 F.3d 14 (1st Cir. 1996) (manslaughter); *Matter of Beato*, 10 I&N Dec. 730 (BIA 1964) (attempted rape).

of a substantial and unjustifiable risk.[58] Recklessly endangering another person with substantial risk of physical injury or death is a crime of moral turpitude even if it does not result in death or serious bodily injury to the victim.[59]

Whereas simple assault does not involve moral turpitude,[60] if injury to a spouse or child is an element of the offense, it may involve moral turpitude.[61] Some sexual crimes, such as prostitution, are considered crimes of moral turpitude,[62] as are some crimes against property, such as theft and robbery.[63]

A conviction of simple DUI or driving while intoxicated ordinarily does not involve moral turpitude.[64] Aggravated DUIs, however, may be crimes involving moral turpitude.[65]

Exceptions

The law contains two categories of exceptions for certain aliens who have been convicted of crimes of moral turpitude or who have made valid admissions regarding such crimes. Of the two exceptions to this inadmissibility ground, the first involves crimes that were committed when the alien was under the age of 18, and the second involves "petty offenses."[66] Aliens who have committed more than one crime of moral turpitude, however, cannot claim either of the exemptions.

The law provides that if the crime was committed while the alien was under age 18 and the alien both committed the crime and was released from prison more than five years before he or she applied for a visa, other documentation, or admission to the United States, then the alien is not inadmissible.[67] This provision is different from the rule that findings of juvenile delinquency are not considered convictions for purposes of immigration law. If the alien had his or her acts adjudicated under juvenile proceedings, or if the foreign proceedings are interpreted as falling within the federal juvenile type of proceedings, then this provision does not apply.[68]

In such a case, the alien would not have been convicted of any crime and would not be inadmissible. On the other hand, if the minor was convicted as if he or she were an adult, or, in the case of foreign convictions, if the minor's conviction does not fall within the type of proceedings that federal law considers necessarily as juvenile proceedings, then this exception comes into play.

The second exception, known as the "petty offense" exception, has two parts. First, the applicant qualifies for this exception only if the crime of moral turpitude under which he or she was convicted, or to which he or she admitted, had a maximum possible penalty of one year of imprisonment.[69] Second, in order not to be inadmissible for such a conviction, an alien must establish that he or she was sentenced to a term of imprisonment of no more than six months, regardless of how much time the convicted alien actually served.[70]

Multiple Criminal Convictions

To be inadmissible under the multiple criminal convictions provision, (1) an alien must have been convicted of two or more crimes (other than purely political offenses), and (2) the aggregate sentences to con-

---

[58] *See Matter of Franklin*, 20 I&N Dec. 867 (BIA 1994); *Matter of Lopez*, 13 I&N Dec. 725 (BIA 1971).

[59] *Matter of Leal*, 26 I&N Dec. 20 (BIA 2012).

[60] *Matter of Short*, 20 I&N Dec. 136 (BIA 1989).

[61] *Compare Matter of Tran*, 21 I&N Dec. 291 (BIA 1996) (finding moral turpitude) *with Matter of Sejas*, 24 I&N Dec. 236 (BIA 2007) (no moral turpitude).

[62] *Matter of Lambert*, 11 I&N Dec. 340 (BIA 1965).

[63] *Matter of de la Nues*, 18 I&N Dec. 140 (BIA 1980) (theft); *Matter of Alarcon*, 20 I&N Dec. 557 (BIA 1992) (robbery).

[64] *Matter of Lopez-Meza*, 22 I&N Dec. 1188 (BIA 1992).

[65] *Id.*

[66] INA §§212(a)(2)(A)(ii)(I), (II).

[67] INA §212(a)(2)(A)(ii)(I).

[68] 22 CFR §40.21(a)(2).

[69] INA §212(a)(2)(A)(iii)(II).

[70] *Id.*

finement must have been five years or more.[71] Under this ground, it is irrelevant whether the convictions occurred in a single trial, whether the offenses arose from a single scheme of misconduct, or whether they involved moral turpitude.

Controlled Substance Violations

Of the two grounds of inadmissibility relating to drug crimes, one is for people who have been convicted or admit commission of drug-related crimes;[72] the other makes inadmissible aliens believed to be drug traffickers.[73] For persons subject to grounds of deportability, the law also classifies drug trafficking crimes as "aggravated felonies," which further drastically restricts possible remedies for people convicted of these crimes.

The provision relating to conviction of a drug-related crime makes inadmissible any alien convicted of, or who makes a valid admission of having committed, certain crimes or the essential elements of those crimes. This inadmissibility ground applies to a violation of, or conspiracy to violate, "any law or regulation of a State, the United States, or a foreign country relating to a controlled substance (as defined in section 102 of the Controlled Substances Act)."[74] This ground covers virtually every type of drug. Furthermore, the use of the words "any law or regulation ... relating to a controlled substance" has been interpreted as being broad enough to encompass convictions for being under the influence of drugs,[75] or facilitating the unlawful sale of cocaine.[76]

Traffickers in Controlled Substances

No conviction—or even valid admission—is necessary to exclude people believed to be drug traffickers. This ground applies to "[a]ny alien who the consular or immigration officer knows or has reason to believe is or has been an illicit trafficker in any such controlled substance."[77] It also applies to persons who knowingly assist, and to abettors, conspirators, and those who collude with others. Spouses and children who knowingly obtained financial or other benefit from the illicit activity within the previous five years are also inadmissible.[78]

An "illicit trafficker" is "a knowing and conscious participant or conduit in an attempt to smuggle" a controlled substance. This broad definition applies not only to persons who smuggle or attempt to smuggle drugs into the United States, but also to people who serve as conduits for the drug trade within the United States.[79] A person can be an illicit trafficker even if he or she has committed only one transgression.[80]

This ground of inadmissibility can follow a person into lawful permanent residency. A person is removable under INA §237(a)(1)(A) for having been inadmissible at the time of entry or adjustment of status pursuant to INA §212(a)(2)(C) as an illicit trafficker in controlled substances where an immigration official knows or has reason to believe that the alien was a trafficker in controlled substances at the time of admission.[81]

Prostitution and Commercialized Vice

Unlike the other grounds included under INA §212(a)(2), prostitution and commercialized vice are not technically "criminal" inadmissibility grounds. They apply even to persons who come from countries

---

[71] INA §212(a)(2)(B).

[72] INA §212(a)(2)(A)(i)(II).

[73] INA §212(a)(2)(C).

[74] INA §212(a)(2)(A)(i)(II).

[75] *Matter of Esqueda,* 20 I&N Dec. 850 (BIA 1994).

[76] *Matter of Del Risco,* 20 I&N Dec. 109 (BIA 1989).

[77] INA §212(a)(2)(C).

[78] INA §212(a)(2)(C)(ii).

[79] *Matter of R– H–,* 7 I&N Dec. 675 (BIA 1958).

[80] *Matter of Rico,* 16 I&N Dec. 181 (BIA 1977).

[81] *Matter of Casillas-Topete,* 25 I&N Dec. 317 (BIA 2010).

Copyright © 2020. American Immigration Lawyers Association.

where prostitution is legal and presumably also to those who are coming to certain states in the United States where prostitution is legal.[82] This ground's three subsections make inadmissible:

- People who are coming to the United States to engage in prostitution or who have engaged in prostitution within 10 years of the date of application for a visa, adjustment of status, or entry into the United States;
- Procurers of prostitutes; or people who attempt to procure, or who receive the proceeds of, prostitution; or people who have done any of these activities within 10 years of applying for a visa, adjustment of status, or entry into the United States; and
- People who are coming to the United States to engage in unlawful commercialized vice, whether it is related to prostitution.[83]

The phrase "engage in prostitution" requires that the person must have been engaged in this type of conduct over a period of time. Similarly, the statute does not cover acts of solicitation of prostitution on one's own behalf.[84] Having been convicted of a single act of prostitution does not make the person inadmissible under this ground.[85] However, those falling into any of these three subsections are inadmissible even if there is no conviction for an offense involving prostitution.

Significant Traffickers in Persons

Under section 111(b) of the Trafficking Victims Protection Act of 2000,[86] a report to Congress identifying publicly foreign persons to be sanctioned under the Act will be prepared by the president. Any alien who is listed in that report, or whom the consular officer or the attorney general knows or has reason to believe is or has been a knowing aider, abettor, assister, conspirator, or colluder with such a trafficker in severe forms of trafficking in persons, is inadmissible.[87] Spouses, sons, and daughters (except unmarried children under 21) of traffickers who have knowingly obtained any financial or other benefit from the trafficker's illicit activity are also inadmissible.[88]

The term "severe forms of trafficking in persons" is defined as either (1) sex trafficking in which a commercial sex act is induced by force, fraud, or coercion, or in which the person induced to perform the commercial sex act is under 18 years of age, or (2) the recruitment, transportation, provision, or obtaining of a person for labor or services, through the use of force, fraud, or coercion, for the purpose of subjection to involuntary servitude, peonage, debt bondage, or slavery.[89]

Crimes and Provisional Waiver Eligibility

USCIS has eliminated the "reason to believe standard," and inadmissibility under the criminal grounds is not a basis for denying a provisional waiver application. Nevertheless, USCIS may still consider criminal history when determining whether an applicant merits a favorable exercise of discretion. We encourage practitioners to include arguments explaining why the applicant was not convicted of a particular offense, or why he or she qualifies for the petty offense or juvenile exceptions. In addition, if the applicant has been convicted of an offense that the BIA has specifically determined does not fall within a crime-based inadmissibility ground, then that should be persuasive evidence that weighs in the applicant's favor. Practitioners should argue that positive discretionary factors–*e.g.*, extreme hardship to the qualifying relative, ties to the United States, involvement in the community–outweigh an applicant's criminal history. Be aware that even if USCIS grants the provisional waiver, DOS will evaluate the applicant's admissibility during the immigrant visa in-

---

[82] 22 CFR §40.24(c).

[83] INA §212(a)(2)(D).

[84] *Matter of Gonzales-Zoquiapan*, 24 I&N Dec. 549 (BIA 2008).

[85] *Matter of R–*, 2 I&N Dec. 50 (BIA 1944).

[86] Pub. L. No. 106-386, §111(b), 114 Stat. 1464, 1485.

[87] INA §212(a)(2)(H)(i).

[88] INA §§212(a)(2)(H)(ii), (iii).

[89] Pub. L. No. 106-386, §103(8), 114 Stat. 1464, 1470.

terview. If an applicant is found inadmissible at the interview, the provisional waiver will be revoked. Thus, a careful analysis of the applicant's criminal record and potential inadmissibility must be assessed before he or she departs.

Illegal Entrants and Previous Immigration Violations

INA §212(a)(6) covers certain immigration-related misconduct. These grounds of inadmissibility apply to numerous categories of aliens, including those who:

- Are present in the United States without being lawfully admitted or paroled;
- Fail to attend removal proceedings;
- Engage in fraud or misrepresentation;
- Falsely claim U.S. citizenship;
- Are stowaways;
- Are smugglers;
- Have been found to have committed civil document fraud; or
- Are foreign students who study at public institutions.

Aliens Present Without Permission or Parole

This ground of inadmissibility applies to aliens who are present in the United States without being admitted or paroled, or who arrive at a place other than a designated port of entry.[90]

This ground does not apply to aliens who leave the United States for consular processing, as they will not then be present in the United States. This ground also does not bar aliens who entered the United States without inspection from adjusting status to permanent residence under the special provisions of INA §245(i).[91]

There is an exception to this ground of inadmissibility for aliens who qualify for immigrant status under the INA's provisions for battered spouses and children.[92] For aliens who first arrive in the United States after April 1, 1997, there are further restrictions on this exception. They must show that the spouse or child was battered or subjected to extreme cruelty by a spouse or parent, or a member of the spouse or parent's family in the household, and that there was a substantial connection between the battery or cruelty and the alien's unlawful entry to the United States.[93]

Failure to Attend Removal Proceedings

Another bar to admissibility applies to aliens who without reasonable cause fail to attend their removal proceedings or are ordered removed in absentia.[94] They are inadmissible for a period of five years following their subsequent departure or removal from the United States. There is no waiver for this ground of inadmissibility; it cannot be cured by filing a Form I-212. This ground applies only to aliens who failed to attend removal proceedings; it does not apply to aliens who failed to attend deportation or exclusion proceedings. In other words, the ground applies only to aliens who fail to attend proceedings that were initiated on or after April 1, 1997, and who were served with Form I-862, Notice to Appear.[95] Moreover, this ground applies only to aliens who departed the United States after failing to attend a removal hearing. Those who did not leave the United States and are seeking to adjust status would need to reopen the removal proceedings.

---

[90] INA §212(a)(6)(A).

[91] *Adjudicator's Field Manual* (AFM) §40.6.2(a)(4)(i).

[92] INA §212(a)(6)(A)(ii).

[93] INA §212(a)(6)(A)(ii)(III).

[94] INA §212(a)(6)(B).

[95] 9 FAM 302.9-3(B)(2); AFM §40.6.2(b)(2)(iv).

It should also be noted that aliens who fail to attend removal proceedings after receiving notice and are ordered removed in absentia will face a separate bar.[96] In situations in which an alien: (1) has received oral notice of the time and place of proceedings and the consequences of failing to appear; (2) fails to appear for less than "exceptional circumstances"; and (3) an in absentia order results, the alien is ineligible to apply for 10 years for cancellation of removal, voluntary departure, adjustment of status, change of status, or registry.[97] This ten-year period could be satisfied through residence in the United States or abroad.

Fraud or Willful Misrepresentation

An alien is inadmissible if he or she commits willful misrepresentation or fraud in attempting to obtain, or in obtaining, a visa, other documentation, admission into the United States, or other benefit.[98] "Other documentation" refers to documents required at the time of the alien's admission to the United States, such as reentry permits, border crossing cards, U.S. Coast Guard identity cards, or U.S. passports. "Other benefit" is understood to include, among other things, adjustment of status applications, all visa petitions, requests for extension of stay, change of nonimmigrant classification, requests for employment authorization, and voluntary departure requests.[99] All such misrepresentations that are material create a permanent bar to admission if they cannot be waived. The BIA has held that "fraud" and "misrepresentation" are the same, except that in cases of "willful misrepresentation" it is unnecessary to prove that the "person to whom the misrepresentation was made was motivated to action because of the misrepresentation."[100]

Under this ground, only misrepresentations to U.S. officials (generally a consular officer or a USCIS officer) are the basis of inadmissibility. Therefore, buying documents from a private individual does not make an alien inadmissible under the ground of procuring a document by fraud or misrepresentation, nor does using false documents to procure an entry into the United States make an alien inadmissible, unless the documents are presented to a U.S. official.[101] However, aliens are inadmissible if they are subject to a final order under the civil document fraud provisions of INA §274C.[102] Note, however, that USCIS is not using its authority under §274C to charge individuals with document fraud, and unless and until this changes, you will not encounter clients with final orders of document fraud.

The fraud inadmissibility ground does not apply if the statements made by the alien were true at the time they were uttered. Thus, the alien's activities after entering the United States do not necessarily indicate that the alien misrepresented his or her intentions at the time of applying for a visa or for admission. For example, if an alien applies for adjustment of status to permanent residence after entering the United States with a tourist visa, this does not necessarily mean that the alien misrepresented his or her intentions at the time he or she obtained the visa. A person may have valid reasons for changing his or her plans after admission.

For many years, DOS consular officers employed a "30/60" day rule to evaluate whether a visa applicant may be inadmissible for material misrepresentation or fraud. Under this rule, a nonimmigrant who was in the United States and engaged in conduct inconsistent with his nonimmigrant status within 30 days of arrival was subject to a presumption that he misrepresented his intentions in applying for the nonimmigrant visa. Violations of status occurring more than 30 days but less than 60 days after entry did not give rise to a presumption of misrepresentation but could be the basis for a reasonable belief that the visa applicant misrepresented his or her intent. The same rule provided that where the inconsistent conduct took place after 60 days, no such presumption applied. In September 2017, DOS replaced this rule with a new standard that provides that an individual who engages in conduct inconsistent with his or her nonimmigrant visa within 90 days of entry is subject to a presumption that he or she made a willful material misrepresentation in applying for the

---

[96] INA §240(b)(5)(A).

[97] INA §240(b)(7).

[98] INA §212(a)(6)(C)(i).

[99] 9 FAM 302.9-4(B)(7); AFM §40.6.2(c)(2)(A)(v).

[100] *Matter of G– G–*, 7 I&N Dec. 161 (BIA 1956).

[101] *Matter of D–L– & A–M–*, 20 I&N Dec. 409 (BIA 1991).

[102] INA §212(a)(6)(F)(i).

nonimmigrant visa or at the time of admission.[103] Examples of inconsistent conduct include working without authorization, enrolling in school without being in a nonimmigrant status authorizing study, and marrying a U.S. citizen or LPR while in B or F status and taking up residence in the United States. Because this is a DOS interpretation, it is not binding on USCIS adjudicators. USCIS officers may look at the 90-day rule for guidance in reviewing whether or not an applicant obtained admission through misrepresentation. According to updated language in the *USCIS Policy Manual*, "After such review, USCIS officers may find that an applicant made a willful misrepresentation, especially if the violation or inconsistent conduct occurred shortly after the consular interview or admission to the United States."[104]

For the misrepresentation to be willful, intent to deceive is not necessary.[105] It is enough that the false statement be made in a deliberate and voluntary manner or that the applicant has knowledge of the falsity of the documentation he or she is employing.[106]

A timely retraction of a misrepresentation can prevent it from being considered a basis for inadmissibility.[107] In general, a retraction should be made at the first opportunity.[108]

Only misrepresentations of material facts may make a person inadmissible. In this context, a misrepresentation can be fairly characterized as material: (1) if the alien was inadmissible on the true facts, or (2) if the misrepresentation tended to shut off a line of inquiry that was relevant to the alien's eligibility, and that line of inquiry might have resulted in a proper determination that the alien not be admitted.[109]

When the true facts would not have made the alien inadmissible, but it has been established that the misrepresentation tended to cut off a relevant line of inquiry, the alien has the burden of persuasion and production to show that the inquiry would not have resulted in a proper determination that he or she was inadmissible.[110] This burden is higher than just showing that the alien is eligible for a visa, because passage of time may have deprived the government of the possibility of making an adequate investigation. Consequently, when available facts indicate the existence of a substantial question as to the alien's eligibility for admission to the United States, a holding that the alien's misrepresentation was material may be warranted. On the contrary, if the record does not contain indications of inadmissibility, the misrepresentation will not be considered material. This holds even when applicants misrepresented their identity, if nothing in the record suggests that by disclosing their true name and identity, they would have revealed an inadmissibility ground.

Misrepresentations on behalf of others do not make an applicant inadmissible under this section. They may, however, lead to inadmissibility due to alien smuggling under INA §212(a)(6)(E).[111]

False Claim of U.S. Citizenship

Any alien who, on or after September 30, 1996, falsely represents himself or herself to be a citizen of the United States for any purpose or benefit under the INA or any other federal or state law is inadmissible.[112] This could include false claims of citizenship to a USCIS agent for purposes of gaining admission to the United States, false claims of citizenship to a state employee for purposes of obtaining a driver's license or public benefit, or voting.

The BIA has held that a false claim to U.S. citizenship requires two elements. First, the false claim must be made with the subjective intent of obtaining a purpose or benefit under the INA or any other federal or

---

[103] 9 FAM 302.9-4(B)(3).

[104] USCIS Policy Manual, Vol. 8, Ch. 3(A)(3).

[105] *Matter of Kai Hing Hui*, 15 I&N Dec. 288 (BIA 1975).

[106] *Falaja v. Gonzales*, 418 F.3d 889 (8th Cir. 2005).

[107] *Matter of M–*, 9 I&N Dec. 118 (BIA 1960).

[108] 9 FAM 302.9-4(B)(3)(f); AFM § 40.6.2(c)(1)(B)(vii).

[109] *Kungys v. U.S.*, 485 U.S. 759 (1988).

[110] *Matter of S– & B– C–*, 9 I&N Dec. 436 (BIA 1961).

[111] 9 FAM 302.9-4(B)(3)(d); AFM § 40.6.2(c)(1)(B)(v).

[112] INA §212(a)(6)(C)(ii).

state law. Second, U.S. citizenship must affect or matter to the purpose or benefit sought.[113] The BIA also distinguished between achieving a "purpose" and obtaining a "benefit" under INA §212(a)(6)(C)(ii)(I). A "benefit" must be identifiable and enumerated in the Act or any other federal or state law, while a "purpose" includes the avoidance of negative legal consequences–including removal proceedings.[114] Three circuit courts of appeal have determined that an individual who marks the box "citizen or national of the United States" on a Form I-9 for the purpose of obtaining employment as a U.S. citizen is inadmissible for having made a false claim to U.S. citizenship.[115] Another circuit court, however, found that falsely claiming to have been born in the United States in the course of an arrest by local police did not constitute a false claim under this section. The court reasoned that it had not been shown that the respondent was subjectively seeking a benefit created by the law and administered by the police, nor was there any objective evidence that the police could confer a "benefit" on him.[116]

DHS and DOS have issued guidance stating that an individual who makes a false claim while under the age of 18 is not inadmissible under this section if she or he lacked the maturity and judgment to understand the nature and consequences of making a false citizenship claim.[117] This is an individualized inquiry and the person who made the false claim has the burden to prove lack of legal capacity.[118] However, the BIA has more recently held that the ground of deportation for false claims of citizenship does not require an intent element.[119] It remains to be seen if the USCIS will amend or update its interpretation of this ground of inadmissibility to incorporate the BIA's holding, since the wording of these two grounds is almost identical.

An exception for certain persons was included in section 201(b)(2) of the Child Citizenship Act of 2000.[120] Under that exception, the inadmissibility ground does not apply if each natural or adoptive parent of the alien is or was a U.S. citizen (by birth or naturalization), the alien permanently resided in the United States prior to reaching age 16, and the alien reasonably believed at the time of making the representation that he or she was a citizen.[121] The exception applies to representations made on or after September 30, 1996.[122]

Timely retraction of a false claim to U.S. citizenship may be used as a defense to this section. The retraction must be both voluntary and without delay in order to be effective, as is the case for timely retractions of general fraud and misrepresentation.[123]

Note that the current version of the Form I-601A does not include a specific question relating to false claims to U.S. citizenship, but it does ask whether the applicant has ever knowingly and willfully given false or misleading information to a U.S. government official while applying for an immigration benefit or to gain entry or admission to the United States.[124] Be sure to address this issue with your client, with reference to any conduct on or after September 30, 1996, in connection with any state or federal benefit that may have in-

---

[113] *Matter of Richmond*, 26 I&N Dec. 776 (BIA 2016).

[114] *Id.*

[115] *Rodriguez v. Mukasey*, 519 F.3d 773 (8th Cir. 2008); *Kechkar v. Gonzales*, 500 F.3d 1080 (10th Cir. 2007); *Crocock v. Holder* (2d Cir. 2012). *See also Theodros v. Gonzales*, 490 F.3d 396 (5th Cir. 2007) (false claim to U.S. citizenship in order to gain private sector employment).

[116] *Castro v. Attorney General of the United States*, (3d Cir. 2012); *see also Valadez-Munoz v. Holder*, 623 F.3d 1304 (9th Cir. 2010) (false claim to citizenship made directly to DHS is to achieve or obtain the purpose or benefit of entry or admission to the U.S.); *See Hassan v. Holder*, 604 F.3d 915 (6th Cir. 2010) (false claim to citizenship on a loan application was not for a "purpose or benefit" where citizenship is irrelevant to the loan application).

[117] DHS, Memorandum from Deputy General Counsel, "False Citizenship Claims by Children: Knowledge and Capacity Elements" (Dec. 6, 2012); 9 FAM 302.9-5(B)(1)(a)(2).

[118] *Id.*

[119] *Matter of Zhang*, 27 I&N Dec. 569 (BIA 2019).

[120] Pub. L. No. 106-395, §201(b)(2), 114 Stat. 1631, 1634.

[121] INA §212(a)(6)(C)(ii)(II).

[122] Pub. L. No. 106-395, §201(b)(3), 114 Stat. 1631, 1634.

[123] AFM §40.6.2(c)(2)(C)(viii).

[124] USCIS, Form I-601A, Application for Provisional Unlawful Presence Waiver, p. 3 (Oct. 20, 2019).

Copyright © 2020. American Immigration Lawyers Association.

volved a false claim to citizenship. Be aware that some consular officers have found visa applicants inadmissible on this ground if they have described being admitted to the United States—such as "waived through"—without documents, based on the assumption that a false claim must have been involved in the admission.

Stowaways

Stowaways are persons who obtain transportation without the consent of the owner or person in command of the vessel or aircraft on which they are traveling.[125] A passenger who travels with a valid ticket is not a stowaway. Stowaways are inadmissible, and there is no specific waiver available for this ground of inadmissibility.[126]

Smugglers and Encouragers of Unlawful Entry

Immigrants and nonimmigrants are inadmissible to the United States if they have at any time knowingly encouraged, induced, assisted, abetted, or aided any other alien to enter the United States illegally.[127] There is no requirement that the smuggling have been for gain.[128] One federal circuit court has found that mere presence in a vehicle with knowledge that an undocumented person was hiding in the vehicle does not constitute alien smuggling without there being an affirmative act to aid or abet the smuggling.[129] The mistaken belief that the smuggled alien was legally entitled to enter the United States may be used as a defense to this ground.[130] Individuals who qualified for Family Unity[131] and who are applying for either Family Unity or an immigrant visa under the immediate-relative or the second-preference family visa provisions of the INA are not subject to this ground.[132]

The consulate may find that where a parent has "co-traveled" with a child to enter the United States illegally, the parent engaged in smuggling, even where the travel is being led by a paid "coyote." In other situations in which an applicant traveled to the United States in the company of others to enter the country illegally, the smuggling ground should not apply unless the applicant's support to the co-travelers was material to their being able to enter. Where a group of individuals is traveling together and each member would have entered illegally regardless of the assistance of the visa applicant, this should not support a smuggling finding.[133]

Congress created a waiver to ameliorate the smuggling inadmissibility ground's possibly harsh results. However, only two groups of aliens can take advantage of this waiver: (1) lawful permanent residents who are returning from a visit abroad, and (2) aliens seeking permanent residence as immediate relatives of U.S. citizens or under the first three family preference categories.[134] In other words, siblings of U.S. citizens do not qualify for the waiver. Even for those individuals who do qualify to apply, the waiver is available only if the alien they encouraged or assisted to enter illegally was, at the time of the smuggling, their "spouse, parent, son, or daughter (and no other individual)."[135] The attorney general is authorized to grant these waivers for humanitarian purposes, to ensure family unity, and when it is in the public interest. It should also be noted that any conviction for smuggling is now an "aggravated felony," unless the smuggling was done only to assist a spouse, parent, son, or daughter.[136]

---

[125] INA §101(a)(49).

[126] INA §212(a)(6)(D).

[127] INA §212(a)(6)(E).

[128] 9 FAM 302.9-7(b)(5); AFM 40.6.2(e)(3)(iii).

[129] *Altamirano v. Gonzales*, 427 F.3d 586 (9th Cir. 2005).

[130] 9 FAM 302.9-7(B)(3); AFM 40.6.2(e)(2)(i).

[131] *See* Immigration Act of 1990, Pub. L. No. 101-649, 104 Stat. 4978.

[132] INA §212(a)(6)(E)(ii).

[133] Minutes from meeting between the author and the chief, Immigrant Visa Section, U.S. consulate, Ciudad Juarez, Nov. 15, 2012.

[134] INA §212(d)(11).

[135] *Matter of Farias-Mendoza*, 21 I&N Dec. 269 (BIA 1997).

[136] INA §101(a)(43)(N).

While the provisional waiver application form does include a question about smuggling, the wording of the question may lead many clients to conclude that the ground does not apply to them if they were only traveling with a family member. A consular officer is likely to conclude that a parent who enters illegally with a child supports a finding of inadmissibility; the officer may also find smuggling in other situations that are not typically considered smuggling. Be sure to review how and with whom your client entered the United States to make sure there isn't a "hidden" inadmissibility ground that will only surface when your client departs for his or her consular interview.

Aliens Previously Removed

INA §212(a)(9) includes three subsections, including the unlawful presence ground of inadmissibility under (a)(9)(B) described in Chapter 2. The other two subsections of this ground of inadmissibility are discussed below.

Prior Removals

INA §212(a)(9)(A) covers aliens previously excluded, deported, or removed. Aliens who have been ordered removed under expedited removal, or ordered removed after proceedings initiated upon the alien's arrival in the United States (in other words, the equivalent of exclusion proceedings under pre-1996 law), are inadmissible for a period of five years after the date of their removal.[137] Other aliens who have been ordered removed, deported, or excluded are inadmissible for 10 years.[138] They are inadmissible for 20 years after a second removal and forever if they have been convicted of an aggravated felony.[139]

These inadmissibility bars do not apply if the attorney general has consented to the alien's reapplying for admission.[140] The inadmissibility periods set in the current statutory provisions went into effect on April 1, 1997, and apply retroactively, in that noncitizens, for example, those who were subject to the prior five-year bar based on a deportation, must now wait 10 years.[141] However, a 1998 DOS memorandum indicated that legacy Immigration and Naturalization Service (INS) would extend "sympathetic consideration" on a case-by-case basis to requests for reentry if the alien served the required period of time outside the United States pursuant to the prior law.[142]

Not every person who has been apprehended by USCIS will be subject to this inadmissibility ground. An alien who (1) was granted voluntary departure—either administratively by USCIS or in deportation proceedings by an immigration judge—and (2) left the United States on his or her own within the period specified in the voluntary departure order is not subject to this inadmissibility ground. However, aliens who leave the United States at their own expense after an immigration judge has entered a deportation or removal order against them are considered to have self-deported or self-removed and are thus also subject to this ground.

Reentering the United States Without Authorization

Under INA §212(a)(9)(C), individuals are inadmissible who:

Enter or attempt to enter the United States after having previously been unlawfully present in the United States for one year, or

Enter or attempt to enter the United States after having been previously ordered removed.

The first of these subsections applies to an alien "who has been unlawfully present in the United States for an aggregate period of one year or more," and who then enters or attempts to reenter the United States with-

---

[137] INA §212(a)(9)(A)(i).

[138] 22 CFR §40.91(b).

[139] INA §212(a)(9)(A)(ii).

[140] INA §212(a)(9)(A)(iii).

[141] DOS Cable, Pub. L. No. 104-208 [IIRAIRA] Update No. 36: 212(a)(9)(A)–(C), 212(a)(6)(A) and (B), 98 State 060539 (Apr. 4, 1998), AILA Doc. No. 98040490.

[142] *Id.*

out being admitted.[143] Because this provision applies only to unlawful presence accruing after April 1, 1997, it applies to persons who enter or attempt to enter illegally on or after April 1, 1998. The same definition of the term unlawful presence as utilized for INA §212(a)(9)(B) purposes applies here.[144] However, the one-year period of unlawful presence requires only an "aggregate period" of one year or more. This means that an alien may trigger inadmissibility under this section with repeated periods of unlawful presence that may each have been too short to trigger the three-year unlawful presence bar, but cumulatively add up to a year or more. While an alien may seek relief from this ground of inadmissibility after remaining outside the United States for 10 years, the bar has no set expiration date, unlike the three– and ten–year unlawful presence bars. For this reason, the bar is termed "permanent."

The second subsection of this inadmissibility ground applies to an alien who has been ordered removed under any provision of law and who then enters or attempts to reenter the United States without being admitted on or after April 1, 1997.[145] This covers persons who were ordered removed, deported, or excluded at any time. Such aliens are permanently inadmissible, although they may seek permission to reapply for admission to the United States 10 years after their last departure. The statutory exceptions to unlawful presence listed in INA §212(a)(9)(B) do not apply to the inadmissibility under §212(a)(9)(C).[146] This means, for example, that a minor who does not accrue unlawful presence for purposes of the three– and ten-year bars prior to age 18 is nevertheless subject to the permanent bar if he or she enters the United States without admission after accruing a year or more of unlawful presence.

Under the statute, only VAWA self-petitioners are eligible to seek a waiver of a permanent bar to inadmissibility immediately. The statute provides that a waiver is available when a self-petitioner can establish a connection between his or her removal, departure from the United States, reentry, or attempted reentry and the battery or extreme cruelty to which he or she was subjected.[147] To date, there is no USCIS guidance on this point to interpret the statutory language.

Although there is no specific question on the Form I-601A application relating to the permanent bar, the applicant must disclose all entries to and exits from the United States. This history, along with information about the immigration status of the applicant and the manner of each entry or admission, would allow USCIS to determine if the permanent bar has been triggered. But the agency would weigh this information only in exercising its discretion whether to grant or deny the application. If the applicant does not fully disclose his or her comings and goings from the United States until consular interview, the issue of inadmissibility under the permanent bar may not surface until after the applicant has departed the country. For this reason, it's critical to obtain an accurate history from your client about his or her travel to and from the United States and make sure your client knows that this is likely to be the subject of questioning at the consular interview abroad.

Reinstatement of Removal

Reinstatement of removal under INA §241(a)(5) is not a ground of inadmissibility, but it is frequently an additional consequence faced by an individual who is potentially inadmissible under INA §§212(a)(9)(A) and 212(a)(9)(C)(i)(II). Aliens subject to this removal provision may be removed from the United States through the "reinstatement" of the prior order of removal and are not eligible for, nor may apply for, any relief. As implemented by regulation, the term "prior removal orders" includes all prior expulsion orders, including orders of deportation and exclusion.[148] Persons whose deportation, exclusion, or removal order has been reinstated are ineligible to apply for a provisional waiver.[149] Customs and Border Protection (CBP) or Immigration and Customs Enforcement (ICE) would first need to have served notice pursuant to 8 CFR §241.8 and

---

[143] INA §212(a)(9)(C)(i).
[144] 9 FAM 302.9-14(B)(1)(a); AFM §40.9(a)(3).
[145] INA §212(a)(9)(C)(i)(II).
[146] AFM §40.9.2(b)(i).
[147] INA §212(a)(9)(C)(iii).
[148] 8 CFR §241.8(a).
[149] 8 CFR §212.7(e)(4)(v).

then have reinstated the order of removal. This could have happened either before the filing of the I-601A or while the waiver application is pending.

Under the statute, reinstatement of removal is triggered by the "illegal reentry" of an individual after she or he has been removed. Decisions in the Second, Fifth, Ninth, and Tenth Circuits have interpreted illegal reentry as including procedurally regular admissions procured through fraud or misrepresentation.[150]

The U.S. Supreme Court has ruled that reinstatement of removal may be applied to a person who illegally reentered the United States before the statute's effective date.[151] Four circuit courts of appeals, however, recognized exceptions to the retroactive application of reinstatement when the individual had applied for discretionary relief[152] or took affirmative steps to legalize his or her status prior to April 1, 1997.[153] The issue of whether reinstatement may be applied retroactively in these situations was expressly not decided in the Supreme Court's decision.

Public Charge

The public charge inadmissibility ground bars entry to any foreign national who, "in the opinion of the consular officer at the time of application for a visa, or in the opinion of the attorney general at the time of application for admission or adjustment of status," is likely to become a public charge.[154] This ground of inadmissibility has recently become a more serious challenge for low-income applicants and a common basis for refusal by the U.S. consulates, especially the consulate in Ciudad Juarez. That challenge is likely to become even more serious once the Department of Homeland Security (DHS) and DOS implement their final rules re-interpreting this ground of inadmissibility.[155]

The 1996 law[156] amended the ground of inadmissibility for individuals likely to become a public charge. The ground requires that consular officers, and the attorney general in the case of adjustment applications, consider several factors, including the foreign national's age, health, family status, assets, resources, financial status, education, and skills.[157] Basically, this statutory change codified the standard that legacy Immigration and Naturalization Service (INS) and DOS previously developed to implement this exclusion ground.

Historically, USCIS and DOS had applied somewhat different standards in determining who is likely to become a public charge. DOS's standard relied heavily on the annual poverty income guidelines of Health and Human Service (HHS). "An immigrant visa applicant relying solely on personal income to [counter public charge inadmissibility], who does not demonstrate an annual income above the income poverty guidelines ... and who is without other adequate financial resources, shall be presumed ineligible" for admission.[158]

After the change in the 1996 law, the emphasis shifted from the immigrant visa applicant to the Form I-130 petitioner, who becomes the sponsor during the consular processing stage. A properly filed, non-fraudulent Form I-864 would normally be considered sufficient to meet the INA §212(a)(4) requirements and

---

[150] *Tamayo-Tamayo v. Holder*, 709 F.3d 795 (9th Cir. 2013); *Cordova-Soto v. Holder*, 659 F.3d 1029 (10th Cir. 2011); *Beekhan v. Holder*, 634 F.3d 723 (2d Cir. 2011).

[151] *Fernandez-Vargas v. Ashcroft*, 548 U.S. 30 (2006).

[152] *Arevalo v. Ashcroft*, 344 F.3d 1 (1st Cir. 2003); *Faiz-Mohammed v. Ashcroft*, 395 F.3d 799 (7th Cir. 2005); *Sarmiento-Cisneros v. Ashcroft*, 381 F.3d 1277 (11th Cir. 2004).

[153] *Valdez-Sanchez v. Gonzales*, 485 F.3d 1084 (10th Cir. 2007).

[154] INA §212(a)(4).

[155] 84 Fed. Reg. 41292 (Aug. 14, 2019). The DHS regulation has been preliminarily enjoined. *See, Make the Road, et al. vs. Cuccinelli*, 19 Civ. 7993 (S.D.N.Y.)(nationwide) and *New York v. DHS*, No. 19-3591(S.D.N.Y.)(nationwide); *Casa de Maryland, Inc. v. Trump*, 19-cv-2715 (D. Md)(nationwide); *Cook County, Illinois v. McAleenan*, 19-cv-6334 (N.D. Ill.) (Illinois); *City and County of San Francisco v. USCIS*, No. 19-cv-4717 (N.D. Cal.) (Plaintiff Counties); *California v. USDHS*, No. 19-cv-4975 (N.D. Cal.) (Plaintiff States and the District of Columbia); *Washington v. USDHS*, No. 19-cv-5210 (E.D. Wash.)(nationwide).

[156] IIRAIRA, Pub. L. No. 104-208, div. C, 110 Stat. 3009, 3009-546 to 3009-724 (Sept. 30, 1996).

[157] INA §212(a)(4)(B).

[158] 22 CFR §40.41(f).

satisfy the "totality of the circumstances" analysis.[159] Only where the immigrant visa applicant evidenced significant public charge concerns—advanced age, physical or mental disabilities, or serious health problems—would the consular agent look beyond the affidavit of support. In those cases, the applicant would need to demonstrate employability or some form of reliable support—e.g., that they have been offered permanent employment in the United States.

The State Department, however, amended the Foreign Affairs Manual (FAM) in January 2018 to increase the burden of satisfying the public charge ground of inadmissibility for immigrant visa applicants.[160] The current language requires the consular officers "in every case" to examine the visa applicant's "age, health, family status, assets, resources, financial status, education, and skills."[161] While the Form I-864 affidavit of support alone used to be sufficient proof of satisfying the public charge test in most cases, it is now merely "a positive factor." Another change in the FAM is the addition of language encouraging the consular officer to consider the likelihood that the sponsor will support the visa applicant. The effect of all of this is to relegate the Form I-864 to a supporting rather than a lead role in the public charge analysis. Current language even states "a properly filed and sufficient, non-fraudulent Form I-864, may not necessarily satisfy the INA 212(a)(4) requirements, but may provide additional evidence in the review of public charge determination."[162]

The FAM goes on to suggest that applicants with health issues submit proof of medical insurance or other ability to pay medical expenses they may incur in the United States. Other evidence that an applicant may submit includes evidence that the applicant has, or will have, personal funds or property at his or her disposal in the United States.

The FAM now puts more emphasis on finding out whether the applicant or a family member in the applicant's household is currently or has received "public assistance of any type" from state, federal, or local sources. While the FAM maintains the distinction between cash and non-cash benefits, and states that the latter should not be considered as public cash assistance or income, it then goes on to add that these supplemental benefits "may only be considered as part of the totality of the applicant's circumstances in determining whether the an applicant is likely to become a public charge." Specifically deleted was prior language prohibiting the consideration of past or possible future use of non-cash or supplemental assistance programs. In other words, receipt of food stamps, the Child Health Insurance Program (CHIP), Women, Infants and Children (WIC), Medicaid, or other health and medical benefits—while not given the same weight as cash assistance programs—may still be taken into account.

More significant is the interim final rule on public chare that the State Department published on October 11, 2019. At the present time, the agency has not implemented that rule nor finalized the necessary Form DS-5540, Public Charge Questionnaire. This final rule mirrors the changes contained in the DHS final public charge rule that was implemented as of February 24, 2020.

USCIS also applies a totality of the circumstances test, which looks at all the circumstances present at the time the foreign national applies for an immigrant visa or for admission to the United States.[163] This ground of inadmissibility is prospective in nature, and the adjudication must be based on whether the applicant is likely to become a public charge in the future. Final DHS regulations that were implemented on February 24, 2020 have substantially altered that totality of the circumstances test.

Under the new regulations, the term "likely at any time to become a public charge" has been redefined in four important ways. First, instead of being applied to those who might become "primarily dependent" on a designated list of state and federal programs, it applies to those who are more likely than not to receive any of these benefits for more than 12 months in the aggregate within any 36-month period.

---

[159] FAM 302.8-2(B) (2017).

[160] "Update to 9 FAM 302.8 Public Charge - INA 212(A)(4)," AILA Doc. No. 18012235. Those FAM changes are being challenged in *Make the Road, et al v. Pompeo, et al*, Case No. 1:19-cv-11633 (S.D. N.Y. 2019).

[161] FAM 302.8-2(B).

[162] *Id.*

[163] *Matter of A–*, 19 I&N Dec. 867 (Comm'r 1988).

Second, DHS has expanded the list of identified programs that can be considered when applying the public charge "totality of the circumstances" test. Under the old definition of public charge, the agency could only consider receipt of three cash assistance programs—Supplemental Security Income (SSI), Temporary Assistance to Needy Families (TANF), and state general relief or general assistance—as well as a Medicaid program that covers institutionalization for long-term care. The final regulation adds five new programs: non-emergency Medicaid; Supplemental Nutrition and Assistance Program (SNAP, formerly food stamps); Section 8 Housing Choice Voucher Program; Section 8 Project-Based Rental Assistance; and Public Housing. Benefits received by the applicant's U.S. citizens children or other family members are not considered in determining whether the applicant is likely to become a public charge. Benefits received by an individual who was not subject to the public charge ground of inadmissibility when the benefits were received would not be considered.

Third, in determining public charge inadmissibility, the regulation has shifted attention away from the petitioning sponsor's income as reported on the affidavit of support and redirected it to the five statutory factors: the applicant's age, health, family status, assets/resources/financial status, and education/skills. Adjudicators will assign weight—negative and positive, as well as heavily negative and heavily positive—to these five factors to determine whether the applicant passes the public charge test. All adjustment of status applicants will need to be complete a declaration of self-sufficiency form and support it with documentary evidence.

Finally, the regulation allows for the posting of a public charge bond for applicants who, in the opinion of the USCIS or State Department, might otherwise fail the public charge test.

Posting of Public Charge Bonds

The statute has allowed for the posting of a public charge bond in situations where the applicant needs to assure the USCIS or State Department that he or she will not become a public charge. But during the last 20 years, the posting of such bonds has been extremely rare. The final rule detailed the procedure for the posting and canceling such bonds with the implication that they may become a common occurrence. Applicants who are initially determined likely to become a public charge by the USCIS may be offered the opportunity to post a public charge bond of at least $8,100. The bond may be cancelled only upon the immigrant's death, permanent departure, five years as a lawful permanent resident, or naturalization. The bond will be considered breached if the immigrant receives any of the nine cash or non-cash programs identified above for more than 12 months in the aggregate within any 36-month period.

Conclusion

Always bear in mind that visa applicants with approved provisional waivers will be departing for their consular interviews with the expectation that they will only be abroad and apart from their families and employment for a brief period. If such an applicant is found inadmissible on another ground, he or she faces an extended separation from family, employment, and other commitments, without having prepared for the psychological and practical impact of this outcome. For this reason, advocates need to take particular care in client interviews and in reviewing any related case records to avoid any surprises when the client attends his or her consular interview. Failure to effectively screen for inadmissibility exposes your client to the risk that you will miss an important issue that affects your client's eligibility to immigrate.

CHAPTER 4
EXTREME HARDSHIP

Demonstrating extreme hardship to a qualifying relative is essential to winning a provisional waiver case. Understanding how extreme hardship is defined will form the basis for advising your client and preparing the case. In this chapter, we will cover how the term "extreme hardship" is interpreted by U.S. Citizenship and Immigration Services (USCIS), the Board of Immigration Appeals (BIA), the Administrative Appeals Office (AAO), and the federal courts. We will also offer practical advice on how to satisfy the standard, because the term "extreme" can be intimidating, as can the courts' pronouncements that extreme hardship must go beyond the hardship normally associated with prolonged separation from close family members. In practice, USCIS does approve waiver applications that demonstrate the kinds of hardships stemming from prolonged separation from close family members if they are well documented and well presented. In other words, the standard that adjudicators use is not as high as you might be led to believe if you relied solely on case decisions.

Along with an overview of the relevant case law, this chapter will provide a guide to evaluating the facts in your client's case, determining which hardship factors to emphasize, and identifying the appropriate documentation to support each alleged hardship. Chapter 6 will discuss how to obtain that documentation. We will stress not only identifying and prioritizing the possible waiver factors, but also applying their cumulative effect. Some waiver applications are based on one overwhelming hardship factor, but in most cases, it is the combined effect of several factors that proves successful. This chapter will focus on the five hardship factors that are most relevant for provisional waivers: family ties, health, financial, social/cultural, and country conditions. In addition to summarizing and including copies of some of the most often-cited administrative and judicial cases, we will provide an extreme hardship worksheet for use in client intake. Appendix 4 is a guide for practitioners when questioning the client on possible extreme hardship factors. Appendix 5 is a series of questions, in English and Spanish, designed for the client to take home and consider.

Extreme Hardship in Unlawful Presence Waivers

Qualifying Relatives in General

The extreme hardship standard is set forth in Immigration and Nationality Act (INA) §212(a)(9)(B)(v). All applicants seeking to waive the three– or ten-year bar triggered by unlawful presence followed by departure from the United States must establish extreme hardship to a U.S. citizen or lawful permanent resident (LPR) spouse or parent. This family member is known as a "qualifying relative." Therefore, a precondition to filing the waiver is the existence of a particular family relationship. Once that is established, the next step is demonstrating that the qualifying relative will suffer extreme hardship if the applicant is not permitted admission or readmission to the United States.

U.S. citizen or LPR children may not be qualifying relatives, nor may the waiver applicant or any other family member. This does not mean that you should ignore the hardship they will suffer should the waiver be denied. Instead, you will need to funnel their hardship through the qualifying relative and make it part of his or her hardship. Show how hardship to the applicant or the applicant's child will result in increased hardship to the qualifying relative. For example, the lack of health care in the foreign country to treat a child's specific medical condition will result in greater stress and suffering to the qualifying relative parent if the family elects to move there. The same could be true for any other non-qualifying family member who will suffer more due to the absence of the waiver applicant. Identify and document that hardship and then explain how it will increase the hardship experienced by the qualifying relative.

Example: Rashid, a citizen of Pakistan, is filing a provisional waiver application based on extreme hardship to his U.S. citizen wife, Joan. They have a ten-year-old U.S. citizen daughter, Ellen. Joan is anxious and depressed about the thought of leaving the United States and relocating to Pakistan, a country she has never even visited. She is worried about many things: cultural and religious differences, the availability of health care, social ostracism, the language barrier, and how they will earn a living. She has also read articles about attacks in Pakistan against young girls seeking an education. Joan is fearful that Ellen could encounter violence, diminished educational opportunities, and discrimination if Rashid's waiver is not granted and the family is forced to relocate to Pakistan. Ellen is not a qualifying relative. However, Ellen's current and potential suffering affects Joan and forms another basis for her argument that she will experience extreme hardship.

Qualifying Relatives for Provisional Waiver

The qualifying relatives for the provisional waiver are the same as for the general unlawful presence waiver under INA §212(a)(9)(B)(v). The provisional waiver regulations used to limit the possible qualifying relatives to the U.S. citizen spouse or parent of the waiver applicant.[1] But the regulatory change in July 2016 expanded the program and eliminated this restriction.[2]

What Is Extreme Hardship?

How has the term "extreme hardship" been defined? Establishing extreme hardship has long been a requirement for many different immigration benefits and forms of relief. In addition to being a necessary element for various waivers of inadmissibility, including for fraud[3] and criminal conduct,[4] it is or was a requirement for suspension of deportation,[5] the Nicaraguan Adjustment and Central American Relief Act (NACARA),[6] relief for self-petitioners under the Violence Against Women Act (VAWA),[7] and a waiver of the joint petition requirement for conditional residents.[8] Despite its prevalence in the immigration laws, the term "extreme hardship" is not defined in the statute or the regulations. Instead, the term remains purposefully fluid and vague. In the words of the BIA, it "is not a definable term of fixed and inflexible content or meaning."[9] But over the course of more than four decades, the legacy Immigration and Naturalization Service (INS), USCIS, the BIA, the AAO, and the federal courts have identified the elements of what this term means and have provided a framework for establishing a successful hardship claim.[10] Most recently, USCIS issued final guidance defining this term.[11]

Possible Extreme Hardship Factors—A Review of Case Law

Because different sections of the immigration statute impose the same extreme hardship requirement, case law from other contexts—suspension of deportation decisions and other sections of the immigration statute—inform what the term means in a waiver of inadmissibility hardship claim.[12] The BIA, in *Matter of Cervantes-Gonzalez,* noted when comparing the term's definition for a fraud waiver with the interpretation used in suspension cases that "we find the factors articulated in cases involving suspension of deportation and other waivers of inadmissibility to be helpful, given that both forms of relief require extreme hardship and the exercise of discretion."[13] *Matter of Anderson*,[14] the seminal extreme hardship case, dealt with eligibility for suspension of deportation and set forth the range of possible factors that the BIA examined to see if the applicant had satisfied the requirement. Suspension of deportation is no longer a defense to deportation under current

---

[1] Former 8 Code of Federal Regulations (CFR) §212.7(e)(3)(vii) (2016).

[2] 81 *Federal Register* (Fed. Reg.) 50243 (July 29, 2016); 8 CFR §212.7(e)(3)(vi). A copy of the regulations is included as Appendix 1.

[3] Immigration and Nationality Act (INA) §212(i).

[4] INA §212(h).

[5] Former INA §244(a)(1996).

[6] Pub. L. No. 105-100, tit. II, 111 Stat. 2160, 2193–201 (1997), as amended.

[7] INA §204(a)(1)(A), (B).

[8] INA §216(c)(4)(C).

[9] *Matter of Cervantes-Gonzalez*, 22 I&N Dec. 560, 565 (BIA 1999*); Matter of Hwang*, 10 I&N Dec. 448, 451 (BIA 1964).

[10] *See, e.g., Matter of O– J– O–*, 21 I&N Dec. 381 (BIA 1996); *Matter of L– O– G–*, 21 I&N Dec. 413 (BIA 1996); *Matter of Anderson*, 16 I&N Dec. 596 (BIA 1978).

[11] USCIS Policy Manual, Vol. 9, Part B.

[12] *Matter of Kao & Lin*, 23 I&N Dec. 45, 49 (BIA 2001).

[13] *Matter of Cervantes-Gonzalez*, 22 I&N Dec. 560, 565 (BIA 1999).

[14] *Matter of Anderson*, 16 I&N Dec. 596 (BIA 1978).

immigration laws, but it required the applicant to prove extreme hardship to himself or herself or to his or her U.S. citizen or LPR spouse, parent, or child. While the qualifying relatives for suspension of deportation are not the same as those for the unlawful presence waiver, the factors the BIA enumerated are nevertheless instructive. The *Matter of Anderson* factors include the following:

- Applicant's age both at the time of entry and at the time of relief;
- Length of residence in the United States;
- Family ties in the United States and abroad;
- Health-related issues;
- Financial situation, including business or occupation;
- Possibility of other means of immigrating;
- Applicant's immigration history;
- Applicant's position in the community; and
- Economic and political conditions in the applicant's home country.

Case law following *Matter of Anderson* further developed and expanded these nine extreme hardship factors as they relate to other forms of relief. Additional relevant hardship factors include:

- Ability to raise children if family members are not available to help[15]
- Quality of life factors in the home country[16]
- Educational opportunities for children who do not speak, read, or write the language;[17]
- Separation from family members, especially in single-parent situations;[18]
- Separation from family members when qualifying relative was ill or elderly;[19]
- Significant health conditions when medical care was unavailable;[20]
- Violence and damage from civil war and disasters in home country;[21]
- Psychological impact, including depression and trauma;[22]
- Political persecution;[23]

---

[15] *Matter of Recinas*, 23 I&N Dec. 467, 470 (BIA 2002) (BIA considered that the noncitizen depended on her legal permanent resident mother to assist her in the care of her U.S. citizen children).

[16] *Matter of Cervante-Gonzalez*, 22 I&N Dec. 560, 566 (BIA 1999*)* (BIA noted that quality of life factors were relevant to the extreme hardship inquiry).

[17] *Matter of Recinas*, 23 I&N Dec. 467, 470 (BIA 2002) (BIA considered whether the U.S. citizen children were able to read, write, and speak in the language of the country of deportation).

[18] *Id*. (BIA considered the fact that the U.S. citizen children were entirely dependent upon the noncitizen because the parents were divorced and the father was not involved in their care).

[19] *Mendez v. Holder*, 566 F.3d 316, 322 (2d Cir. 2009) ("Petitioner's daughter suffers from severe asthma. Petitioner testified that she has about 25 asthma attacks a year and that her condition requires the use of a home nebulizer as well as an inhaler. She also requires regular visits to the emergency room for serious attacks. ... Petitioner's son was diagnosed with Grade II Vesicoureteral Reflux. This disease causes urine to reflux from the bladder back [**5] to the kidneys and liver, causing staph infections, scarring, and tissue damage. Ultimately, the condition can lead to kidney or liver failure.").

[20] *Matter of Cervantes*, 22 I&N Dec. 560, 566 (BIA 1999) (BIA reviewed expanded hardship factors following *Matter of Anderson* in §212(i) waiver application).

[21] *Matter of L–O–G–*, 21 I&N Dec. 413, 420 (BIA 1996) ("Nicaragua is an extremely poor country, still in political turmoil, with a shattered economy, very high unemployment, and minimal government.").

[22] *Lam v. Holder*, 698 F.3d 529, 534 (7th Cir. 2012) ("Lam submitted a letter from his wife's psychologist, who stated that Ms. Lin suffered from 'severe' postpartum depression and that she was 'truly psychologically unable to care fully' for their children. Her psychologist also stated that Lam's removal would place Ms. Lin 'in extreme psychological distress.'"); *Ravancho v. INS*, 658 F.2d 69 (3d Cir. 1981) ("[p]sychological trauma may be a relevant factor in determining whether a United States citizen child will suffer 'extreme hardship' within the statute.").

Copyright © 2020. American Immigration Lawyers Association.

- Contributions to the community;[24]
- Acculturation and integration into U.S. society;[25] and
- Severe personal consequences and non-economic hardships flowing from economic ones.[26]

Case law requires that each of these factors be analyzed in the context of the facts and circumstances specific to each case.[27]

Example; Carlos, a Mexican citizen, is married to Rosie, a U.S. citizen. The couple has two U.S. citizen children. Carlos provides great emotional, financial, and parental support to Rosie. Carlos is an attentive father, and the children would greatly miss him if he were required to leave and reside in Mexico for 10 years. In the past, when Carlos's work took him away for long periods, their eldest son didn't eat well, became rebellious, and performed poorly at school. Rosie became depressed, experienced difficulty sleeping, and was unable to properly care for her children. A psychological report found that Rosie suffers from separation anxiety and is susceptible to depression. Rosie has no family in Mexico but has strong family and community ties in the United States. She speaks very little Spanish. She has worked as a filing clerk at the same job for the past 16 years and worries about the poor employment opportunities she would experience in Mexico. Rosie is also worried about other things that would happen were she and the children to relocate to Mexico with Carlos: the reported violence in northern Mexico, where Carlos is from; the loss of health insurance for her children, which is currently paid for by her employer; the lower qualify of educational and health care options; and the expected difficulty adjusting to life in Mexico.

This fact pattern is very similar to a waiver case that was originally denied by USCIS but later approved by the AAO.[28] It demonstrates the range of inter-related factors that typically compose a waiver case. Although none of these factors standing alone would probably be enough to establish extreme hardship to Rosie, in combination, they are likely to rise to the level of extreme hardship.

---

[23] *Gutierrez-Centeno v. INS*, 99 F.3d 1529, 1534 (9th Cir. 1996) ("Gutierrez and her family have had a history of conflict with the Sandinistas. In light of the political instability in Nicaragua and the power which the Sandinistas continued to wield after the election of the Chamorro government, the political situation in Nicaragua is also a factor that should have been considered. *See In re O–J–O–*, 21 I&N Dec. 381 (BIA 1996), at 5 ('In light of the respondent's family's history of conflict with the Sandinistas, the current political situation in Nicaragua should be factored into the hardship assessment.')"; *Blanco v. INS*, 68 F.3d 642, 646 (2d Cir. 1995) ("incidents of violence that have been and would be directed at her in El Salvador. Her affidavit in support recounted the killing of her common-law husband, her father, and her uncle; the murder of a neighbor; threats against her by guerrillas; injury to her child from a bomb blast outside her home; and child kidnapping from a school attended by one of her children. This evidence was relevant to a claim of hardship more personally directed and more severe than the claim that might be made by any deportee to such a strife-torn nation.").

[24] *Urbina-Osejo v. INS*, 124 F.3d 1314, 1318–19 (9th Cir. 1997) ("Urbina worked as a volunteer telephone counselor for the San Francisco Aids [sic] Foundation, teaching AIDS prevention to Spanish-speaking callers."); *Matter of O–J–O–*, 21 I&N Dec. 381 (BIA 1996) ("He is deeply involved in church activities, attending services regularly and serving as a voluntary deacon in his congregation.… The hardship related to community involvement, however, derives from the loss of the personal and social bonds established during the course of such activities.").

[25] *Ramos v. INS*, 695 F.2d 181, 184 (5th Cir. 1983) ("[his] speech, choice of toys, knowledge, and interest were typical of American boys. … [His] choice of toys and drawings were typical of American children. … He would be particularly vulnerable to a move at this age because he is just now developing relationships outside the home … Once a child has adopted the culture of a country, he is subject to rejection by peers if he is forced to readjust to the new culture. The child at age six and onward is particularly vulnerable to this."

[26] *Tukhowinich v. INS*, 64 F.3d 460, 464 (9th Cir. 1995) ("Because the loss of financially comparable employment would create not only an economic hardship for Ms. Tukhowinich but would severely frustrate what she regards as the overriding mission in her life—to provide for her parents and siblings—we think the BIA should have considered the implications of her economic loss.").

[27] *Jara-Navarrete v. INS*, 813 F.2d 1340 (9th Cir. 1987); *Zavala-Bonilla v. INS*, 730 F.2d 562 (9th Cir. 1984); *Ramos v. INS*, 695 F.2d 181 (5th Cir. 1983); *Matter of Hwang*, 10 IN Dec. 448, 451 (BIA 1964).

[28] AAO Decision, Mexico City, Mexico, (Mar. 26, 2012). The AAO found that the applicant established extreme hardship.

Extreme Hardship and Regulations

In addition to the hardship factors enumerated by the BIA, the AAO, and the federal courts, USCIS has in its regulations set forth factors that it will consider in determining whether an applicant for suspension of deportation or cancellation of removal under NACARA has satisfied the extreme hardship standard. These factors, many of which overlap with those found in case law, include:

- Age of the applicant;
- Age, number, and immigration status of the applicant's children and their ability to speak the native language of the foreign country and adjust to life there;
- Health conditions of the applicant or of his spouse, parents, and children, and the availability of required medical treatment in the foreign country;
- Ability of the applicant to obtain employment in the foreign country;
- Length of residence in the United States;
- Family members residing in the United States and their immigration/citizenship status;
- Financial impact of the applicant's departure;
- Disruption of educational opportunities;
- Psychological impact of the applicant's departure;
- Current political and economic conditions in the foreign country;
- Family and other ties in the foreign country;
- Contributions to and ties to the community in the United States;
- Immigration history; and
- Availability of other means of obtaining LPR status.[29]

The agency has expanded this list to include abuse-related hardship factors for applicants for VAWA suspension of deportation or cancellation of removal:

- The nature and extent of the physical or psychological consequences of abuse;
- The impact of loss of access to the U.S. courts and criminal justice system (including, but not limited to, the ability to obtain and enforce orders of protection, criminal investigations and prosecutions, and family law proceedings or court orders regarding child support, maintenance, child custody, and visitation);
- The likelihood that the batterer's family, friends, or others acting on behalf of the batterer in the home country would physically or psychologically harm the applicant or the applicant's child(ren);
- The applicant's needs and/or needs of the applicant's child(ren) for social, medical, mental health, or other supportive services for victims of domestic violence that are unavailable or not reasonably accessible in the home country;
- The existence of laws and social practices in the home country that punish the applicant or the applicant's child(ren) because they have been victims of domestic violence or have taken steps to leave an abusive household; and
- The abuser's ability to travel to the home country and the ability and willingness of authorities in the home country to protect the applicant and/or the applicant's children from future abuse.[30]

The hardship factors for VAWA-related cases, while not binding in non-VAWA cases, are still relevant in all waiver cases and should be included when they exist.

---

[29] 8 CFR §1240.58(b).
[30] 8 CFR §1240.58(c).

Example: Miriam, a citizen of Mexico, is married to John, a U.S. citizen. They reside together in Tucson with their one-year-old child. Miriam came to the United States to escape an abusive relationship with an ex-boyfriend, and she fears returning to Mexico where he continues to live. John has two children from a prior marriage and would be unable to financially support the children or meet his childcare obligations if he were to accompany Miriam to Mexico. John is also distraught that he would be subject to the drug-related violence that pervades Mexico.

These facts formed the basis for a waiver application that was originally denied by USCIS but was granted by the AAO on appeal.[31] The decision reflects the sensitivity of the agency to domestic violence claims.

USCIS Final Guidance on Extreme Hardship

On November 20, 2014, DHS Secretary Jeh Johnson issued a memo directing USCIS to expand eligibility for the provisional waiver program to include other family-based categories and provide additional guidance on the definition of extreme hardship. The intended purpose of the guidance is to "provide broader use of this legally permitted waiver program." In addition to clarifying the factors to be considered, the secretary directed the agency "to consider criteria by which a presumption of extreme hardship may be determined to exist." On October 7, 2015, the agency issued draft guidance that proposed significant changes to the existing assessment of extreme hardship but did not incorporate the presumption of hardship criteria. Following a public comment period, USCIS released the final guidance, which is found in the Policy Manual, Vol. 9, Part B.

Should I Stay or Should I Go?

Adjudicators had been requiring waiver applicants to demonstrate that the qualifying relative would suffer extreme hardship in two scenarios: if he or she were to relocate to the applicant's country, *and* if he or she were to remain in the United States separated from the applicant. This requirement was set forth in the adjudicator's training manual (Standard Operating Procedures, or SOP) and was boilerplate language in written decisions, even though it was not explained to the applicant in the instructions to the Form I-601 or I-601A. One of the most significant changes is the reduction in this burden of demonstrating extreme hardship to the qualifying relative. The final guidance allows the applicant to decide whether the qualifying relative would either relocate or remain in the United States.[32] The applicant now has to establish extreme hardship in only one of those scenarios rather than in both.

The guidance still allows the qualifying relative to show that extreme hardship would result from both separation and relocation. But if the applicant submits evidence related to both possible outcomes and demonstrates extreme hardship only to one of them, USCIS will likely issue a request for evidence (RFE) asking "whether the qualifying relative has established which scenario is more likely to result" from a denial of the waiver.[33]

The qualifying relative is required to submit a statement certifying under penalty of perjury the decision either to relocate with, or to separate from, the waiver applicant in the event the waiver is denied. The statement should be "sufficiently detailed" and "credible," and should explain the reasons for the decision. The qualifying relative is encouraged to submit any documentation that would support the basis for the decision, although due to its subjective nature, the statement itself may be the best available evidence. In most cases, "in the absence of inconsistent evidence, a credible, sworn statement from the qualifying relative of his or her intent to relocate or separate would generally suffice to demonstrate what the qualifying relative plans to do."[34]

Prior to the final guidance and the elimination of having to show both relocation and separation hardship, written decisions on unlawful presence waivers revealed that it was easier to establish that the qualifying relative would suffer extreme hardship due to relocating to the applicant's country. Decisions often cited the

---

[31] AAO Decision, Ciudad Juarez, Mexico, Mar. 6, 2012. The AAO found that the applicant established extreme hardship.
[32] USCIS Policy Manual, Vol. 9, Part B, Ch. 4.
[33] *Id.*
[34] *Id.*

qualifying relative's lack of foreign language skills, unfamiliarity with the foreign country, inability to find comparable employment, the stress in relocating to a different culture, and any health-related factors that would be exacerbated by such a move. In most cases, it will be more difficult to establish that the qualifying relative would suffer extreme hardship due to separation from the waiver applicant. The final guidance may encourage applicants to show why it is reasonably foreseeable that the qualifying relative would accompany them to the foreign country in order to maintain family unity and why such a move would result in extreme hardship.

In the Aggregate

The final guidance reminds adjudicators that the hardship factors must be considered in the aggregate and that no single hardship, taken in isolation, needs to rise to the level of extreme. This principle is already set forth in administrative appeal decisions and is codified in the SOP. But accentuating it in the guidance may encourage applicants to set forth all the possible hardship factors if, taken together, they add up to extreme hardship.[35]

While the applicant needs to demonstrate extreme hardship only to one qualifying relative, two qualifying relatives–for example, a spouse and a parent–may be present in some cases. The applicant can combine the hardships that both qualifying relatives might experience. This may be helpful if neither qualifying relative alone would be able to establish extreme hardship, but if taken together, the aggregate of their hardships would meet that standard. For example, the qualifying relatives may each experience the common results of separation or relocation that when taken alone do not rise to the level of extreme hardship, but the combination of those hardships, or their cumulative impact, may meet the necessary standard.

The BIA has consistently stressed that hardship factors must be considered cumulatively: "Relevant factors, though not extreme in themselves, must be considered in the aggregate in determining whether extreme hardship exists."[36] Although one particular hardship factor may not be extreme on its own, the hardship faced by the qualifying relative may become extreme in combination with other factors. A legacy INS General Counsel memorandum on extreme hardship in the battered spouse context notes that "[f]actors which may not alone be determinative should be considered, and may become a significant or even critical factor when weighed with all the other circumstances presented."[37] An applicant's inability to reside in the United States may have a ripple effect that causes hardship in many aspects of the qualifying relatives' lives. The range of consequences, both small and large, must be evaluated in their totality in an extreme hardship evaluation.[38] In the cover letter accompanying the waiver application and supporting documents, advocates should therefore craft a strong argument explaining how the various factors fit together and amplify each other. In Chapter 5, we discuss how to create a central "theory of the case" that ties all the hardship factors together.

Example: Priya, a citizen of India, came to the United States in 2009, flying first from India to Mexico and then entering the United States without inspection. In 2010, she married U.S. citizen George, who owns a modest restaurant that the couple operates together. George has diabetes and depends on Priya to run the restaurant whenever he is not feeling well. Priya is from a small village in the Punjab where her family still resides. Her family pooled their money to enable her to come to the United States after she was abused by a wealthy landowner in her village. George is anxious and depressed about Priya's history of abuse and the possibility that she will have to return to India. He is currently taking medication to deal with insomnia. He has lived his whole life in Winesburg, Ohio, where his parents and siblings also reside. The couple has a one-year-old daughter, Ritu. Priya is eligible to file for the provisional waiver for unlawful presence.

---

[35] *Id.*

[36] *Matter of Ige*, 20 I&N Dec. 880 (BIA 1994).

[37] INS General Counsel's Office, Memorandum from Paul W. Virtue, "'Extreme Hardship' and Documentary Requirements Involving Battered Spouse and Children" (Aug. 16, 1998).

[38] *Matter of O-J-O-*, 21 I&N Dec. 381 (BIA 1996) at 383, quoting *Matter of Ige*, 20 I&N Dec. at 882. ("The adjudicator must consider the entire range of factors concerning hardship in their totality and determine whether the combination of hardships takes the case beyond those hardships ordinarily associated with deportation.")

Priya can employ all of the five factors to support her hardship claim. The potential extreme hardship to her husband as a result of her absence would touch on all of the following: his health and psychological state, the financial difficulties that would result, the loss of economic opportunities for Ritu, George's family ties in the United States and the other personal factors, and the social conditions in India that forced Priya to leave. While none of these factors may be compelling in isolation, taken together they are likely to constitute extreme hardship. Note that in order to make a compelling argument for extreme hardship, they would need to carefully document each of these factors, as well as articulate a strong "theory of the case" that would tie their story together.

"Ordinary" Hardship Insufficient

The final guidance underscores that extreme hardship means "more than the usual level of hardship that commonly results from family separation or relocation."[39] Case law has stated repeatedly that extreme hardship means something more than the "ordinary hardship" one would suffer in being separated from family members or from a country and lifestyle to which one has become accustomed.[40] These common hardships include the difference in standards of living between the United States and Mexico or other Latin American countries. They also include economic hardship,[41] difficulty in finding employment, and inability to find employment in a chosen trade or profession.[42] Difficulty in readjusting to life in one's home country after residing in the United States will not, in and of itself, be found to constitute extreme hardship,[43] nor will reduced educational opportunities and medical facilities in the home country.[44] Another common consequence of relocation includes inferior quality of medical services and facilities abroad. While none of these "common" results taken alone would be enough to satisfy the extreme hardship standard, their combination may be enough.[45]

Hardship to a Non-Qualifying Relative

Children cannot be qualifying relatives for unlawful presence, nor can hardship to the waiver applicant be considered. Nevertheless, "the hardship experienced by non-qualifying relatives can be considered as part of the extreme hardship determination, but only to the extent that such hardship affects one or more qualifying relatives."[46] For this reason, the guidance encourages applicants to describe the emotional or other hardship that the qualifying relative parent would experience due to the suffering of a child who must either relocate to a foreign country or remain separated from the applicant. This "derivative hardship" is one of the factors that adjudicators must consider in weighing the totality of the circumstances.

The Five Factors

The guidance points out that any factor that the applicant presents should be considered. It then sets forth the five most common factors and their impact: family ties, social and cultural issues, economic issues, health conditions and care, and country conditions.[47] It then spells out examples of what hardships might fall within each of the five categories. For example, social and cultural impact could be evidenced by loss of access to U.S. courts, the criminal justice system, and the protection of family law proceedings (protection orders, child support, or visitation). It could also be demonstrated by fear of persecution or social ostracism and lack of access to social institutions and support networks. Other examples include the more obvious: lack of language

---

[39] *Id.* at Ch. 2.

[40] *Matter of Pilch*, 21 I&N Dec. 627, 631 (BIA 1996).

[41] *Palmer v. INS*, 4 F.3d 482, 488 (7th Cir. 1993).

[42] *Hernandez-Patino v. INS*, 831 F.2d 750, 754 (7th Cir. 1987) (Petitioner "claims he would not be able to secure steady employment other than subsistence-level seasonal sharecropping.").

[43] *Matter of Ige,* 20 I&N Dec. 880 at 883 (BIA 1994).

[44] *Matter of Kim*, 15 I&N Dec. 88, 90 (BIA 1974) (Diminished educational opportunities and medical facilities without other strong hardship factors did not tip the scales toward a finding of extreme hardship.).

[45] *Id.* at Ch. 5.

[46] *Id.* at Ch. 4.

[47] *Id.* at Ch. 5.

skills, quality of educational opportunities, assimilation into U.S. culture, and community ties in the United States versus in the foreign country. The country conditions category could include the designation of Temporary Protected Status (TPS), civil unrest or generalized level of crime and violence, and State Department travel warnings or alerts. These will be analyzed and illustrated below.

No Presumption but "Likely to Support" Finding of Extreme Hardship

The final guidance also identifies five factors that "often weigh heavily in support of a finding of extreme hardship."[48] While the existence at the time of adjudication of one or more of these "particularly significant factors" would not create a presumption of extreme hardship, they are "often likely to support findings" of it. The five particularly significant factors are:

1. Qualifying relative was granted Iraqi or Afghan Special Immigrant Status, T nonimmigrant status, or asylee or refugee status from the waiver applicant's country of relocation. This is not likely to occur in many waiver cases, but if it does, it would "often weigh heavily," regardless of whether the qualifying relative is alleging separation or relocation hardship. This would also be true if the qualifying relative had been granted withholding of removal or deferral of removal under the Convention Against Torture.

2. The qualifying relative is on active duty with any branch of the U.S. Armed Forces. These are defined as the Army, Navy, Air Force, Marine Corps, the Coast Guard, and the Selected Reserve of the Ready Reserve. The premise here is that being in the Armed Forces already includes "stresses, anxieties, and other hardships" that would be exacerbated by the psychological and emotional harm caused by separation from the applicant.

3. Either the qualifying relative or a member of the household who is dependent on the qualifying relative's care is disabled or suffers from a medical/physical condition that makes travel to or residence in the foreign country detrimental to his or her health or safety. The applicant may submit a formal finding of disability by a government agency or, if none has been made, other evidence that the family member suffers from a medical condition. The hardship to the qualifying relative could be due to either separation or relocation. If it is due to relocation, it could be in situations in which the disabled person is the qualifying relative or is a family member who will accompany the qualifying relative. In that situation, the applicant should submit evidence that "the services available to the disabled individual in the country of relocation are unavailable or significantly inferior to those available to him or her in the United States." If it is due to separation, the applicant will need to submit evidence that the qualifying family member or the household member requires the applicant's assistance for care due to the disability.

4. The Department of State has issued either a country-wide travel warning or one for a region of the country where the applicant or the qualifying relative would likely relocate. Travel warnings vary in severity from urging against travel because of safety concerns to advising U.S. citizens currently in the country to depart. If the travel warning is for only a part of the country, the applicant will need to establish that the qualifying relative would relocate to that part. If the qualifying relative has elected to remain in the United States, the separation may result in extreme hardship due to the increased danger to the applicant in the relevant country or region. At the present time, the Department of State has issued travel warnings for all or parts of Honduras, Nicaragua, El Salvador, and Guatemala. It has also issued various warnings for many of the 32 states in Mexico. In addition, Nicaragua, Honduras, and El Salvador have been designated for TPS. To access current travel warnings, click on: *https://travel.state.gov/content/travel/en/traveladvisories/travel advisories.html/*.

5. Separation would result in the qualifying relative becoming the primary caretaker--and possibly income-earner–for the couple's children or otherwise taking on significant parental or other caregiving responsibilities. This factor would apply in situations in which the separation would result in a substantial shift in caregiving responsibilities from the applicant to the qualifying relative. It assumes that the qualifying relative is responsible for the welfare of a child. The applicant will need to establish a bona fide relationship between the child and either the applicant or the qualifying relative. For purposes of this hardship factor, the immigration status of dependent children is irrelevant–they may be U.S. citizens, LPRs, or undocumented. This factor would not be relevant in situations in which the qualifying relative and applicant will relocate and remain together.

---

[48] *Id.*

Employing the Five Factors

With the final extreme hardship guidance, USCIS has reworded and slightly modified the five factors that it has been using for more than a decade to guide adjudications of waiver applications. The factors are now labeled: (1) family ties and impact; (2) social and cultural impact; (3) economic impact; (4) health conditions and care; (5) and country conditions.[49] We will describe and illustrate these in greater detail.

Family Ties and Impact

The focus here is on the relationship between the qualifying relative and the applicant, as well as the qualifying relative and family members here in the United States. The agency typically looks to issues such as the following: how long the couple has known each other, how long they have been married, how many family members the qualifying relative has in the United States and their citizenship and immigration status, how many family members the qualifying relative has in the foreign country where the couple would relocate, and existence of children or elderly parents who rely on the care provided by the qualifying relative.

Make sure you describe how long the couple has known each other and how long they have been married. Include in the declarations examples illustrating the strength of their bond and their daily interactions. This is particularly important if the couple indicates they will separate. But it is also critical in explaining and supporting their decision to relocate and remain together.

Similarly, indicate where the qualifying relative's extended family members reside and how often they interact with the qualifying relative. If the qualifying relative is providing care for elderly parents, explain why other siblings are not able to provide this level of care.

If the qualifying relative is from the same country as the applicant, explain why relocation would still create difficulties. Compare how long the qualifying relative has lived in the United States versus in his or her home country. If the qualifying relative is an LPR, point out that residence abroad will likely cause abandonment of permanent resident status. If the qualifying relative is a naturalized U.S. citizen, explain how he or she has made the formal commitment and sworn allegiance to this country. Some LPRs must give up citizenship in their home country when they naturalize.

Adjustment–either to separation or relocation–is theoretically harder as one gets older. If the qualifying relative is middle-aged or older, point this out.

Be creative, since the list is by no means exhaustive. In documenting these hardship factors, you will be relying on statements in the declarations of the applicant and qualifying relative, in addition to declarations from other family members, friends, neighbors, employers, teachers, and church or civic leaders.

Example: "The applicant's spouse is the custodian for her grandson due to the mental health condition of her own daughter, and based on this, the applicant's spouse would experience extreme hardship upon relocation and separation. Counsel asserts that, upon relocation, the applicant's spouse would experience hardships due to her age, and that relocation would be additionally burdensome because she is the custodian for her grandchild. He explains that the applicant's spouse would have to give up her career in the United States and would be separated from her other daughters and grandchildren."[50]

Example: "The qualifying spouse has lived in the United States her entire life and has close family ties to the United States, including her parents, siblings, and friends. The record contains several letters indicating the closeness of the qualifying spouse's relationships with her friends and family and the importance of her relationships, in light of the mental and medical issues that she suffers."[51]

In both cases, the AAO considered the existence of strong family ties and relationships to be an integral part of the overall extreme hardship narrative. In neither case was this the only hardship factor, but in both instances, it served to amplify significant medical hardship, both physical and psychological, to the qualifying relative. The applicants in both cases provided strong supporting documentation, including letters from family

---

[49] *Id.* at Ch. 5.

[50] AAO Decision, Bloomington, MN, p. 4, Mar. 26, 2012. The AAO found that the applicant established extreme hardship.

[51] AAO Decision, Denver, CO, p. 5, Oct. 25, 2011. The AAO found that the applicant had established extreme hardship.

members, medical records and doctors' letters, and in the case of the grandmother who had custody of her grandchild, court records awarding custody; any asserted hardship factors must be documented.

Social and Cultural Impact

The final guidance lists several examples of hardship to the qualifying relative due to relocation: the community ties developed here in comparison to those in the foreign country; any inability to speak the foreign language, which would impair developing friends and associates; and loss of educational opportunities. Be sure to indicate the qualifying relative's involvement in the community, such as church, school, or sports clubs.

The guidance also emphasizes U.S. laws and institutions that protect workers' rights, defend against domestic violence, allow for victim's compensation, support criminal investigation and prosecution, and ensure the enforcement of orders regarding child custody, maintenance, and visitation. Compare these protections against those in the foreign country, if there is a disparity.

Relocation may also cause the qualifying relative to be socially ostracized due to a culture clash: the religion or western values practiced in the United States versus those in the foreign country. It could also result in the qualifying relative fearing possible persecution or societal discrimination.

Laws and institutions in the United States also protect against discrimination based on gender, sexual orientation, religion, race, national origin, and disability. Compare these protections against those in the foreign country, if there is a disparity.

In every case that includes children, there are likely to be educational hardships. Most of these anticipated hardships will be due to the child's relocating to the foreign country. Typical hardships could include the child's lack of foreign language ability, loss of grade, poorer quality of education in the foreign country, lack of access to tutors, lack of access to special education, or loss of potential internship or externship programs. But educational hardship could also result if the child is going to remain in the United States. These could include the inability to afford private school, after-school educational counseling for special needs, or tutors.

The educational hardships may also be experienced by adults who are in college or training programs, are working on advanced degrees, or were planning to take advantage of internship programs.

Remember to funnel the anticipated hardship to the child through the qualifying relative. The loss of educational opportunities to U.S. citizen children of the qualifying relative often results in financial, emotional, and psychological hardship to the qualifying relative. Have the qualifying relative explain how he or she would suffer watching her child be disadvantaged due to receiving a poorer quality education.

Economic Impact

Every waiver case will involve some negative economic impact, both in relocation and separation cases. These could include the following: anticipated loss of job by the applicant or the qualifying relative, or both; unemployment or reemployment at a reduced salary; termination of a professional practice; sale of business, house, or other property; loss of health insurance coverage; increased costs due to relocation; travel costs by the qualifying relative to visit the applicant; additional child care costs resulting from loss of the applicant; additional education-related costs in the foreign country, including special education or training; and additional costs in providing care to elderly, sick, or disabled parents. The possible financial factors will depend on the particular facts in your client's case, but make sure you explore and identify all of them.[52]

It is important to understand how to document and present financial considerations. Be detailed and include a budget showing current revenue and expenses. Don't just submit bills; itemize all major financial costs and forms of income. Then, explain and demonstrate how the family would be unable to meet expenses or would suffer financially due to the applicant's absence or the qualifying relative's relocation. This will be covered further in Chapter 6.

---

[52] For a practice advisory on this issue, see "Tips for Arguing Financial Hardship in I-601A Waiver Cases," AILA Doc. No. 14122342.

The BIA has favored applicants who have not amassed savings or who do not have substantial equity in a house or other property they will be selling. Credit card or other debt is viewed as a positive factor. Qualifying relatives who have had to rely on public assistance or church hand-outs after the applicant has departed have been viewed sympathetically. With provisional waiver applications, speculate how the qualifying relative would be able to care for himself or herself without the applicant's financial support, and indicate the potential need and eligibility for food stamps, Temporary Assistance for Needy Families, or other federal or state needs-based assistance programs.

Example: In an unlawful presence waiver in Mexico that was sustained by the AAO, the applicant submitted car titles, bank statements, pay stubs, an employment letter for the applicant, property records, and insurance documentation. In this case, the applicant's spouse asserted that she was suffering anxiety over financial issues following her husband's departure from the United States. The application included a psychological evaluation that discussed these anxieties and how they connected to her diagnosis of major depression, anxiety, and post-traumatic stress disorder. Note that in this case, not only were financial hardships clearly delineated and documented, but financial hardships were also clearly connected to another set of hardship factors—psychological factors. Strong waiver applications draw connections between the various hardship factors.

Health Conditions and Care

Many of the strongest waiver applications include health-related factors, so start with an examination as to whether there are any medical problems in your client's family. These could include serious medical conditions, physical or mental disabilities, psychological abnormalities, or relatively minor and treatable conditions. They could be suffered by the qualifying relative or the child, parent, or other family member, as long as you can demonstrate that the health condition causes or will cause hardship to the qualifying relative. The qualifying relative needs to indicate how he or she would suffer if the child/parent/sibling in turn would suffer because of the waiver applicant's absence, as well as the lack of treatment options or adequate medical care in the applicant's home country should the family elect to relocate.

Common health-related conditions include heart disease, strokes, cancer, diabetes, high blood pressure, lack of mobility, allergies, asthma, and physical disabilities. Chronic health-related afflictions generally pose stronger hardships than acute ones, which flare up and then subside. In the same way, long-term conditions are often stronger than short-term. Common mental or psychological conditions include Alzheimer's and other forms of senility, depression, anxiety, schizophrenia, and bipolar disorder. Ask your client for a description of all illnesses or health-related problems in the family, no matter how minor. It may take some investigation and follow-up questioning to uncover them.[53]

It is also very important to describe how the applicant's anticipated absence or the qualifying relative's relocation will make the health-related problem worse. For example, it is not enough to state that the qualifying relative suffers from a heart condition; explain how the applicant's departure and extended absence or the qualifying relative's relocation will aggravate the problem. Include documentation about the availability of treatment facilities and affordable medication in the foreign country where the family member would reside. This will be covered in greater detail in Chapter 6.

Example: "The applicant's older daughter's physician states that [the older daughter] was diagnosed with eczema and asthma and she requires bronchodilators and preventative medication. He states that she was hospitalized. The applicant's older daughter's physician states that a prolonged separation from her father could make her vulnerable to more frequent and severe asthma exacerbations. The record includes a psychological evaluation of the applicant's spouse, which reflects that she is suffering from Major Depressive Disorder with accompanying features of Anxiety. Several family and friends of the applicant's spouse have detailed the emotional difficulty that she is experiencing."[54]

---

[53] For a helpful article on this issue, see "Practice Pointer: Health Related Hardship Grounds and the Use of Experts in the I-601A Provisional Waiver Process," AILA Doc. No.15043060.

[54] AAO Decision, Ciudad Juarez, p. 5, Mar. 28, 2012. The AAO found that the applicant established extreme hardship.

Example: "The AAO finds the psychological report demonstrates the applicant's spouse has inadequate coping skills and stressful situations negatively contribute to mental and emotional well-being. The record allows us to find that her separation from the applicant has pushed her into a mental state in which she cannot function well and care for her children."[55]

In both AAO decisions above, the psychological well-being of the qualifying relative is considered a significant factor, in combination with other health-related factors. The waiver applications in both cases contained psychological evaluations that identified the mental condition. The first example also included a doctor's letter verifying ongoing treatment for eczema and asthma that required bronchodilators and preventative medication and stated that separation from the waiver applicant could result in additional and more severe asthma episodes.

Psychological reports can play an important role in establishing and verifying anticipated hardship, especially where the subject of the report has an ongoing treatment relationship with the therapist. Most U.S. citizen spouses will experience anxiety and depression, or both, when faced with the real possibility of their partner leaving the country for an extended period of time. The challenge is to show how this reaction is different or more severe than that experienced by others. Do not overlook the psychological impact on the qualifying relative due to suffering–economic, social, physical, psychological, or other health-related hardship–by the applicant.

While we do not want to discourage you from using psychological reports, we do want to point out that a report based on a single visit of an hour or less may not carry much weight with the adjudicator. The strongest reports and applications indicate a history of psychological problems or treatment so that the applicant's absence would aggravate a preexisting condition.

Country Conditions

Country conditions in the applicant's home country could include political, financial, cultural, religious, and even environmental factors. The final guidance on extreme hardship suggests including evidence of civil unrest or generalized levels of violence, designation of TPS, withdrawal of Peace Corps from the country for security reasons, and issuance of State Department travel warnings. Investigate how strong the central government is: Can the police or security forces protect the safety of its citizens? Would religious customs and requirements make it difficult for someone from another faith to be accepted? Has a recent environmental disaster made life there a challenge?

Gang- and drug-related violence is rampant in parts of Mexico and in certain Central American countries. Unlike in asylum cases, where the applicant must show a well-founded fear of persecution throughout the country, the waiver applicant has the choice of where he or she will reside. It is the conditions in that specific locale that are important. Applications that indicate high levels of violence, mortality, or lawlessness in the particular city or state where the applicant intends to reside have resulted in favorable decisions. As described in Chapter 6, it is more effective to submit articles, reports, or declarations detailing the violence in the region or town where the applicant lives or intends to live, rather than general country condition reports.

Example: In a Honduran case that succeeded at the AAO, the qualifying relative (the applicant's U.S. citizen mother) detailed the problems she would face in relocating to Honduras. When she visited Honduras in the past, she became ill with parasites caused by unsanitary conditions. She would be separated from family in the United States, her Spanish is not sufficiently good for her to work in Honduras, and she fears crime and gang violence in Honduras. The fact that Honduras has been designated for TPS contributed significantly to the AAO's finding that relocating would cause extreme hardship to the applicant's U.S. citizen mother.[56]

---

[55] AAO Decision, Mexico City, p. 5, Mar. 26, 2012. The AAO found that the applicant established extreme hardship.

[56] AAO Decision, Tegucigalpa, Honduras, p. 6, Sept. 1, 2011. The AAO found that the applicant had established extreme hardship.

Think creatively about how to give the adjudicator a strong sense of the hardships your clients would face. In an appeal of a decision from Ciudad Juarez, the AAO noted approvingly that the applicant had submitted photographs of the poor conditions in which her spouse was residing in Mexico, saying that the photos "lend credence to his spouse's suspicion that she could become a target of crime if she resided there with the applicant based on her possession of a car and perceptions of her as an American with a job in the United States."[57]

When you do include documentation of country conditions, try to focus it as closely as possible on the region in which the qualifying relative would actually live. In a decision in which the AAO denied an appeal, the AAO found that "although ... Pakistan is not a western country and ... its primary religion is Islam, general materials on national human rights statistics are not enough to demonstrate that a qualifying relative will experience discrimination or be a victim of religious crime simply because they do not adhere to Islam."[58]

Discretionary Factors

Do not forget to address discretionary factors in your client's case; these are often unrelated to the extreme hardship factors. Every AAO decision discusses whether the applicant has met this burden, assuming he or she has established extreme hardship. They can often tip the balance in either direction: strong cases can lose if negative discretionary factors are not addressed, and borderline cases can turn into approvable ones by stressing the positive factors.

We have compiled a list of the positive and negative factors that emerge from a reading of numerous AAO decisions. Documenting these will be addressed in further detail in Chapter 6.

Positive factors include the following, some of which may have already been brought out in demonstrating extreme hardship:

- U.S. citizen children;
- Aging parents that depend on the care of the qualifying relative or applicant;
- Immigration history;
- Community involvement;
- Volunteer activities;
- Payment of taxes;
- Steady employment history;
- Entry into the United States as a young child;
- No prior marriages and divorces; and
- Other evidence of good moral character.[59]

Negative discretionary factors include the following:

- Criminal convictions or activity;
- Prior marriage to a U.S. citizen or LPR that may or may not have led to the filing of an I-130 petition;
- Multiple illegal entries;
- Prior arrests by the Department of Homeland Security resulting in grants of voluntary departure;
- Evidence of failure to pay child support; and
- Evidence of domestic violence.

---

[57] AAO Decision, Mexico City, Mexico, p. 6, Jan. 3, 2011.

[58] AAO Decision, New Delhi, India, p. 5, June 29, 2011. Almost all AAO decisions state this two-fold requirement.

[59] *See Matter of Mendez-Moralez*, 21 I&N Dec. 296, 301 (BIA 1996).

Conclusion

A review of administrative decisions demonstrates that even strong waiver cases can be denied, both by USCIS and the AAO. Similarly, those that are relatively weak can be approved if they are well documented. As many practitioners can attest, inconsistent adjudications of hardship exist at all levels. However, the first step in preparing a winning waiver application requires an understanding of and familiarity with how extreme hardship has been defined and interpreted by the agency. Follow the guidelines and tips we have set forth, but do not predict the outcome to your client or raise expectations, since this is an imperfect science.

That same review also reveals that what often tips the scales from "ordinary" to "extreme" hardship is a thorough and specific examination of a particular family's circumstances, coupled with careful documentation of all the hardship factors asserted in each case. Each family's circumstances are unique, and the more that an advocate can paint a picture of a specific family and what prolonged separation will mean for this individual family, supporting that portrait with documentation, the stronger the hardship argument will be.

An AAO decision from 2012, in which the AAO sustained the appeal, notes that some of the most important hardship factors included the fact that the applicant's wife, his qualifying relative, was suffering major depressive disorder, but also that she was "further burdened by [their] children's sadness and aggressive behavior, which she attributes to the absence of their father [and] her inability to spend more time with them due to her work schedule. ... Evidence in the record establishes that in spite of her full-time work, the applicant's wife has relied on emergency food assistance every three months to feed her family since her husband left the country."[60] A wife's feeling depressed, children being sad and aggressive, a wife's having to rely on public assistance to feed her children—none of these is a startling or unusual outcome when a spouse is removed from a family. But in this case, the applicants (who represented themselves) were able to clearly articulate and document all of these painful, but not out-of-the-ordinary, results of family separation.

---

[60] AAO Decision, Ciudad Juarez, Mexico, Mar. 9, 2012, p. 6.

CHAPTER 5
WORKING WITH THE CLIENT

In the previous chapters, we discussed eligibility for provisional waivers, unlawful presence and other grounds of inadmissibility, and the extreme hardship standard. With an understanding of the legal principles that govern provisional waivers, you now have the tools to work with your client to gather the information you will need to meet the requirements for the provisional waiver process. This chapter will discuss best practices for working with your clients to elicit information, screen for eligibility, develop the theory of the case, and prepare their statements or declarations.

Developing the Facts of the Case

The first step in obtaining the information you will need for the waiver application is a well-structured interview with your client. The information from the interview will enable you to determine if your client has a viable hardship claim, is inadmissible on grounds other than unlawful presence, and has enough positive discretionary factors. A good client interview with follow-up questionnaires and conversations will point you toward problem areas and sources of documentation. A sample intake form for use in immigration cases is included as Appendix 3.

The second step in acquiring information necessary for the waiver involves double-checking that your client is inadmissible only for unlawful presence. It is crucial that you identify any other inadmissibility issues before your client leaves the United States for consular processing. Carefully screen your client regarding past arrests, charges, and criminal convictions, as well as any immigration violations.

The third step is using the information you obtained through interviews and record checks to develop a theory of the case, prepare effective declarations, and identify supporting documentation. The declarations by the applicant and the qualifying relative(s) should be the heart of the case. In this chapter, we will discuss how to prepare effective declarations. Supporting documentation is discussed in the following chapter.

Interviewing the Client

There is no one-size-fits-all approach for interviewing clients, and practitioners use a range of options. No matter which approach you use, it is critical that you build trust with your client to ensure that your client reveals his or her full story.

Building Trust with Your Client

It is impossible to obtain the information you need for a successful waiver application without establishing a rapport with your client and securing his or her trust. You will need to ask your client extensive and often deeply private questions about his or her life. You will also need your client to be willing to answer honestly and speak freely. Without understanding every aspect of your client's current situation, background, and activities—both good and bad—it will be very difficult to construct a winning case. Your client has to feel comfortable disclosing past traumas, hopes, and fears. This is the type of information that makes your client's story come alive and allows you to pull together the evidence that will persuade the adjudicator that your client has established extreme hardship. The following are suggestions of ways to create a trusting relationship with your client.

Explain Confidentiality

You will be more likely to obtain essential information if you advise your client that all information he or she discloses to you will remain confidential. Knowing that you will not share your client's private information with others outside your legal team without your client's knowledge and consent will encourage him or her to relate all information, whether embarrassing or discomforting. Explain your commitment to confidentiality during the first intake meeting with potential clients. Some practitioners incorporate information about confidentiality into their retainer or client agreement.

Private space for client interviews is vital to confidentiality and to building and maintaining client trust. Waiver cases are very fact-intensive and fact-specific, and often involve questions about intimate details of your clients' lives. When interviewing clients about waiver cases, it is essential that you use a private meeting space, where you will not be interrupted or overheard during the interview.

Explain the Process

Give your client an overview of the waiver application process and acknowledge your client's expectations. Your client may have unrealistic expectations, but it is important to recognize them and describe the procedure. Explain the waiver process, including processing times, the legal requirements for provisional waiver eligibility, and the risks and benefits of submitting an application. Well-informed clients will be more trusting and better able to fully participate in the waiver process.

Describe What You Are Looking for

Let the client know what you are looking for before your client describes his or her hardship claim. Clients may be hesitant to admit to challenging situations and you will need to let them know this is exactly the type of information you need. Remind the client that proving extreme hardship involves describing difficult circumstances—the "bad" things in their life may actually make their case stronger.

Make sure the client understands how important it is not to conceal any information out of embarrassment. Clients need to know that you cannot provide adequate representation if you do not have all the facts. The information of which clients are most ashamed may well be the most helpful to their hardship case. You must be willing to ask very personal questions and address your client's hesitancy in answering them.

Example: Claudia is reluctant to admit to her representative that her eldest son, a U.S. citizen, is serving time in prison. After much prodding, Claudia finally indicates that her son cannot provide a declaration because he is incarcerated at a facility five hours away and is allowed visitation only once per month. Claudia's representative can use this information as evidence of why Claudia would suffer hardship were she to accompany her husband, the waiver applicant, to Mexico. The high cost of travel would prevent Claudia from visiting her son if she left the United States.

Probe all facets of the five extreme hardship factors with your clients. In some cases, it will be clear what the hardships are, but in other cases, you will need to delve into your client's lives to fully understand the impact on the qualifying relative. Remember to consider the consequences if the qualifying relative remains in the United States without the applicant and if the qualifying relative accompanies the applicant abroad.

Ask your client about factors that will help merit a favorable exercise of discretion. For example, does your client perform volunteer work, help with activities in his or her church, make monetary contributions, or pay taxes?

Ask questions about other grounds of inadmissibility. How many times has your client entered and left the United States? Has your client ever had any contact with the Immigration Service or border officials? Has your client ever been in proceedings before an immigration judge? Has your client made a misrepresentation to the consulate in an effort to obtain a tourist visa or border crossing card? Has your client ever been arrested, detained, or convicted of a criminal offense? Has your client ever used illegal drugs? Did your client ever enter the United States illegally with another family member or a friend, and in the process provide assistance?

Make the questions related to crimes understandable to your client. Rather than using legal terms such as "arrest" or "conviction," ask the client questions such as the following: Have you ever been stopped by the police? Ever been in the back of a police car? Ever had fingerprints taken? Ever been handcuffed? You will get more useful information about your client's experiences with the criminal justice system if you phrase the questions in this manner.

Listen Carefully to Your Client's Story and Ask Questions

Listen carefully to your client in order to get a clear picture of the case. Good listening skills include maintaining eye contact with your client, encouraging your client to continue speaking by nodding, being alert for nonverbal cues, and repeating back what was said.

Asking appropriate questions is another essential element of the interview process. Some practitioners do this by asking broad questions, such as: "Tell me about your situation." Other practitioners begin with specific questions to help focus the categories of the client's hardship factors. For example: "Tell me the names of every family member, including your extended family, who lives in the United States, and describe your relationship with that family member." Practitioners also vary the type of questions they ask based on the client's level of sophistication, whether the elements of the client's hardship are less obvious, and whether the client is reticent.

One interviewing technique that can help uncover hardship factors is asking your client to describe a typical day, or a typical week, in his or her household. Even the most mundane details can contribute to an extreme hardship argument. Figuring out individual components of your client's life can uncover the ways in which the applicant is essential to the life of the qualifying relative, or vice versa.

Some of the questions that prompt an examination of your client's life, particularly if they have children, include the following:

- If there are children in the household, who feeds them and gets them ready for school?
- Who brings them to school, or cares for them if they are sick or are too young for school?
- How and when do the children get home from school, and who cares for them?
- Who prepares the children's meals and supervises their homework?
- If any family member has a medical condition requiring regular treatment, how and when does that take place? Who helps out with it?
- Which family members are working, and what are their hours?

Questions like these can help to paint a picture of what role the waiver applicant plays in the household unit and how important that role is. They can also help you to uncover hardship factors that your clients may not have recognized or considered.

Retain the Information

It is critical to keep track of all of the client's information. Some practitioners use intake sheets to record client information and notes from interviews. Some practitioners request that clients complete a questionnaire with detailed questions related to hardship and grounds of inadmissibility. Other practitioners use checklists to record information. Some use a list of the five hardship factors identified in the provisional waiver instructions and note the factors relevant to the client as the client answers questions during the interview. Appendix 4 is a guide for practitioners when questioning the client on possible extreme hardship factors. Appendix 5 is a series of questions, in English and Spanish, designed for the client to take home and consider.

Review your notes after the interview has ended to determine the strongest hardship claim and where gaps in the case may pose problems. Determine where you need more information and whether to obtain statements from your client's extended family, friends, employer, or neighbors. Consider whether your client has disclosed possible grounds of inadmissibility and seek additional information to confirm that your client is inadmissible only for unlawful presence.

Team Review of Case

If you have colleagues and co-workers, review the case notes with them to help spot issues and look for gaps in the evidence. Through discussion with your colleagues, you may identify weaknesses in the case and determine additional forms of documentation. If your colleagues identify a line of questioning you have not considered, you can follow up with your client to pursue those issues.

Interviews—How Much Is Enough?

Practitioners use a variety of interview practices to obtain the information they need to prepare a waiver application. Some practitioners schedule the first in-person meeting to be a one-hour interview and then use questionnaires, telephone calls, and a longer follow-up meeting. Some practitioners schedule back-to-back client interviews throughout the day and do not plan for long three– or four-hour appointments with one client. Some practitioners build in multiple meetings with clients. Others report that they do not settle on the key hardship factors until they have met with the clients more than once. This is particularly true if the client has been in an abusive relationship.

The calculus of "how many interviews" is based on the special circumstances of your own practice. You will need to elicit information from your client to understand all the elements of the extreme hardship claim. You will need to understand the hardship claim so that you can request evidence from your client, from the qualifying relative(s), from other family members, and from experts. Your understanding of the hardship claim allows you to seek the appropriate documentary evidence. Your client is the primary person who can provide this crucial information, though sometimes other family members and experts can help supply different perspectives. Whether you are able to obtain this information from a single interview in conjunction with questionnaires or from multiple interviews will depend on your office's structure, organization, and preferences.

Inadmissibility Issues

Eligibility for the provisional waiver requires that the applicant is inadmissible *solely* because of the accrual of unlawful presence. It is essential that you know whether your client may be subject to other potential grounds of inadmissibility before you begin working on the waiver case. After your interview indicates that there may be another potential ground, you should follow up by obtaining criminal history or immigration records.

Accessing Records Regarding Criminal History

FBI Record Check

If an interview indicates that your client has had contact with police or other law enforcement, it is important to know the exact nature of that interaction. The criminal justice system is complex and can be confusing. Your client may not understand whether he was arrested or stopped, charged, or convicted. In those cases, it is crucial that you obtain an FBI record check or a state criminal record check.

If your client has lived in many different locations or is unsure of where—or even if—he or she was arrested, or if it is difficult to obtain information from the local police department or courts, you can request an FBI record check. The FBI "rap sheet" may identify where and when arrests, charges, and convictions occurred, indicating where you should look to obtain complete police or court records. FBI criminal record checks will frequently—but not always—reveal any order of removal. If your client indicates any uncertainty about the type of interaction he or she has had with the criminal justice system, it is a good idea to request a FBI record.

You can request an FBI criminal record check by completing the form available on the FBI website,[1] including a hard copy (not electronic) fingerprint form FD-258, and enclosing a money order or cashier's check in the amount of $18. Review the FBI record request instructions and checklist to ensure that you have included all of the required information.[2] Send the form, fingerprint card, and fee to:

FBI CJIS Division – Summary Request
1000 Custer Hollow Road
Clarksburg, WV 26306

The current processing time for FBI record checks is approximately 12 to 14 weeks.

State Record Check

Each state maintains its own system of criminal records checks. Some states maintain an online system, while others require that individuals must submit a form, fingerprint images, and a processing fee to the state department of justice to obtain a copy of the record. In order to determine the requirements to obtain a state record check, look online to find out the steps to complete and request a state criminal record check.

---

[1] FBI Identity History Summary Checks Review Form, https://forms.fbi.gov/identity-history-summary-checks-review/q384893984839334.pdf.

[2] FBI Identity History Summary (instructions on how to submit a request), https://www.fbi.gov/services/cjis/identity-history-summary-checks; FBI Identity History Summary Checklist, https://www.fbi.gov/file-repository/identity-history-summary-request-checklist.pdf/view.

If your client is certain of the arresting agency or the court where he or she appeared, the client can go directly to that location. Ask your client to request a certified copy of the record of conviction from the court or the arrest record from the police department. This information will allow you to evaluate whether there are any immigration consequences to the conduct or conviction and whether your client qualifies to apply for the provisional waiver.

Accessing Information Through FOIA

A Freedom of Information Act (FOIA) request provides information about immigration records—"A" files—that practitioners need to determine whether a client has been ordered removed, ordered to depart voluntarily, or arrested by U.S. Immigration and Customs Enforcement (ICE). A copy of an "A" file will also reveal whether the client previously applied for an immigration benefit. Under the FOIA statute, the government is mandated to provide a copy of the respondent's documents within 20 days of the request.[3] Unfortunately, it often takes many months to get a response to a FOIA request. However, a 1992 national class action settlement agreement states that government agencies will expedite a FOIA request if the requestor shows exceptional need or urgency, such as potential infringements on due process rights.[4] The settlement continues to govern the processing of these FOIA cases.[5]

Form to Use for a FOIA Request

If you are requesting information from U.S. Citizenship and Immigration Services (USCIS) or ICE under FOIA, it is recommended that you use Form G-639, Freedom of Information/Privacy Act Request. Although the form is not required, it is helpful to make sure you have included all the information that is necessary to process the request.

Agencies under the Department of Justice (DOJ), such as the Executive Office for Immigration Review (EOIR), do not use Form G-639. If you are requesting information from the immigration court or the Board of Immigration Appeals (BIA), you should instead make the request in writing with specific facts identifying the information you seek. The request should include the full name and "A" number of the subject of the records, their country of citizenship, and the location of the immigration proceeding. When requesting one's own records, the requestor must verify his or her identity. This can be done by submitting DOJ Form DOJ-361, Certification of Identity.[6] When requesting EOIR records on behalf of a client, you may submit either a notarized authorization signed by that individual or a sworn statement made by that individual authorizing disclosure of the records to you.

Rules regarding filing a FOIA request are subject to change. To access the most recent FOIA rules, review the relevant sub-agency website.[7]

Filing the FOIA Request

In order to know where to file a FOIA request, you must identify the information or record you require and the agency or sub-agency most likely to have that information. For example, if you are seeking a copy of a previously filed I-130 petition for a client, the USCIS FOIA unit is the best place to look. If, however, you are searching for information regarding an expedited removal order, U.S. Customs and Border Protection (CBP) is the sub-agency most likely to possess this record.

Your client's A-file could be in the possession of USCIS, ICE, or CBP. However, within that single file, there could be documents controlled by and in the possession of the different sub-agencies. Also, some

---

[3] 5 U.S. Code (USC) §552(a)(6)(A)(i).

[4] *Mayock v. Nelson,* 938 F.2d 1006 (9th Cir. 1991*); Mayock v. INS,* 714 F. Supp. 1558 (N.D. Cal. 1989).

[5] *Hajro v. USCIS,* 832 F. Supp. 2d 1095 (N.D. Cal. 2012).

[6] Form DOJ-361 is available at https://www.justice.gov/sites/default/files/oip/legacy/2014/07/23/cert_ind.pdf.

[7] FOIA information on the U.S. Citizenship and Immigration Services (USCIS) website is available at https://www.uscis.gov/about-us/freedom-information-and-privacy-act-foia/uscis-freedom-information-act-and-privacy-act.
FOIA information on the Immigration and Customs Enforcement (ICE) website is available at http://www.ice.gov/foia/request.
FOIA information on the Customs and Border Protection (CBP) website is at https://www.cbp.gov/site-policy-notices/foia#.

noncitizens do not have an A-file, but only receipt files. However, all noncitizens in removal proceedings will have an A-file. Because of the various sub-agencies that maintain A-files, it may be useful to submit FOIA requests to multiple locations. The various locations to request A-files include the following:

For almost all USCIS records, FOIA requests should be sent to:

U.S. Citizenship and Immigration Services
National Records Center FOIA/PA Office
P.O. Box 648010
Lees Summit, MO 64064-8010

Or, by overnight delivery, send to:

U.S. Citizenship and Immigration Services
National Records Center, FOIA/PA Office
150 Space Center Loop, Suite 300
Lees Summit, MO 64064-2139

Via email, requests may be sent to uscis.foia@uscis.dhs.gov. Or, via facsimile, send to National Records Center FOIA Division at fax number (816) 350-5785, and then place a copy with an original signature in the mail to the post office box address listed above.

USCIS instituted a processing-time report for FOIA requests and maintains that the processing times for Tracks 1-3 range between 31 and 112 days. Processing times are subject to change, and it can be helpful to check with other practitioners for information on processing times for various agencies. Each DHS immigration sub-agency has its own email inquiry address available on the agency's website.[8]

For ICE records, requests should be sent to the addresses below. It is best to check the websites for USCIS, ICE, and CBP prior to sending the FOIA request to ensure that the addresses have not changed.[9]

FOIA Office
U.S. Immigration and Customs Enforcement
Freedom of Information Act Office
500 12th Street, S.W., Stop 5009
Washington, D.C. 20536-5009
Fax number: (202) 732-4265

Requests may be emailed to ICE-FOIA@dhs.gov.

FOIA requests for documents controlled by CBP must be made by submitting an online FOIA request. The FOIA request to CBP can be filed by following this link and completing the online form: https://foiaonline.regulations.gov/foia/action/public/request/publicPreCreate.

For EOIR records, the FOIA request for documents is sent to:

U.S. Department of Justice
Executive Office for Immigration Review
Office of the General Counsel – FOIA Service Center
FOIA Request/Privacy Act Requests
5107 Leesburg Pike, Suite 1903
Falls Church, VA 22041
Phone: (703) 605-1297

---

[8] USCIS website on FOIA: https://www.uscis.gov/about-us/freedom-information-and-privacy-act-foia/uscis-freedom-information-act-and-privacy-act; ICE website on FOIA: http://www.ice.gov/foia/submitting_request.htm; CBP website on FOIA: http://www.cbp.gov/site-policy-notices/foia.

[9] *Id.*

Email: EOIR.FOIARequests@usdoj.gov

FOIA requests are processed on a first-come, first-served basis. It is not necessary to make a FOIA request on the G-639 form, and it may be advisable to make your request in a letter if you do not wish to respond to particular questions on the form.

Building a Strong Theory of the Case

You have interviewed your client, evaluated the interview, and confirmed that he or she is not inadmissible for a ground other than unlawful presence. To build a strong waiver case, you will need to create a "theory of the case." A theory of the case encapsulates your central argument; it is the essence of your case. A good theory should be fairly short—no more than a sentence or two—and should comprise a paragraph in a cover letter. All the evidence in your case should connect to the theory of the case.

To demonstrate extreme hardship, the theory of the case must be more specific than "this qualifying relative would suffer extreme hardship if her spouse were unable to live in the United States," or if "the qualifying relative had to live in the noncitizen's home country with her or him." That is the underlying situation for every extreme hardship waiver application. Your theory of the case needs to pinpoint and explain the nature of the hardship that this particular qualifying relative would face.

Examples of Case Theories

"Disabled Afghan war veteran Kevin Ortega would suffer greatly without his wife Serena, whose financial, physical, and emotional help is essential for his well-being."

"Diana Rodriguez, a lawful permanent resident, is a divorced mother of four U.S. citizen children, and is married to the applicant. Because her custody agreement prohibits her from taking the children outside the United States, she cannot accompany the applicant to Mexico, and will default on her mortgage if the applicant, the main breadwinner, is not admitted to the United States."

"Alejandra Munoz works hard to earn money and obtain health insurance for her family. She would not be able to care for her youngest son, Travis, who suffers from severe asthma, without the constant support of her daughter Luisa. Luisa is the primary caregiver for her three younger siblings."

"Karen Roberts was deeply traumatized by the sexual abuse she suffered as an adolescent. She depends now on the psychological and emotional support of her husband, Achill Farouk. She would suffer greatly if he had to return to Egypt, and she would face harassment and possibly persecution if she were to live there with him."

How and When to Create a Theory of the Case

Working closely with your client is essential to building a strong case theory. Using the information you obtained from your interview(s), questionnaires, and checklists, you and your client will put together an overall narrative for the case. Extreme hardship waivers will often include a range of issues and facts, but a good case theory will pull all of these together.

Preparing Effective Declarations

What Is a Declaration?

A "declaration" is a written statement by a person about matters of which he or she has personal knowledge. The person writing the declaration is called the "declarant." The declarant should begin with a statement that he or she is signing the declaration under penalty of perjury and should then sign and date the declaration.

How are declarations different from affidavits? An affidavit is also a statement written by a person with personal knowledge of the matters included in the affidavit. Affidavits are also signed under penalty of perjury, but they are signed before a notary public. The notary witnesses the signing of the affidavit, checks the ID of the affiant, and verifies the affiant's identity with a seal and a signature. In immigration matters, it is generally sufficient to submit declarations.

Whose Declaration?

Declarations from the waiver applicant and from the qualifying relative(s) who would suffer extreme hardship form the heart of a waiver case. A declaration can be a very powerful and persuasive document, laying out your client's story in detail, and making her or his voice come alive on the page. Because waivers are adjudicated based on a paper record, without an in-person interview of your client, it is especially important that the declarations you submit convey your client's unique voice and story.

The waiver applicant and the qualifying relative should both submit a detailed declaration. Remember that all of the hardship factors must be channeled through and tied to the qualifying relative. That person must establish that he or she is unable to accompany the waiver applicant to the foreign country *and* is unable to reside in the United States without the applicant's continued support.[10] Make sure the qualifying relative indicates how any current hardship will be aggravated by the absence of the applicant or by the qualifying relative's residing in the foreign country. Declarations or letters from other documented relatives, such as children or parents, can also be very useful. You will need to evaluate in each case whose declarations are necessary to the case.

In some cases, you will also want to include the declaration of an expert witness, such as a doctor or mental health professional, who can speak to any medical or psychological issues. We cover use of expert testimony at greater length in Chapter 6.

What Makes Declarations Effective

The most effective declarations convey coherent, personal stories. A declaration should convey your client's voice to the reader. Declarations are important advocacy tools, allowing your client to plead his or her case to the adjudicator by creating sympathy and a sense that this particular family is different from all other families. Details are very important and are what will make your client's case stand out.

Example: Look at these two statements and determine which one is more effective:

"My husband picks up our children after school every day. I would not be able to manage this on my own without his help."

"My husband picks up our three children after school every day. Two of the children go to a charter school almost five miles from our house, and he takes two public buses to get there. It takes him close to an hour when the buses run on time, and more time when the buses are slow. After he picks up the two younger children, he takes them by bus to our eldest daughter's school, a fifteen-minute walk away. Then they all take the city bus home. Because I work full time to support our family, there is no way that I could pick the children up. Without my husband there to pick up the children, my younger children would have to leave the special charter school they are enrolled in now."

Declarations should generally be written and organized around the theory of the case, supporting and substantiating that theory. Declarations are sometimes written chronologically, but need not be, as long as they are coherent.

Declarations should always be written in the voice of the declarant; they are the declarant's own written testimony. Avoid putting words in your client's mouth. Unless he or she is a lawyer, you will want to make sure the statement is not full of legalese. Grammar, spelling, and English mistakes are fine—in fact, they can help convey your client's own natural speech—unless they impede the reader's comprehension. If the client's English is too limited to be comprehensible, have the declaration written in his or her native tongue and translated into English. The interpreter must complete a certification indicating that he or she is fluent in English and the declarant's language, and that the declaration has been faithfully translated. The certification must be dated, and the interpreter's full name must be listed.

If the declarant cannot read or write in any language, include a statement at the end of the declaration indicating that it was dictated to him or her, that he or she has personal knowledge of the facts and statements

---

[10] For an excellent article on I-601 waivers, see L. Scott with contributions from J. Ovink, "How to Make the AAO Happy: Avoiding Mistakes When Appealing an I-601 Denial," *Immigration & Nationality Law Handbook* (AILA 2010–11 Ed.).

contained in the declaration, and that they are true and correct to the best of his or her knowledge. Identify the person who assisted with the preparation of the declaration.

Declarations do not have to be typed. In fact, hand-written declarations may be more personal and convincing. However, because adjudicators have limited time, always ensure that the writing is clearly legible.

Appendices 10A and 10B are sample declarations written by the qualifying relative. Appendix 10C is an example of a declaration written by a waiver applicant.

How to Prepare Declarations

There are a number of ways to prepare effective declarations, and you may choose different methods depending on the client and the circumstances. Some clients may be able to write their own declarations, while others may need more help and guidance from the advocate. There is no one right way. Use whatever method conveys your client's voice and supports the theory of the case.

Having your client write the declaration, or at least a first draft, can be very time-efficient, cutting down significantly on the number and length of in-person meetings. If you decide to ask your client to write a first draft, give your client specific instructions. It is a very good idea to talk beforehand about what to include in the declaration and how to describe it. Rather than giving your client a sample declaration, give him or her a list of questions or issues to address in the declaration. Questions getting at the specific elements of the hardship can often keep your client on track. This also helps to make the client's declaration more unique.

Once your client has written a first draft, review and edit it to include more pertinent details or take out irrelevant ones. You can draw a line through the information you think your client should remove and add an asterisk to a topic that she or he forgot to cover. Encourage your client to rework the declaration on his or her own time. This will promote the efficiency of the process and enhance the authenticity of the declaration.

With some clients, you may need to work on the declaration together. The easiest way to ensure that the declaration is written entirely in your client's own words is to type while your client talks, so that you are transcribing your client's exact words. This method is more laborious than having your client write a first draft, but it allows you to direct the flow of the narrative and question your client at times to elicit more details.

Some advocates draft their clients' declarations for them, using their interview notes as a guide. If you do choose this method, realize that it may lead to a declaration that is not fully in your client's own voice and therefore is not as convincing. You will also need to review it carefully with your client to make sure that it is accurate.

Whichever of these methods you use, it is essential to review the declaration over with your client to identify any errors or omissions. Reading it over will often trigger the recollection of additional facts or details that were overlooked in the first draft.

Incorporating Non-Qualifying Relatives

Children are not qualifying relatives for unlawful presence waivers, but that does not mean that they are irrelevant. You can, and often should, incorporate a statement or declaration from the child.

Children are relevant insofar as hardship to them affects or would affect the qualifying relative. For example, assume a family consists of a U.S. citizen wife, a noncitizen husband (the waiver applicant), and two minor U.S. citizen children. The applicant's departure from the United States would adversely affect the children—financially, psychologically, and academically—which would in turn cause hardship to their mother. Assume the father is the one who takes them to school and picks them up. If he is gone for 10 years, the mother will have sole responsibility for the children. Explain in her declaration the hardship that she will suffer if she is left as the sole care provider. In addition, if the children accompany their father to Mexico, they will suffer different hardships. Tie those hardships to the qualifying relative, and spell them out in her declaration.

Other non-qualifying relatives may also be vital to establishing extreme hardship to the qualifying relative. For example, assume the qualifying relative has elderly parents who require regular care and support from both the waiver applicant and the qualifying relative. They will suffer if either the applicant or the qualifying relative leaves the United States. The parents can describe the hardship they would experience in their own declarations. But, make sure that the qualifying relative also reflects this hardship in his or her own declaration. The qualifying relative might state "it would pain me to know that my parents are no longer receiving the type of care we used to provide for them."

Appendix 8 includes instructions for the client in gathering declarations from non-qualifying relatives. Appendix 9 includes letters for clients to give to doctors, employers, teachers, or other persons who will be writing a declaration.

Qualifying Relative Can't Leave and Can't Live Without Applicant

Remember that you must demonstrate hardship to the qualifying relative based on his or her inability to leave the United States and reside in the foreign country *or* on his or her inability to remain in the United States without the applicant. It is no longer necessary to prove both elements, although establishing both remains an option.[11]

Establish a Nexus Between Hardship and Absence or Residence Abroad

Describe the nexus between the applicant's residing abroad and the qualifying relative's increased suffering. A common mistake is describing and documenting a health-related hardship without linking it to the applicant's absence. Make sure you also describe the role the applicant currently plays in alleviating that hardship and the support he or she currently provides. In addition, make sure you describe and document how this health-related condition will be aggravated by the qualifying relative's living in the foreign country.

Be Consistent

No matter how your client prepares his or her declaration, you must read it for consistency. Is the declaration internally consistent? Is it consistent with the other evidence you will be presenting? If you discover inconsistencies, discuss them with the client to understand why they are there, and either correct them (if they are due to error), remove them (if they are not legally necessary to include), or explain them (if they are not due to error and are necessary to include).

Inconsistencies do not necessarily indicate that your client was untruthful, but they can undermine your client's credibility. Your client will not be able to explain them to the adjudicator during an interview, so it is necessary either to avoid or explain them at the time of submission.

---

[11] *See Matter of Calderon-Hernandez*, 25 I&N Dec. 885 (BIA 2012) (remanding for determination of hardship based only on separation after immigration judge had rejected hardship based on relocation); *Matter of Recinas*, 23 I&N Dec 467 (BIA 2002) (consideration of hardship based only on relocation); *Cerrillo-Perez v. INS*, 809 F.2d 1419 (9th Cir. 1987) (ordering consideration of extreme hardship based on separation after BIA found no hardship based on relocation). *See also* USCIS Policy Manual Vol. 9, Part B, Ch. 4.

CHAPTER 6
DOCUMENTING THE CASE

In Chapter 4, we defined extreme hardship and stressed the need to prove either that the qualifying relative is unable to live in the waiver applicant's home country or that the qualifying relative is unable to live in the United States without the waiver applicant.[1] We also discussed the importance of showing that the waiver applicant merits a favorable exercise of discretion. In Chapter 5, we discussed how to work with your client to conduct an effective interview, create the theory of the case, and prepare persuasive declarations. This chapter provides practical advice on how to identify other supporting statements; locate and use experts; and obtain reports, articles, or other documentation that will support your client's hardship claims.

Supporting documentation can be divided into two groups. One consists of personalized evidence specific to the qualifying relative's current living situation, including his or her day-to-day routine, community involvement, health concerns, employment status, and relationship with the waiver applicant and other family members. It is crucial to demonstrate that relationships and responsibilities bind the qualifying relative to the United States and to the waiver applicant. By creating this picture, the applicant is better able to demonstrate the hardship that would result if the family were ripped apart.

The second group of documentation addresses what life would be like should the qualifying relative accompany the waiver applicant to the foreign country. This documentation addresses the current financial, political, cultural, and societal factors in the part of the country where the family would reside. Safety concerns, likelihood of employment, quality of education, and availability of health care are all issues that should be emphasized. Strong documentation is key in demonstrating how conditions in the home country create extreme hardship for the qualifying relative.

This chapter focuses on documentation that will support the five extreme hardship factors identified by U.S. Citizenship and Immigration Services (USCIS) and the administrative appellate courts: (1) family ties; (2) social and cultural issues; (3) economic; (4) health conditions and care; and (5) current country conditions.

The Importance of Personal Documents

Every hardship claim must be supported by specific, personalized evidence regarding the applicant, the qualifying relative, and the applicant's family. The Administrative Appeals Office (AAO) frequently states that assertions of hardship unsupported by documentary evidence are not enough to meet the applicant's burden of proof. One of the most common bases for denial is the applicant's or qualifying relative's failure to adequately document the alleged hardship.

If you are unable to obtain the necessary documentation that supports the alleged hardship claim, then consider omitting it from the declaration and cover letter. If you do include hardship factors that are not supported by documentation, U.S. Citizenship and Immigration Services (USCIS) will likely send a request for evidence asking for the documentation that is unavailable. Responding that the documentation is not available will weaken your client's case.

Declarations from the Applicant and the Qualifying Relative

Every waiver application should include a detailed declaration from both the applicant and the qualifying relative. These declarations—particularly the qualifying relative's—will form the backbone of the application. You may decide to include additional declarations from other relatives, friends, and employers. Each declaration should address at least one of the five hardship categories that apply to the qualifying relative(s).

A declaration should be detailed and include only facts that the declarant knows firsthand. If the declarant does not have that knowledge, then locate the person who does. The declaration of the qualifying relative should include the following:

---

[1] For an excellent article on I-601 waivers, see L. Scott with contributions from J. Ovink, "How to Make the AAO Happy: Avoiding Mistakes When Appealing an I-601 Denial," *Immigration & Nationality Law Handbook* (AILA 2010–11 Ed.).

- Biographical information;
- Any relevant childhood or adolescent information;
- How he or she is related to the applicant;
- If the qualifying relative is a spouse, how long they knew each other before marrying;
- Important marital facts;
- Names and ages of children;
- Names, addresses, and immigration status of all close family members;
- A description of the family's daily routine; and
- A description of all hardship factors asserted in the application.

The applicant and the qualifying relative will need to decide whether the qualifying relative will remain in the United States or relocate if the applicant is denied the waiver. The applicant is only required to show that extreme hardship to the qualifying relative would result from one of those scenarios, not both. A credible statement from the qualifying relative in his or her declaration is typically the best evidence in establishing the option the family would likely choose, but it may be helpful to support that statement with declarations from other family members.

While the applicant may argue that extreme hardship would result from both separation and relocation, it may be more effective to focus on the scenario that is most likely to occur in a specific case. If you argue that extreme hardship will result from both separation and relocation, be prepared to provide supporting evidence for each possibility. If the statement is not plausible or credible (including because it is inconsistent with the hardship evidence presented), USCIS may request additional evidence.[2]

The qualifying relative should express his or her feelings as much as he or she is able to. These might include love for the applicant, fear about upcoming separation or relocation, anxiety about the unknown, and concern for other family members. Hardships that would not be considered extreme by themselves can add up to extreme hardship. Personal factors like an individual's history, temperament, health, and age may also make "ordinary" hardships appear more compelling for the adjudicator. Remember that all hardship must be channeled through the qualifying relative, so a child's hardship must be expressed in terms of its impact on the qualifying relative.

The applicant should address his or her unlawful presence and any previous entry without inspection. The declaration is an opportunity to explain why he or she came to the United States. The possible reasons are varied—a better or higher-paying job, educational opportunities, personal safety, or to reunite with family members—but they should be explained. The applicant should include a statement indicating that he or she regrets having entered without inspection and should explain why the applicant merits a favorable exercise of discretion.

Be detailed. In countless AAO decisions, the difference between what could be considered "ordinary" hardship versus "extreme" hardship lies in how much detail is provided. A statement such as "I suffer from migraine headaches that are caused by stress," without more, is vague and weak. Instead, indicate exactly how severe the headaches are, how debilitating they can be, what the declarant is forced to do when they happen, how long they last, how often they occur, the types of situations that trigger them, whether medication is effective in controlling or relieving them, the side effects of the drugs, how the impending separation or relocation is aggravating the condition, etc. Make sure to do this for every alleged hardship. Unique personal details help to distinguish the case from the many others that the adjudicator has reviewed.

The applicant's declaration should generally discuss the same issues as the qualifying relative's but be told through his or her point of view. This declaration should include the same type of biographical information. The applicant should stress the favorable discretionary factors and address all the negative ones. See Chapter 5 for a longer discussion on preparing declarations.

---

[2] USCIS Policy Manual, Vol. 9, Part B, Ch. 4.

Objective Evidence Regarding Hardship Conditions

In addition to using evidence prepared by the family, friends, and members of the applicant's community, it is also important to obtain objective evidence that will corroborate the applicant's hardship claims. An expert's report or statement can be used to prove: (1) conditions and characteristics specific to the applicant and his or her family; (2) living conditions for the applicant in the United States, such as education, health conditions and services, employment qualifications and job market; and (3) living conditions in the applicant's home country, including employment prospects, access to health care and its cost, quality of education, and level of violence. For example, a statement from a doctor who has treated the qualifying relative provides expert analysis regarding the individual's circumstances and the hardships he or she will face. A more generalized expert report—for example, a government study on health care in the home country—can support the hardship claim by providing additional context.

Personal Documents

Personal documents can confirm the facts in the case and support the applicant's hardship claims. Examples of personalized evidence include marriage certificates, birth certificates, doctor's reports and statements, report cards, financial statements, and income tax returns. They include statements from a range of individuals who have personal knowledge of the hardship facts or circumstances. Individuals who have personal knowledge of the objective conditions in the applicant's home town in the areas of education, availability of medical treatment, employment, drug-related violence, etc., may also provide important evidence for the hardship claim. If the applicant has any close friends or family members who have been killed in the home country, a death certificate, along with a statement explaining the relationship and the circumstances surrounding the death, can be powerful evidence.

Other personal evidence might include one or more of the following:

- Rent receipts indicating long-term residence in the community;
- Title to property indicating home ownership;
- Correspondence from a bank or lender stating his or her home is facing foreclosure;
- Letter from a school indicating participation in volunteer work and parent-teacher conferences;
- Letter from a church indicating participation in church activities, evidence of attending church, and evidence of donating to the church;
- Letter from community organizations indicating volunteer activity;
- Records from a hospital indicating hospitalization for illness or injury;
- Letter from an employer indicating long-term employment, job title, and employment benefits, as well as check stubs;
- Letters from family members or civic leaders, such as a town mayor in the applicant's home country, indicating the difficulty of finding employment;
- Letters from family members or civic leaders in the applicant's home country concerning the location and availability of primary and secondary schools, as well as institutions of higher learning;
- Letters from teachers describing a U.S. citizen child's participation in the class, academic strengths, special education needs, relationships with other children, fluency, and literacy in English; and
- Evidence of the family's income through a tax preparer's statement, outstanding bills, credit card debt, and other evidence that a qualifying relative may be unable to pay everyday expenses should the applicant be required to depart.

Appendix 6 is a list of possible documents that the client should consider gathering. This list is in English and Spanish.

Personalized Expert Evidence

Who is an expert? An expert is anyone who is qualified by knowledge, skill, experience, training, or education in a particular subject whose statements or opinion will help the adjudicator understand the evidence or a fact in the case.[3]

Are experts necessary? Many practitioners, especially those who serve low-income clients, do not use experts because they are too expensive. Other practitioners only use experts who are connected to the applicant's or the qualifying relative's life, such as social workers or school counselors. In some situations, it may be extremely important to have an expert report, and it may be possible to obtain that report for free. Where the qualifying relative or applicant has a history of psychological problems, an evaluation or report from the treating mental health professional is critical. If the qualifying relative or applicant has some other health-related problem, then include any medical reports or documentation the doctor or treating facility can provide. Teachers, social workers, job counselors, or others who have assisted the qualifying relative in dealing with issues or problems may also be able to provide expert declarations.

Working Directly with an Expert

Trying to find an expert who is available to assist you directly can be frustrating. However, when hardship claims require additional proof, expert declarations, statements, or reports can often make a difference. Expert statements may be obtained from family doctors, psychologists, teachers, community workers, accountants, job counselors, and members of the clergy. Experts in the applicant's home country or home town might include the mayor, the town's leading employer, doctors or hospital administrators, teachers, and military or police officials. Statements by experts in the fields of health, environment, family relations, psychology, economics, religion, employment, education, or politics might support the hardship claim with objective facts. Professionals in various fields and academics at colleges and research institutions, both in the United States and abroad, may also be a good source of expert reports, statements, or declarations. By contacting the relevant department and specific faculty at academic institutions, government agencies, or nonprofit organizations, you may find an expert who is willing to provide a detailed statement or declaration regarding the country conditions that will affect the waiver applicant. If one expert is unable to provide assistance, you may be able to get recommendations for others who are able to do so.

After locating an expert who is willing to assist you, it may be helpful to orient him or her to the facts of the case and the type of evidence you are seeking. In most instances, it is useful to provide the expert with the qualifying relative's declaration, any statements from the applicant or family members, and other helpful background information. It may also be helpful for you to write up a short statement explaining the facts that you would like the expert to address. This will enable the expert to focus his or her expertise on the facts most relevant to the hardship claim. See Appendix 9 for sample letters to experts requesting assistance.

It is important to review the expert's declaration, statement, or report after it is completed to ensure that incorrect or contradictory information is not included. If you believe the expert made an error, it is critical that you discuss the issue with the expert in the most diplomatic way possible. Unfortunately, there may be circumstances in which it is not possible to use the expert's work because the error is too significant.

Note that if the expert already has a confidential relationship with the applicant, particularly in the case of a psychologist or medical doctor, you will need to obtain a signed release of information from the applicant and furnish the expert with it. This will ensure that the expert is able to discuss the case openly with you.

Expert Evidence on Living Conditions

Academics, government agencies, research institutions, and other experts generate reports and articles that can support the applicant's hardship arguments. While these types of documents may not be personalized to the applicant and his or her family, they corroborate and provide context for hardship claims. The most persuasive evidence will have a targeted connection to the qualifying relative and the applicant. For example, an article describing the treatment for a specific medical condition may be more persuasive than an article on the

---

[3] This definition is based on Rule 702, Federal Rules of Evidence.

treatment of medical conditions generally in the country of relocation. A study on general economic outlook in the country of relocation is not as compelling as a report outlining employment prospects for women in a particular region.

Documenting Hardship Claims

The following section offers guidance on gathering evidence for each of the extreme hardship categories. Note that some types of documentation may fit into several hardship categories. See Appendix 7 for additional resources on locating expert reports and expert witnesses.

Family Ties and Impact

Personal factors are specific to the applicant and his or her family. These factors typically include the qualifying relative's age, length of residence in the United States, country of origin, foreign language abilities, history of travel or residence in the applicant's home country, family members residing in the United States and their citizenship or immigration status, and membership in the U.S. military. If the qualifying relative is a spouse, personal factors also include how long the couple has known each other, how long they have been married, how many children they have, and their responsibilities as caregivers for children, elderly, or disabled relatives. Other ties to their community should also be documented.

These personal factors should be detailed in the declarations of the qualified relative and applicant. They may also be supported by statements from other family members, neighbors, employers, friends, religious leaders, or members of the community. Other documentation might include birth certificates of children and siblings; the marriage certificate of the couple; documentation indicating U.S. citizenship or lawful immigration status of parents, in-laws, or siblings; documentation indicating that the qualifying relative was previously granted Iraqi or Afghan special immigrant status, T nonimmigrant status, asylum status, or refugee status from the country of relocation; photos of the couple in various stages of their marriage or courtship; photos of the children or other family members; any awards or formal recognition of community involvement; and proof of military service.

Social and Cultural Impact

Social, cultural, environmental, and safety-related conditions in the home country may contribute to extreme hardship. Considerations include the extent to which the qualifying relative has integrated into U.S. culture and the degree of difficulty in integrating into the country of relocation; the inability to speak the language; and difficulty in understanding or adopting cultural and societal norms, including gender roles or moral codes. It also includes the availability and quality of educational opportunities in the foreign country and lack of access to social institutions.

These issues can be documented through declarations from the qualifying relative, applicant, and others describing the social and cultural challenges that are present in a specific case. Friends or relatives who live in the home town or region may be able to provide details from their direct, personal experiences. Expert reports from academics, research institutions, nonprofit organizations, and government agencies may provide objective information regarding relevant issues.

Waiver applicants who have children will experience education-related hardships. These may include a range of factors, depending on the particular circumstances. Should the child remain with the qualifying relative in the United States, the absence of the waiver applicant will likely result in financial loss, which could in turn result in the child's loss of private school education, tutoring, counseling, or after-school instruction. If the child relocates to the applicant's home country, the hardship could manifest in a setback in academic grade level, an inability to understand instruction due to language barriers, poorer quality of instruction, loss of access to special education or other treatment for learning disabilities, loss of access to internships, loss of access to loans and grants, and any additional costs that are covered through public education in the United States. Adults, including the qualifying relative and the applicant, may also experience education-related hardships.

Personalized, unique hardship factors are more persuasive than general claims. When documenting education-related hardship, be sure to consider statements and evaluations from teachers and report cards, any certificates or honors that the student has earned, and declarations from any counselors or learning specialists.

Does the student have unique educational issues? Does he or she receive special education in the United States that would be unavailable in the country of relocation? Expert information from schools, teachers, and medical professionals may be available. Also include records of English as a Second Language (ESL) classes, GED credentials, enrollment in classes, scholarships, aptitude test results, etc.

Information about access to education and statistics on illiteracy in the foreign country may be available on the websites of newspapers or international nongovernmental organizations and in academic studies and articles. Be sure to tailor your research to the specific region, state, or town where the individual will reside.

Financial and Economic Hardship

Financial hardship will exist in almost every waiver case whether the qualifying relative remains in the United States or accompanies the applicant to the home country. The applicant's—and possibly the qualifying relative's—relocation will likely result in any of the following: loss of employment; reduction in salary due to relocation; expenses related to moving to the foreign country; selling a business, home, or other personal property at a loss; travel expenses related to visiting the applicant in the foreign country; and expenses related to additional child care or care for elderly parents. Be creative and thorough in your evaluation of all possible financial effects.

It may be helpful to include a detailed financial statement showing current income and expenses. Such a profit/loss statement gives context to claims of financial hardship and is preferable to simply submitting copies of bills, which does not provide a complete understanding of both income and financial obligations. Include a list of assets in the United States. Summarize the financial impact by listing all current income and expenses and compare those with the anticipated income and expenses should the qualifying relative remain in the United States or accompany the applicant abroad. See Appendix 11 for a sample financial statement.

Information on employment opportunities may be available online. Research may reveal the absence of any job openings. If there are openings, you may find the salaries that are offered. This can be useful evidence for assertions about the applicant's or qualifying relative's employment prospects or likely salary in the home country.

Differences between standards of living in the United States and the home country will not in themselves constitute hardship, but an inability to find work, the loss of a home or business, and other significant economic losses may constitute special hardship. The loss of scholarships, loans, and grants that are available in the United States but not in the relocation country may also be hardship factors. Information on unemployment rates, wage stagnation, and poverty income levels in the relocation country is available on the websites of the government, nonprofit organizations, and international nongovernmental organizations.

Health Conditions and Care

For those with medical conditions, the inability to access quality medical care can result in great suffering and even premature death. Yet hardship related to health factors is not limited to the individual who is ill. It affects the entire family in economic, psychological, and other ways. The qualifying relative need not be the family member with the health problem. The problems of other relatives may cause the qualifying family member to suffer hardship if the provisional waiver application is not granted. Note that a qualifying relative's or related family member's disability can be a particularly significant factor that weighs heavily in support of extreme hardship.

The types of documentation that support a health-related hardship claim include, for the individual:

- Personal declarations, expert declarations from medical professionals, and medical records;
- Information describing the health condition, standard course of treatment, and the consequences of the failure to provide treatment;
- Prognosis for recovery;
- Whether the conditions are acute or chronic and short-term or long-term;
- Prescribed medication or therapy;
- Whether the condition is common or rare;

CHAPTER 6: DOCUMENTING THE CASE

- Factors that may aggravate the condition; and
- Formal disability determination from medical professionals and/or government agencies.

When describing health conditions, use layman's terms instead of medical jargon. The declaration from the qualifying relative or other family member should likewise use words the adjudicator can readily understand and relate to. Describe how the medical condition affects the sufferer on a day-to-day basis, including what limitations or difficulty it causes in mobility, activity, sleeping, eating, or working; pain and suffering; dietary restrictions; and medication schedule. The same is true for those who are caring for the family member with the health condition; describe a typical day in food preparation, pill administration, exercise supervision, medical appointments, etc. Documentation supporting a health-related hardship claim in context includes:

- Reports on the availability of medical treatment in the applicant's home country or home town;
- Reports on the number of doctors and hospital beds in the applicant's home country or home town;
- Cost of medical treatment for the specific condition and access to health insurance in applicant's home country or home town;
- Information about availability of health care treatment based on gender;
- Reports on infant mortality statistics;
- Reports on the leading causes of death in the applicant's home country; and
- Information on environmental conditions, including the availability of clean water sources, sanitation issues, and pollution, which affect health.

Country Conditions

Safety and security concerns may raise fears that the applicant and/or the qualifying relative will be in danger in the home country. Civil unrest, generalized levels of violence, law enforcement's inability to address significant crime, environmental catastrophes, and other socio-economic or political conditions can jeopardize safe repatriation and lead to a fear of physical harm upon relocating. For Mexican or Central Americans, gang- or drug-related violence and corruption in the state, region, or city where the applicant will reside is often a significant issue.

Information about safety concerns and dangerous conditions in the home country can be gathered from numerous sources. Articles from periodicals covering a specific region can help illustrate current dangers. Always include an English translation of anything that is in a foreign language. Include the dates of articles and colored photos if they are available. Expert reports documenting country conditions can often be found online. For example, reports on drug-related violence in Mexico involving kidnappings, disappearances, and murder are available on the websites of government agencies, academic institutions, and nonprofit organizations. The Department of State (DOS) may issue travel warnings for a particular region and/or recommendations against travel to the area. Issuance of DOS travel warnings can be evidence of a "particularly significant factor" that weighs heavily in support of an extreme hardship finding. To assess current DOS travel warnings, go to this link: *https://travel.state.gov/content/travel/en/traveladvisories/traveladvisories.html/*. Recent reports, news articles, studies, or testimonials related to the geographical area where the applicant or family will reside are more persuasive than lengthy, overly broad, or highly technical reports. Use excerpts or highlighting to direct the reader to the portion of a report that is most relevant.

Declarations from relatives in the home country can be used to describe the personal impact of crime, violence, or environmental disasters in their own lives.

Documenting Discretionary Factors

Don't overlook the need to document the positive discretionary factors in the applicant's case. A range of possible positive factors is laid out in Chapter 4. Emphasize factors that will tip the balance in the applicant's favor, even if they do not relate directly to extreme hardship. Consider including the following documents, if they are not already included:

- Birth certificates of U.S. citizen children;

- Tax returns;
- Employment history;
- Police clearance letters or an FBI fingerprint report indicating no arrests;
- Evidence indicating care for elderly parents;
- Donations and volunteer activities;
- ESL or GED classes;
- Participation in children's schools; and
- Community involvement.

If the applicant has been arrested for infractions or crimes that do not qualify as a ground of inadmissibility, then these should be addressed. Examples could include public intoxication, disorderly conduct, simple assault, or non-DUI traffic-related offenses. These must be addressed and explained in the applicant's declaration and possibly supported with evidence of remorse or rehabilitation. Be sure to note the details of the applicant's unlawful entry. However, make sure you address and highlight any sympathetic factors.

Documentation in Action

Let's see how we can take the information presented in this chapter and apply it to a hypothetical case.

Example: Martha, a 25-year-old U.S. citizen, is married to Hector. They have been married for two years and have a four-month old child, David. Martha was born in the United States and has lived her whole life in Tulsa, Oklahoma. She has three siblings, two of whom live in Tulsa and one who lives in Oklahoma City. Her parents also live in Tulsa. Martha speaks only a few words of Spanish. Martha suffers from diabetes. She is currently enrolled in a community college and is hoping someday to get her nursing degree. Hector is from the Mexican state of Guerrero. He is 29 years old and has lived in the United States continuously for the last seven years after entering the country illegally. He has never returned to Mexico since. He has never been arrested nor had any contact with the police. He has held the same job for the past five years. In addition to declarations from Martha and Hector, consider submitting the documents below to support Martha's claim of extreme hardship and Hector's positive discretionary factors. Remember that Martha will need to show hardship were she to stay in the United States or to leave with her husband and reside in Mexico.

Health-Related Hardship

- Doctor's report, physician's letter, and or/medical record verifying Martha's diabetes condition, medication she is prescribed for treatment of condition, prognosis for recovery or worsening of condition, risks of change in symptoms, factors that could result in change in condition, and how diabetes limits her activity;
- Declarations from other individuals who assist Martha in administering prescribed drugs;
- Declaration from doctor or health facility in Hector's home town specifying ability of the hospital to treat diabetes, availability of prescribed drugs, and their cost; and
- Other articles or reports concerning diabetes treatment in Guerrero.

Financial-Related Hardship

- A monthly budget showing that the couple can meet expenses using their current income but would be unable to do so if separated or forced to move to the foreign country. Include sample debts, bills, and receipts;
- Verification of Hector's employment status, title, employment history, employment skills, and salary;
- Bank statement indicating the balance in the family's checking and savings account;
- Statement from mortgage company indicating balance of principal owed;
- Appraisal of house indicating equity value;

- Statement from Hector's brother explaining difficulty of securing employment in his home town in Mexico; and
- Reports on unemployment statistics and joblessness in Mexican state of Guerrero.

Education-Related Hardship
- Proof of Martha's current enrollment in community college;
- Declarations from professors on Martha's educational aptitude;
- Evidence of the tuition cost for community college, financial aid she is receiving, and student loans she has taken out that she might be unable to repay;
- Information regarding quality or affordability of nursing programs in Guerrero and her employment opportunities as a nurse in Guerrero;
- Articles on quality of public education in the Mexican state of Guerrero with respect to David; and
- Reports on Martha's likelihood of attending college in the Mexican state of Guerrero.

Family Ties and Impact
- Declarations from siblings and parents verifying Martha's family ties in Oklahoma, including their birth certificates;
- Family photos;
- Proof of family relationships and family's U.S. citizenship and lawful immigration status;
- Birth certificate of their son, David;
- Declarations from friends and others who can verify Martha's community involvement; and
- Declarations from friends and family who can support Martha's and Hector's statements about their close relationship.

Country Conditions
- Declaration from a member of Hector's family indicating the level of drug-related violence, including kidnappings, in his home town;
- Articles from Mexican periodicals on drug-related murders, shootings, and kidnappings in the Mexican state of Guerrero;
- Color photos of the house where the applicant would reside, the local school, the hospital, or other typical scenes; and
- Other reports and articles concerning drug-related violence in the Mexican state of Guerrero.

CHAPTER 7
PUTTING THE CASE TOGETHER

In this chapter, we will give advice on how to present the documents for your client's waiver application in a persuasive and organized manner. At this point in a waiver case, your clients will have decided whether they are going to separate or relocate should the waiver be denied, you will have developed the theory of the case, and you will have identified the hardship factors you want to address. You have prioritized those factors based on their relative strength. You have helped prepare the declarations of the qualifying relative and the waiver applicant and obtained the documents that support each hardship claim. You have also obtained any documents that support a favorable exercise of discretion for your client. You have reviewed all of this evidence for consistency and accuracy. You have determined which pieces of the evidence you need to highlight or emphasize. The next step is summarizing the case in a convincing cover letter, identifying the documentation in an index, and assembling all the documents in an organized manner.

Exhibit Basics

Make sure that the documents you submit with the waiver application are the correct size: 8.5 by 11 inches. You may need to shrink the size of an original document by copying it into this format. It is not necessary to submit originals of documents; photocopies are sufficient and in fact advisable. Any document you submit will remain a part of your client's file and will be difficult to retrieve later.

Verify that you have a full English translation of any document in a foreign language and that the translation contains a certification stating that the translation is complete and accurate, and that the translator is competent to translate from the foreign language into English. All declarations by individuals who do not speak, read, or write English must contain a certification that the document was translated into their native language and an affirmation that they understood the contents of the declaration. In the alternative, include a copy of the declaration in the person's native language together with an English translation.

If you are submitting a report, declaration, or letter from an expert, attach a copy of that person's résumé or curriculum vitae (c.v.). The expert's c.v. should include information about his or her education and experience. If the expert is a family member or friend, include information within the declaration explaining why he or she is qualified to give his or her opinion.

Reviewing Exhibits

Reviewing the exhibits and considering whether you have all the documents you need is not your task alone. Work with your client and with any experts who have contributed to the case to ensure that you have gathered all the necessary documents to prove hardship. There may be a piece of evidence that the client is aware of that you would not have considered. Before you package the case, review all the documents with your client and discuss the possibility of including any other evidence.

An Organized Approach

An easily accessible, reader-friendly, well-organized waiver packet quickly points the U.S. Citizenship and Immigration Services (USCIS) adjudicator to the compelling nature of the hardship claim. By organizing the waiver application, you will ensure that the strongest components of your waiver case jump out from the page. Be sure that you make the adjudicator's job as easy as possible by directing the adjudicator to the documents that prove extreme hardship to the qualifying relative and indicating why discretion should be exercised favorably. The adjudicator wants to know which document is the most important one to read or which part of the document is most relevant. You can provide that answer by organizing your documents in a way that presents the heart of the hardship claim in a clear manner.

Using Placement of Documents to Reflect Importance of Evidence

Consider how best to organize the documents. The Form I-601A Instructions specifically require that a copy of the Department of State immigrant visa fee receipt and of the Form I-797 approval notice for the I-130 visa petition accompany the provisional waiver application.[1] It is advisable to place the declarations from the qualifying relative and the waiver applicant after those. Decide the order of the remaining documents by strategically placing evidence that displays the strongest hardship claims ahead of weaker ones. Before you can decide which document presents the best hardship claim, it is important to evaluate the documents from the vantage point of the theory of the case.

Example: Elena is the U.S. citizen spouse of Enrique, a waiver applicant and citizen of Mexico. Enrique is a waiter at a unionized restaurant and receives health insurance for himself and Elena through his employer. Their health insurance covers the medical treatment that Elena needs to manage her diabetes. You have obtained a letter from Elena's doctor about the severity of her diabetes and the medical treatment she receives regularly. You also have copies of Elena's medical records showing hospital visits, the couple's tax returns, bank statements, a letter from the community college that Elena attends, documents showing student loans, a letter from Enrique's employer confirming health insurance coverage for the couple, and a letter from Enrique's cousin in Mexico stating that there is no medical clinic in Enrique's home town in Mexico where the cousin currently lives. In addition, you have a report from the Pan American Health Organization stating that diabetes is the leading cause of death in Mexico. You also have other documentation showing financial hardship, personal hardship, and the crime rate in the town where Enrique is from.

The theory of Enrique's case is that the qualifying relative, Elena, will lose her crucial medical care and suffer untreated diabetes if Enrique is not granted a waiver. She will suffer hardship if she relocates and accompanies Enrique to Mexico. Her case rests heavily on her diabetes, the treatment she is receiving here, her access to Enrique's health insurance, and the lack of convenient and affordable medical treatment in Mexico. But her case also uses the cumulative effect of educational, financial, personal, and special factors. The organization of the documents for this waiver application should mirror the theory of the case. Prioritize and arrange the documents with this theory in mind, placing the health-related evidence first. Then decide which of the other factors is the next strongest, and so forth. An index of exhibits might look like this:

- Exhibit 1: Immigrant visa fee receipt
- Exhibit 2: Form I-797, I-130 approval notice
- Exhibit 3: Declaration from qualifying relative
- Exhibit 4: Declaration from applicant

Health-Related Evidence for Elena

- Exhibit 5: Letter from Elena's doctor explaining her medical condition, prognosis, and treatment
- Exhibit 6: Medical records regarding Elena's hospitalizations
- Exhibit 7: Letter from Enrique's employer confirming medical insurance coverage

Health-Related Evidence: Medical Care in Mexico

- Exhibit 8: Letter from Enrique's cousin stating health care unavailable in home town
- Exhibit 9: *Health in the Americas 2015 Edition – Regional Outlook and Country Profiles, Mexico*, Pan American Health Organization: Page 446: Table I (leading cause of mortality in Mexico, 2005–09, is diabetes)

The other possible documents in this example—tax returns, bank statements, a letter from the community college that Elena attends, documents showing student loans, evidence of community ties in the United States, lack of family ties in Mexico, and drug-related violence in the region of Mexico where Enrique is

---

[1] U.S. Citizenship and Immigration Services (USCIS), "Instructions for Application for Provisional Unlawful Presence Waiver, Form I-601A (Oct. 20, 2019)," http://www.uscis.gov/i-601a.

from—are also important and address the other hardship factors. These documents should be included in the order of their relative strength and be listed in the index in a similar manner.

Readability and Legibility Matters

An organized waiver packet allows the adjudicator to focus on the most important documents and hardship claims quickly and efficiently. Prepare your waiver packet by keeping in mind that adjudicators do not want to search through the application looking for documentation that supports the hardship claims. A readable, legible, and organized waiver packet invites the adjudicator to approve the application quickly. Put yourself in the position of the adjudicator who must review numerous waiver applications every day. A clear and structured waiver application that provides a roadmap to the case makes the adjudicator's job easier and the likelihood of approval greater. For example, identifying each exhibit with a number on a colored piece of paper and paginating throughout makes it simpler to locate a particular document. This is especially important when you are including a large number of documents.

We recommend including a cover letter and an index of the exhibits. Some practitioners also include a summary of the hardship-related facts as a separate document. Other practitioners include a legal brief if there are complex legal issues. The index should include topical headings that segregate and identify the evidence by subject type. The headings will allow the adjudicator to focus on the topics he or she thinks are the most important, and glance at those that are not central to the application. For example, the topical heading in the example above of Elena and Enrique is "Health-Related Evidence for Elena." Examples of other topical headings might be "Evidence of Community Ties," "Evidence of Financial Hardship," or "Evidence of Positive Discretionary Factors."

Cover Letter

An effective cover letter captures the essence of your client's case and lays out the heart of the hardship claim. The cover letter will help the adjudicator see quickly who the applicant and qualifying relative are, why the qualifying relative or relatives would experience extreme hardship, and why the applicant is deserving of a discretionary waiver grant.

The cover letter should summarize the basic elements of the waiver application and discretionary factors, and then request that the waiver be granted. Include a reference to the positive equities in the applicant's case and note that the applicant merits a positive exercise of discretion. Use the cover letter to identify the U.S. citizen petitioner and qualifying relative, assuming the petitioner is not the qualifying relative. Explain the theory of the case and the reasons why, in summary form, the qualifying relative will experience extreme hardship if the applicant is not granted a waiver. Explain why the qualifying relative will suffer extreme hardship if he or she accompanies the applicant to the home country and, alternatively, if the qualifying relative remains in the United States.

If the applicant has a criminal history, admits to fraud or smuggling, or has a history of immigration violations, the cover letter should also explain why the applicant warrants a favorable exercise of discretion.

Format of Cover Letter

A cover letter should be written in standard business format. The letterhead should contain the practitioner's name, address, phone number, fax, and email. The date of the letter should be placed directly under the practitioner's letterhead address. The USCIS address for provisional waivers should follow below the date. Currently, the USCIS address is the USCIS Chicago lockbox,[2] but always consult the USCIS website to verify the correct address.

Under the USCIS address, put "Re:" and include the waiver applicant's name and the number assigned to the approval notice of the I-130 petition. According to the I-601A instructions, USCIS will use this number as iden-

---

[2] The current USCIS Chicago lockbox address is: USCIS, P.O. Box 4599, Chicago, IL 60680 for U.S. Postal Service delivery, and USCIS, Attn: I-601A, 131 S. Dearborn, 3rd Floor, Chicago, IL 60603-5517 for Express Mail and courier delivery. Be sure to verify the address at www.uscis.gov.

Copyright © 2020. American Immigration Lawyers Association.

tification if the waiver applicant does not have an "A" number. If the waiver applicant has an "A" number, that number should also be referenced. Also, include "Form I-601A" in this section of the cover letter.

Some simple writing rules will make the cover letter more readable. Use a size 12-point font. The text of the letter should be single spaced with one blank line between each paragraph. Do not overuse capitalization. Avoid long paragraphs; they should be no longer than a few sentences.

Send the waiver application packet by either certified, return-receipt mail or by a courier service such as UPS or FedEx in order to have proof that the application was mailed and received. After you receive proof that the application was received, maintain that in the client's file with a copy of the application and supporting documents.

If the waiver applicant is in removal proceedings that have been administratively closed, you may need to provide a copy of the waiver application packet and proof of receipt to the immigration court and Office of the Chief Counsel.

Length of Cover Letter

Remember that the cover letter should be concise while still conveying the principal facts of the case. Although some practitioners prepare lengthy cover letters that review the evidence in some detail, others insist that a well-crafted cover letter should be no longer than one or two pages. See Appendices 12A–C for samples of cover letters. Other practitioners submit a short cover letter in conjunction with a more detailed summary of the facts and the law. As you practice, you will decide which style of cover letter you prefer and find the most effective.

Legal Arguments

When would it be useful to include a legal argument in conjunction with the cover letter and waiver packet? In many cases, it is not necessary for the cover letter to contain a legal argument. USCIS adjudicators review hardship based on the five factors identified in the final guidance on extreme hardship. However, in certain waiver applications, it may be useful to include a legal argument in the cover letter or in a separate legal brief. Practitioners seeking to emphasize a particular tenet of the case law on extreme hardship in a challenging case may address the facts of the case and the relevant legal principle in a cover letter or brief. See Appendix 13 for a sample legal brief. The case law regarding extreme hardship is discussed in Chapter 4.

> ***Example:*** If the primary hardship factor is financial hardship and the secondary factors are personal and special factors, some practitioners include a short review of case law on the importance of considering the cumulative effect of the hardship factors. The USCIS instruction manual focuses on the difficulty of proving extreme hardship when financial factors or community ties constitute the hardship factors, in and of themselves.[3] A cover letter that included this legal argument or a short legal brief would serve to clarify the current interpretation of extreme hardship.

Practitioners may find it helpful to explain why the applicant is not inadmissible based on a separate ground of inadmissibility, such as the "permanent" bar for illegal entry after more than one year of unlawful presence, or a crime involving moral turpitude.

Index of Exhibits

An index of exhibits is a listing of all the documents and evidence that are part of the waiver packet. The index should identify and briefly state the relevance of each document. The index facilitates access to the documents and helps the adjudicator navigate the evidence to locate those documents he or she wishes to review more closely. The index acts like a table of contents and a summary of the evidence, as well as a guide for the adjudicator. Producing an index of exhibits is standard legal practice for cases in state and federal courts and those before administrative agencies.

---

[3] USCIS, *Immigrant Waivers: Procedures for Adjudication of I-601 for Overseas Adjudication Officers,* at 50 ("In other cases of extreme hardship, it has been found that the mere loss of employment, the inability to maintain one's present standard of living or to pursue a chosen profession, or separation of a family member or cultural readjustment, in and of themselves, do not constitute extreme hardship.").

The index of exhibits is one of the first documents that the adjudicator will see and may color his or her perception of the case. A well-prepared index of exhibits adds credibility and coherence to the waiver application, while no index or a sloppy one may give the impression that the hardship factors are weak or unclear.

Contents of Index of Exhibits

Categorize the documents by the hardship factor that they address or the person they relate to. Some practitioners include just the title or name of the document, while others include a phrase or short description of the document. Each document or exhibit should be numbered, and that number should be used in the index. Staff at the USCIS lockbox will remove any tabs before they scan the application and documentation. For that reason, we recommend that exhibits be separated by colored paper that contains the exhibit number.

The USCIS website recommends paginating the exhibits. For example, a document can be paginated as "Page 1 of 11." Or, the entire packet of documents may be paginated consecutively after it is assembled. In addition, the USCIS website states that each document should include the waiver applicant's name and either the I-130 or I-360 receipt number or "A" number.

Neither the USCIS website nor the I-601A instructions specifies the type of binding to use to connect the exhibits and the application. Staff at the USCIS lockbox will remove any staples or two-hole ACCO binding before they scan the application and documentation. Therefore, we recommend not including any binders other than a clip that can be easily removed and returned after the scanning.

Preparing the Index of Exhibits

The first step in preparing the index of exhibits is collating all of the documents and grouping them into one file. Ensure that all of your documents are in one location and not scattered in various places. Review all of the evidence to verify that the document you are attaching contains correct information that is not inconsistent with other documents you are submitting.

Example: If you are attaching tax returns, confirm that the number of dependents is correct, the filing status or designation as either head of household or married is correct, and that the child that is claimed as a dependent qualifies as a dependent. The IRS website includes a Form 1040 instruction sheet with simple, clear information on completing the Form 1040 at www.irs.gov.

After gathering all the documentation you wish to submit and ensuring that the information is accurate, you are ready for the second step, which is dividing the exhibits into categories and possibly subcategories. Use the legal theory of your case and the relative weight you have assigned to each hardship factor to help to create the exhibit categories. An index of exhibits without categories may appear chaotic and disorganized.

The categories can be delineated by the type of hardship. The final guidance on extreme hardship identifies five separate categories of impact: family, social, health, economic, and country conditions. Remember that USCIS can consider hardship that falls outside of these five categories.

Example: The theory of the case is that Mina, U.S. citizen spouse, will experience social and economic hardships if her husband, Miguel, is not granted a waiver. The couple has decided they will relocate together. You will be submitting a copy of the immigrant visa fee receipt and the I-130 petition approval notice as the first exhibits. You have decided to group the following documents in these categories:

Economic Hardship to Mina xxx

- Exhibit 3: Declaration of Mina xxx, qualifying relative
- Exhibit 4: Declaration of Miguel xxx, waiver applicant
- Exhibit 5: Audited statement from restaurant that Miguel owns indicating income from restaurant and list of names of employees
- Exhibit 6: Joint tax return of Miguel and Mina indicating Michael's salary
- Exhibit 7: Restaurant review from *Chronicle* reviewing Michael's restaurant and noting Michael is considered one of Oakland's 10 best chefs
- Exhibit 8: Declaration from Gerald Puck, owner of The Tides restaurant, stating that Michael's position as a chef is critical to the continued success of his restaurant

- Exhibit 9: Letter from mortgage company indicating that Michael and Mina are two months in arrears on their mortgage payment
- Exhibit 10: Copy of mortgage showing amount of principal due and names of Michael and Mina on mortgage document
- Exhibit 11: Copy of most recent bank statement showing $200 balance remaining in joint bank account
- Exhibit 12: Copy of Mina's student loan indicating she owes $54,000

Social Hardship to Mina xxx

- Exhibit 13: Letter from Norman Nursing School stating that Mina is a full-time student and will complete her registered nursing course of studies in one year
- Exhibits 14: Copies of Mina's transcripts from Norman Nursing School showing she has been enrolled in the school for two years

The exhibit list categories can also be defined based on hardship to a particular qualifying relative. The categories can be further divided into subheadings for each qualifying relative and include the type of hardship that each qualifying relative would experience. In cases in which there are other qualifying relatives in addition to the petitioner, this may be particularly useful. The Form I-601A instructions require that where the applicant claims hardship to qualifying relatives who are not the petitioner, there must be evidence included that shows the qualifying relationship between the waiver applicant and the qualifying relative.[4]

Example: Jordan is the U.S. citizen spouse of waiver applicant Guadalupe. Arturo and Maria are the lawful permanent resident (LPR) parents of Guadalupe. Jordan, Arturo, and Maria, and are all qualifying relatives. You will be submitting the evidence of hardship in the following categories:

Economic Hardship to Jordan xxx

Family Hardship to Jordan xxx

Social Hardships to Jordan xxx

Health-Related Hardship to Arturo xxx

- Exhibit xx: Copy of Guadalupe's birth certificate listing Arturo as her father
- Exhibit xx: Copy of marriage certificate of Arturo and Maria
- Exhibit xx: Copy of LPR card of Arturo
- Exhibit xx: Letter from Dr. Cohen, Arturo's radiologist, stating that Arturo suffers from thyroid cancer
- Exhibit xx: Letter from Dr. Joyce, Arturo's psychologist, stating Arturo is suffering from generalized anxiety disorder
- Exhibit xx: Letter from Jean Jones, social worker, stating that Guadalupe drives Arturo to his radiology appointments and serves as his interpreter during doctors' appointments

Health-Related Hardship to Maria xxx

- Exhibit xx: Copy of LPR card of Maria
- Exhibit xx: Letter from Dr. Lu stating that Maria suffers from heart failure
- Exhibit xx: Hospital records dated March 1, 2016, indicating that Maria was hospitalized from February 25, 2016, to March 1, 2016, for treatment following a stroke

A well-organized index of exhibits, together with a carefully constructed cover letter that summarizes the hardship claims and the positive equities of the case, should greatly improve your chances of obtaining an approval. Appendices 12A–B contain sample cover letters with tables of exhibits.

---

[4] U.S. Citizenship and Immigration Services (USCIS), "Instructions for Application for Provisional Unlawful Presence Waiver, Form I-601A (Oct.20, 2019)," http://www.uscis.gov/i-601a.

Chapter 8
Filing Procedures

In the world of immigration law and practice, adhering to procedural requirements is critical. The failure to follow the proscribed procedure will result in the denial of an otherwise meritorious application. This rule is equally true for the filing of a provisional waiver application.

This chapter describes the requirements and procedures for filing the provisional waiver application packet. There are two main steps in applying for the provisional waiver. The first step in preparing the waiver is completing the application, Form I-601A, Application for Provisional Unlawful Presence Waiver. The second step in organizing the waiver application is ensuring that the packet contains the necessary documents and fees and comports with the filing requirements. In this chapter, we will walk through the questions on the application form, address questions that raise "red flags," and discuss practice tips.

Completing the Form I-601A

While the Form I-601A appears straightforward, many of the questions have important eligibility ramifications. For example, the form asks if the applicant has committed fraud or smuggling, engaged in drug trafficking, or been convicted of a crime. It then states that if the applicant answers in the affirmative, "your application for a provisional unlawful presence waiver may be denied as a matter of discretion."[1] But it fails to add that being subject to a separate ground of inadmissibility also makes the applicant ineligible for the provisional waiver. U.S. Citizenship and Immigration Services (USCIS) is no longer empowered to deny an application if it has "reason to believe" that the applicant is inadmissible under a ground other than unlawful presence; it may only take that into consideration when it weighs the positive and negative factors as part of its discretionary analysis. Nevertheless, it should have included the warning that if the applicant is found to be inadmissible for any of the listed actions in Part 1, questions 32-45, an approved I-601A waiver will simply be revoked by the Department of State (DOS) during the consular interview. In that case, the applicant would need to file a Form I-601 to waive both the unlawful presence and the separate ground of inadmissibility while waiting abroad, assuming the separate ground is waivable.

Some of the questions ask for biographic data and others request technical responses. If the question does not apply, then answer "N.A."; if the question requires a numeric response and the answer is zero, then write "none."

Type or use black ink to complete the form. The waiver applicant must sign the form; a copied or typed signature will not be accepted. If you need additional space to answer any of the questions, go to "Part 5" on page 5 of the Form I-601A, and use the space provided to answer the question. In Part 5, indicate the number of the question that you are answering.

Most applicants will be using the fillable form that is available on the USCIS website or on case management software programs. If printing the form out, then type or use black ink to complete the form. The waiver applicant must sign the form; a stamped or typewritten signature will not be accepted. If you need additional space to answer any of the questions, go to "Part 9, Additional Information" or attach a separate sheet of paper. Type or print the applicant's name and "A" number at the top of each page; reference the page number, part number, and item number to which the answer refers; and sign and date each page.

Remember that all the information provided must be true to the best of your client's knowledge. The U.S. Department of Homeland Security (DHS) warns that an individual who commits fraud on the application is subject to the issuance of a notice to appear (NTA), which is the initiation of removal proceedings.[2]

---

[1] USCIS, Application for Provisional Unlawful Presence Waiver, p. 3 (Oct. 20, 2019), http://www.uscis.gov/i-601a.
[2] 78 *Federal Register* (Fed. Reg.) 554 (Jan. 3, 2013).

Part 1—Information About the Applicant

Question 1, Alien Registration Number: This number, called an "A" number, identifies individuals who have a record in the immigration system. If the applicant has ever been in removal, deportation, or exclusion proceedings, or been issued a notice to appear, an order to show cause, or a notice to applicant for admission detained for hearing before an immigration judge, he or she will have an "A" number. If the applicant previously applied for an immigration benefit such as deferred action, Deferred Action for Childhood Arrivals (DACA), adjustment of status, or asylum, or was granted certain benefits such as Temporary Protected Status (TPS), he or she may also have an "A" number.

Red Flag: An "A" number is a red flag that the applicant *may* be inadmissible based on a prior removal, deportation, or exclusion order, which may make him or her ineligible for a provisional waiver. If the applicant has an "A" number, you need to know the reason for the issuance of the "A" number and whether the "A" number reflects that the applicant is inadmissible for a ground other than unlawful presence. Chapter 5 discusses working with your client and using screening tools to ensure that the applicant qualifies for a provisional waiver.

Practice Tip: You can investigate whether the applicant's "A" number points to a ground of inadmissibility in several ways:

- *Call the Executive Office for Immigration Review (EOIR) 800 Number:* If you have the applicant's "A" number, you can call the EOIR toll-free number at (800) 898-7180 to determine whether the immigration judge or Board of Immigration Appeals (BIA) issued an order of removal. You will also be able to determine whether a removal proceeding is ongoing.

- *File an FBI Criminal Record Check:* An FBI criminal record check will frequently—but not always—reveal an order of removal. You can request an FBI criminal record check by completing the form available on the FBI website, including a hard copy (not electronic) fingerprint Form FD-258 and a money order or cashier's check in the amount of $18. Review the FBI record checklist to ensure that you have included all of the required information. Send the form, fee, and fingerprint card to:

    – FBI CJIS Division – Record Request
    1000 Custer Hollow Road
    Clarksburg, WV 26306

    – The FBI record check response time is approximately two to four weeks.

File a Freedom of Information Act (FOIA) Request: You can file a request to obtain a copy of the applicant's immigration file through a FOIA request. The response to a records request under FOIA varies widely. Practitioners have reported that it takes between three to four months to get requested records back from the National Records Center. The USCIS uses a three-track system to process FOIA requests for A-File material and has provided the following average response times: Track One (simple requests): 35 days; Track Two (complex inquiries that normally require additional search and review time): 44 days; and Track Three (requests by individuals scheduled for a hearing before an immigration judge): 37 days. The agency uses a two-track system to process FOIA requests for non-A-File material: Track One: 33 days; and Track Two (processing time impacted by sensitivity of records, volume of records and extent of review process): 294 days. The agency uses a three-track system to process FOIA appeals: Track One: 7 days; Track Two: 24 days; and Track Three: 28 days.[3]

Question 2, Social Security Number: If the applicant has a valid Social Security card issued to him or her by the Social Security Administration, you may list this Social Security card number. USCIS states in the Form I-601A instructions and on the Form I-601A itself that Question 2 is an optional field and need not be answered. Do not include fictitious numbers.

Question 3, USCIS Online Account Number: If the applicant has previously filed an application or petition with USCIS using the online filing system, he or she will have been issued an account number.

---

[3] https://first.uscis.gov/#/check-status.

CHAPTER 8: FILING PROCEDURES

Question 4, Full Name: This is the applicant's legal last, first, and middle name. This may be the name on the applicant's birth certificate, but it may also be the applicant's married name, or the name obtained through a legal name change.

Question 5-6, Other Names Used: If the applicant has used other names, including a maiden name, a name given to an employer, a nickname, or a name given to law enforcement officials when stopped, detained, or fingerprinted, those names should be added to this section. If the applicant has never used another name, state "N.A." in this section.

> *Practice Tip*: Check to see if all other documents you are submitting in support of the waiver application use the applicant's name as listed in Question 4. If the employer's letter, bank statements, tax returns, etc., use names other than the applicant's current legal name, make sure that you add those names to Question 5-6.

Question 7, Mailing Address: Write the address where the applicant would like to receive any correspondence from USCIS regarding this application. This is where the decision or any request for evidence will be sent. The applicant should feel comfortable that this is a secure address for the receipt of mail. USCIS indicated that applicants should make sure that apartment numbers are included in the mailing address.

Questions 8-9, Physical Address: This question asks for the physical address where the applicant resides, even if he or she does not receive mail at this address. Do not provide a post office box. In order to be eligible for the provisional waiver, this address must be in the United States.

> *Practice Tip*: Make sure the address on the applicant's supporting documents is the same as the addresses listed in Questions 7-9.

Question 10, Gender: Indicate whether the applicant is male or female.

Question 11, Date of Birth: List the applicant's birth date in month/day/year format.

> *Practice Tip*: Confirm that the date listed in Question 11 is the same as the birth date on the applicant's birth or marriage certificates, passport, or other identification documents provided.

Questions 12–13, City and Country of Birth: Write the place where the applicant was born, including the city and country of birth.

Question 14, Country of Citizenship: List the applicant's country of citizenship or nationality. If the applicant does not have citizenship in any country, write "stateless" and provide an explanation in Part 9.

Question 15–16, Mother's and Father's Name: Put the full legal name of both parents.

Question 17-18, Last Entry into the United States: State the date of the applicant's last entry into the United States in month/day/year format. Include port of entry or the nearest city or town, and state where the applicant entered the United States.

Question 19, Immigration Status: If the applicant entered the United States without inspection or parole, write "EWI."

> *Practice Tip*: If an immediate relative entered the United States with authorization, he or she is likely eligible for adjustment of status. Almost everyone who enters as a nonimmigrant, as well as those who were paroled into the United States, is eligible for adjustment of status if they are an immediate relative. The nonimmigrant categories that do not qualify for adjustment of status include those in C and D visa status, and K-1 visa holders who failed to marry the U.S. citizen petitioner within 90 days. Individuals who are applying for adjustment of status are ineligible for a provisional waiver. If the applicant entered the United States with inspection and admission, you should evaluate whether adjustment of status, in lieu of consular processing, is the preferred alternative. For those who are immigrating in one of the preference categories, entry with inspection is only one of the eligibility requirements for adjustment of status. The other is that they must have always maintained lawful immigration status, which means not working without authorization and not overstaying the period of time allowed by the I-94.

Question 20-26, Previous Entries into the United States: If the applicant entered the United States on other occasions, write the Port of Entry (or approximate city), and state of the applicant's prior entries, the dates that the applicant was present in the United States, and the applicant's immigration status at the time of entry. If there are more than two previous entries, then include them in the space provided in Part 9.

Red Flag: An answer to this question may indicate that the applicant is inadmissible under Immigration and Nationality Act (INA) §212(a)(9)(C) for accruing more than one year of unlawful presence on or after April 1, 1997, departing the United States, and then returning to the United States without inspection and admission. An individual subject to this ground of inadmissibility is not only ineligible for a provisional waiver but is also subject to the "permanent" bar.

Practice Tip: Carefully review all of the applicant's travel to and from the United States, especially trips on or after April 1, 1997. If you see more than one entry into the United States since that date, calculate the total period of unlawful presence in the United States to ensure that the applicant did not accrue more than one year of unlawful presence followed by a departure and illegal reentry. Do not file a provisional waiver for an individual inadmissible under INA §212(a)(9)(C).

Question 27-45, Immigration or Criminal History:

Question 27: If the applicant is currently in removal, exclusion, or deportation proceedings in which no final order has been issued, check box "Yes." If the applicant is not in proceedings or a final order has already been issued, then check "No" and proceed to Question 29a.

Practice Tip: An applicant is in proceedings if an Order to Show Cause or an NTA has been lodged with the immigration court and the case has not been terminated. Persons whose proceedings have been terminated are no longer in proceedings. In this case, they should include a copy of all documents relating to the proceedings and an order of termination. A person is still in proceedings even if the proceedings have been administratively closed. If the immigration judge has not issued a final order, or if the case has been appealed to BIA, and the BIA has not issued a final order, then the applicant is considered in proceedings. In that case, the applicant only qualifies to file a provisional waiver if the proceedings have been administratively closed and not re-calendared. The ability to move for administrative closure was curtailed, however, with the Attorney General's decision in *Matter of Castro-Tum,* which held that immigration judges and the BIA lacked the authority to administratively close cases, with some exceptions.[4]

Question 28.a: If the applicant is in immigration proceedings where no final order has been issued and was successful in getting the immigration judge to administratively close the case, check this box. Persons in proceedings may file for the provisional waiver if they have had their case administratively closed and, at the time of filing, their case has not been placed back on EOIR's calendar. They will need to include a copy of the administrative closure order.

Question 28.b: Applicants who are in proceedings and whose case has not been administratively closed, or whose case was closed but EOIR subsequently placed the proceedings back on its calendar, should check this box. These persons are ineligible to file for the provisional waiver until they administratively close their case and, if so, the case has not been placed back on EOIR's calendar.

Question 29.a: If the applicant is currently in removal, exclusion, or deportation proceedings in which a final order has been issued, check box "Yes." Persons who have departed the United States after a final order was issued have affected or executed the order. These persons are no longer considered in immigration proceedings and they should check "No."

Practice Tip: An applicant has a final order if the immigration judge ordered the person deported, excluded, or removed and the order was not appealed to the BIA, or it was appealed and the BIA upheld the order. This includes persons who were granted a period of voluntary departure in lieu of deportation or removal, and that period has now elapsed. Departure and execution of the deportation, exclusion, or removal order would then make the person inadmissible for a period of five or 10 years (20 years in some situations).[5] Persons who have executed the order by departing the United States and

---

[4] *Matter of Castro-Tum*, 27 I&N Dec. 271 (A.G. 2018). *But see, Jesus Romero v. Barr*, No. 18-1850 (4th Cir. 2019).
[5] INA §212(a)(9)(A).

then reentering without inspection on or after April 1, 1997, have triggered a separate ground of inadmissibility called the "permanent bar."[6] This ground may not be cured through the provisional waiver process. Instead, the person must reside abroad for 10 years and then obtain a waiver (consent to reapply) by filing a Form I-212, Application for Permission to Reapply for Admission into the United States After Deportation or Removal. Persons who have a final order but who have not departed the United States and executed the order may apply for a waiver of this ground of inadmissibility before they leave. This is done by filing the Form I-212 with USCIS in the jurisdiction where the person was ordered removed.[7] If the I-212 is approved, the individual's order of removal, deportation, or exclusion would no longer bar him or her from obtaining an immigrant visa abroad. After obtaining such consent, the person would then be eligible to apply for the provisional waiver. Otherwise, persons subject to a final order of deportation or removal who have not been granted a Form I-212 would be ineligible to file for the provisional waiver.[8]

Red Flag. Persons who without "reasonable cause" fail or refuse to attend or remain in attendance at an immigration hearing commenced on or after April 1, 1997, will be issued a final order of removal in absentia. When that order is executed by departing the United States, the person will trigger a separate ground of inadmissibility that renders him or her inadmissible for a mandatory five-year period.[9] There is no waiver eligibility for this ground of inadmissibility. The five-year period begins upon departure from the United States, though the five years does not have to be spent outside the United States. The granting of a Form I-212 would waive the five- or ten-year bar under INA §212(a)(9) but would not cure the separate ground of inadmissibility under INA §212(a)(6)(B). For that reason, persons subject to an in absentia removal order would not be eligible for the provisional waiver. They would need to reopen their case and have the order vacated.

Question 29.b: Those persons who are still in proceedings, have been issued a final order, and apply for a "consent to reapply" on Form I-212, and whose Form I-212 is granted, may then apply for the provisional waiver. They will enter the USCIS receipt number for the Form I-212 that was approved. The applicant can also submit a copy of the I-212 approval notice in lieu of entering the receipt number.

Question 30.a: Indicate whether the applicant has been served with a DHS Form I-871, which is notice that the agency intends to reinstate a prior order of deportation, removal, or exclusion.

Red Flag: Most persons who have reentered the United States illegally after April 1, 1997, have triggered the "permanent" bar under INA §212(a)(9)(C) and thus are ineligible for the provisional waiver until they have resided abroad for 10 years and have then been granted a "consent to reapply" on Form I-212. But persons who reentered the United States illegally prior to April 1, 1997, would not have triggered that bar. Nevertheless, they may be ineligible for the provisional waiver based on a separate statutory provision. Illegal reentry to the United States after a deportation, removal, or exclusion order renders the person subject to reinstatement of removal.[10] In order for persons to be ineligible for the provisional waiver based on this provision, U.S. Immigration and Customs Enforcement (ICE) or U.S. Customs and Border Protection (CBP) must have formally reinstated the order.[11] Evidence of the agency's formal reinstatement begins with service of a Form I-871, Notice of Intent/Decision to Reinstate Prior Order. If the applicant has been served with a Form I-871, it will put USCIS on notice that the person will be ineligible for the provisional waiver as soon as the prior order is formally reinstated.

Question 30.b: Indicate if the applicant has been served with a final decision reinstating a prior order of deportation, removal, or exclusion.

---

[6] INA §212(a)(9)(C).
[7] 8 CFR §212.2(j).
[8] 8 CFR §212.7(e)(4)(iv).
[9] INA §212(a)(6)(B).
[10] INA §241(a)(5).
[11] 8 CFR §212.7(e)(4)(v).

Red Flag: If the applicant checks box "Yes," do not file the provisional waiver since the applicant is ineligible.

Question 31: Persons who were issued a grant of voluntary departure by the immigration judge, and that period of voluntary departure has not expired, are still considered in proceedings and have not been issued a final order. Such persons would not be eligible to file for the provisional waiver until the proceedings are administratively closed. To accomplish that, they would first need to reopen their proceedings and withdraw their request for voluntary departure. Then, they would be able to request administrative closure. Or, alternatively, they would need to overstay and thus terminate their period of voluntary departure. They would then still be considered in proceedings but subject to a final order or deportation, exclusion, or removal. In that case, they would follow the procedure set forth in Question 29.b and apply for a "consent to reapply" on Form I-212. If that is approved, they would then be eligible to file for the provisional waiver.

Question 32-45: Other Grounds of Inadmissibility

Red Flag: The following questions ask if the applicant is possibly inadmissible based on a number of grounds. Being found inadmissible on a ground separate from unlawful presence makes the applicant ineligible for the provisional waiver. Unfortunately, the form only warns applicants that admission of any of the actions listed in questions 32-45 will be taken into consideration as a possible adverse discretionary factor. In fact, applicants who are likely to be found inadmissible at the consular processing stage should not file for the provisional waiver. If USCIS were to exercise favorable discretion and grant the I-601A, the applicant would then be subject to revocation when DOS makes a formal finding of inadmissibility on a ground separate from unlawful presence. Therefore, if it appears that the applicant is inadmissible for fraud, false claim of citizenship, smuggling, drug trafficking, conviction of a crime of moral turpitude, or a health- or security-related ground, do not file for the provisional waiver. It serves no purpose for someone to apply for the provisional waiver when he or she is ineligible for it, but it is far worse for a person to apply, be granted a provisional waiver, and then depart the United States only to be denied by the consulate and stranded abroad with possibly limited options.

Question 32: Fraud or Misrepresentation: If the applicant knowingly and willfully gave false information to a DOS, DHS, or other government official to gain entry or admission to the United States or to obtain an immigration benefit, check "Yes." If not, check "No." Do not file the application for a provisional waiver if the applicant checks "Yes."

Red Flag: The applicant is inadmissible under INA §212(a)(6)(C) if he or she by fraud or misrepresentation knowingly or willfully gave false information to a government official to obtain an immigration benefit. The misrepresentation must have been material, *i.e.*, the applicant would have been denied the benefit if he or she had told the truth. Immigration benefits include adjustment of status, advance parole, employment authorization, asylum, withholding of removal, DACA, TPS, naturalization, and employment authorization. It does not include employment itself, however. Thus, misrepresentations on a Form I-9—other than a false claim of citizenship—would not constitute misrepresentation for immigration purposes. This ground of inadmissibility makes the applicant ineligible for a provisional waiver. However, the applicant may apply for an I-601 waiver under INA §212(i) after a finding of inadmissibility by the consulate. Applicants who made a false claim of U.S. citizenship on or after September 30, 1996, in order to gain an immigration benefit or any benefit under state or federal law are inadmissible. There is no waiver for this ground of inadmissibility, although there is a narrow exception. Children below a certain age may be found to have lacked the legal and mental capacity to have triggered this ground of inadmissibility.

Practice Tip: Applicants who entered without inspection and admission did not seek to enter or be admitted to the United States by fraud or misrepresentation. For applicants who entered with inspection, review their passport and discuss any trips the applicant made to the U.S. consulate to obtain or try to obtain a nonimmigrant visa. Discuss whether the applicant attempted unsuccessfully to enter the United States with documents not his or her own.

Question 33, Smuggling: If the applicant helped anyone else to enter the United States in violation of law, check "Yes." If not, check "No." Do not file the application for a provisional waiver if the applicant checks "Yes."

Red Flag: The applicant is inadmissible under INA §212(a)(6)(E) if he or she knowingly encouraged, induced, assisted, abetted, or aided any noncitizen in entering or trying to enter the United States in violation of the law. The U.S. consulates are vigilant in asking immigrant visa applicants if they ever entered the United States illegally accompanied by a family member. If the applicant's child has entered the United States illegally, the consulate will ask if the applicant assisted in this illegal entry in any significant way. You should be asking your client detailed questions about how he or she and any other family members entered the United States to determine if smuggling was committed. This ground of inadmissibility is currently one of the most common reasons the consulate revokes provisional waivers. Applicants may be eligible for an I-601 waiver of this ground of inadmissibility under INA §212(d)(11) following a finding of inadmissibility at the consulate.

Question 34, Arrested, Cited, Detained by DHS or Law Enforcement: If the applicant has been arrested, cited, or detained in the United States or abroad for any reason other than a traffic violation, check "Yes." In that case, attach a description of the event, including the date and location. This includes arrests at the border where the applicant was processed and voluntarily returned to Mexico. If the applicant was arrested but not charged with any offense, provide a statement or other documentation from the arresting authority, prosecutor's office, or court to show that the applicant was not charged with any crime or offense.

Red Flag: You should obtain a certified copy of the records relating to the event to determine if the applicant is inadmissible under INA §212(a)(2) for crime-based inadmissibility grounds or INA §212(a)(3) for security-related inadmissibility grounds. In addition, obtain a copy of the state statute to determine whether the criminal offense falls within the "petty offense" exception under INA §212(a)(2)(ii). In most but not all cases, an arrest, citation, or detention without a conviction is not enough to make the applicant inadmissible.

Practice Tip: Remember that the applicant will be submitting biometrics, and USCIS will be examining the results of the background check, which would typically include the applicant's criminal history and possible immigration violations. Make sure you carefully screen the applicant for arrests and contact with law enforcement. Remember to obtain FBI and state criminal record checks before starting the waiver process. If the applicant is admissible despite a criminal conviction, include a copy of the certified record of conviction, the state statute, and any other information that explains that the offense does not constitute a crime involving moral turpitude. While the form indicates that criminal-related conduct or prior immigration violations will be weighed as possible negative discretionary factors, they may also result in findings of inadmissibility and thus ineligibility for the provisional waiver.

Question 35, Charged, Indicted, Convicted, Imprisoned, Jailed: If the applicant has been charged, indicted, convicted, imprisoned, or jailed for any crime or offense in the United States or abroad, check "Yes." In that case, attach a description of the event, the date of the event, and a certified copy of the court charging documents and dispositions. See the red flag and practice tip above for Question 34.

Questions 36-37, Drug Trafficking: Check "Yes" if the applicant is currently trafficking in any controlled substance or has trafficked in the past. Check "Yes" if the applicant is currently or has ever knowingly assisted, abetted, conspired, or colluded with others in trafficking controlled substances. Do not file the application for a provisional waiver if the applicant checks "Yes."

Red Flag. There is a separate ground of inadmissibility for persons believed to be drug traffickers.[12] No conviction—or even valid admission—is necessary. This ground applies to "[a]ny alien who the consular or immigration officer knows or has reason to believe is or has been an illicit trafficker in any such controlled substance."[13] It also applies to persons who knowingly assist, and to abettors, conspirators, and those who collude with others. Spouses and children who knowingly obtained financial or other benefit from the illicit activity within the previous five years are also inadmissible.[14] An "illicit trafficker" is "a knowing and conscious participant or conduit in an attempt to smuggle" a controlled

---

[12] INA §212(a)(2)(C).
[13] INA §212(a)(2)(C).
[14] INA §212(a)(2)(C)(ii).

substance. This broad definition applies not only to persons who smuggle or attempt to smuggle drugs into the United States, but also to people who serve as conduits for the drug trade within the United States.[15] A person can be an illicit trafficker even if he or she has committed only one transgression.[16]

Question 38, Prostitution: Check "Yes" if the person is currently or has ever been engaged in prostitution. See below to determine if the applicant meets the definition of "engaged in prostitution." Make sure the applicant is not inadmissible to file the application for a provisional waiver if the applicant checks "Yes."

Practice Tip: The phrase "engaged in prostitution" requires that the person must have been involved in this type of conduct over a period of time. Having been convicted of a single act of prostitution does not make the person inadmissible under this ground.[17] The ground of inadmissibility does not cover acts of solicitation of prostitution on one's own behalf.[18] No conviction for an offense involving prostitution is required. Those falling into either of these two categories are inadmissible: (1) coming to the United States to engage in prostitution or who have engaged in prostitution within 10 years of the date of application for a visa, adjustment of status, or entry into the United States; and (2) procurers of prostitutes, or those who attempt to procure or who receive the proceeds of prostitution, or people who have done any of these activities within 10 years of applying for a visa, adjustment of status, or entry into the United States.[19]

Question 39, Human Rights Violations: If the applicant ever ordered, incited, called for, committed, assisted, helped with, or otherwise participated in human rights violations involving torture, genocide, killing, or intentionally and severely injuring any person; engaged in any sexual conduct or relations with any person who was being forced or threatened; or limited or denied any person's ability to exercise religious beliefs, check "Yes." Do not file the application for a provisional waiver if the applicant checks "Yes."

Red Flag. If the applicant checks "Yes," he or she may be inadmissible under INA §212(a)(3) and will not be eligible for a provisional waiver.

Questions 40-45, Terrorist Activity and Possible National Security Threats: These questions ask about prior service in military units, paramilitary groups, and guerilla groups; work in jails, prison camps, detention facilities; use of weapons, sale of weapons, or receipt of weapons training; and use of children under 15 in service of armed forces or to take part in hostilities. Check "Yes" if the applicant engaged in any of these and provide a complete explanation in Part 9.

Practice Tip: These questions were added to the I-601A to comply with the Intelligence Reform Terrorism Prevention Act[20] and the Child Soldier Accountability Act.[21] They relate directly to inadmissibility grounds at INA §§212(a)(3)(B), (F), and (G). The effect of checking "Yes" will depend largely on the particular circumstances and the explanation for the admitted conduct. For example, former police officers or members of the military who received weapons training in their home country as part of mandatory military service should not be found inadmissible. nor should that training be a negative discretionary factor.

Part 2—Information About the Applicant

Questions 1-6, Biographical Information: Provide the information requested regarding ethnicity, race, height, weight, and eye and hair color. Do not use the metric system for height and weight.

---

[15] *Matter of R H*, 7 I&N Dec. 675 (BIA 1958).
[16] *Matter of Rico*, 16 I&N Dec. 181 (BIA 1977).
[17] *Matter of R*, 2 I&N Dec. 50 (BIA 1944).
[18] *Matter of Gonzales-Zoquiapan*, 24 I&N Dec. 549 (BIA 2008).
[19] INA §212(a)(2)(D).
[20] Act of Dec. 17, 2004, Pub. L. No. 108-458, 118 Stat. 3638.
[21] Act of Oct. 3, 2008, Pub. L. No. 110-340, 122 Stat. 3735.

Part 3—Information About the Immigrant Visa Case

Questions 1.a-e, Basis on Which Applicant Is Immigrating: Check the appropriate box indicating whether the applicant is immigrating as a family-based (immediate relative or preference category) beneficiary, employment-based beneficiary, Diversity Visa (DV) selectee, widow, or Violence Against Women Act (VAWA) grantee.

Question 2.a-d, DV Selectee or Derivative: If the applicant is a DV selectee or derivative, enter the Department of State (DOS) DV case number. This number is found on the print-out from the DV Entrant Status Check page of the DOS Electronic Diversity Visa system website, www.dvlottery.state.gov. If the applicant is a derivative, enter the DV selectee's full name in 2.b-2.d.

Question 3.a-f, Approved Visa Petition Information: If the applicant is the beneficiary of a family-based petition, an employment-based petition, a widow self-petition, or a VAWA self-petition, provide the USCIS receipt number of the underlying approved petition (I-130, I-140, or I-360). USCIS requests that the applicant also submit with the waiver packet a copy of the Form I-797 approval notice, if available. Failure to include a copy of the approval notice "may result in processing delays or in the rejection of your application."[22] Also, provide the National Visa Center (NVC) Consular Case number. This is located on the receipt for the DOS immigrant visa processing fee. For a sample copy of a fee receipt, see Appendix 14A. This case number should correspond to the USCIS approved petition. Provide the full name of the I-130 petitioner or company that filed the I-140 petition. If the applicant is a widow or VAWA recipient who filed a self-petition, write "Self." If the applicant is a derivative of a widow or VAWA petition, put the name of the self-petitioner.

Part 4—Information About the Qualifying Relative

Question 1.a-c, Qualifying Relative's Name: Provide the last, first, and middle name of the qualifying relative. The qualifying relative is the applicant's U.S. citizen or lawful permanent resident (LPR) parent or spouse.

Question 2.a-d, Relationship to Applicant: Check the box to indicate if the qualifying relative is the applicant's U.S. citizen or LPR spouse or parent.

> *Practice Tip:* Include a copy of the U.S. citizen spouse or parent's proof of citizenship and proof of relationship to the applicant (birth certificate or marriage certificate) with the waiver packet.

Questions 3-5, Other Qualifying Relative: If the applicant has another qualifying relative in addition to the one listed in Question 1, check "Yes." Provide the second qualifying relative's name and indicate his or her relationship to the applicant.

> *Practice Tip*: Include a copy of the U.S. citizen or LPR spouse or parent's proof of citizenship or proof of LPR status and proof of relationship to the applicant (birth certificate or marriage certificate) with the waiver packet.

Part 5—Statement from the Applicant

A statement from the applicant describing why the qualifying relative would experience extreme hardship and why the applicant merits a waiver in the exercise of discretion is required.

> *Practice Tip*: This statement, in conjunction with one from the qualifying relative(s), will form the basis for approving the application. See Chapter 5. Attach detailed declarations from both the applicant and the qualifying relative to the waiver packet.

In this section, write "See attached declaration of _____ (name of applicant)." The declaration, as well as all of the other supporting documents for the waiver packet, must include the applicant's name and either the USCIS receipt number or the applicant's "A" number.

---

[22] USCIS, Instructions for Application for Provisional Unlawful Presence Waiver, p. 11 (Oct. 20, 2019), http://www.uscis.gov/i-601a.

Part 6—Applicant's Statement, Contact Information, Certification, and Signature

Questions 1-6: The applicant must sign this section of the form under penalty of perjury. This must be an original signature; a copy of the signature will not be accepted. A parent or legal guardian may sign the form if the applicant is mentally incompetent. The applicant must also indicate that he or she reads and understands English or used an interpreter who read every question and instruction to the applicant, as well as the answer to every question. If the applicant is using someone to help prepare the answers on the application, check that box and have the preparer complete Part 8. The applicant certifies to the accuracy of photocopied documents and authorizes the release of information contained in the application or from any of the applicant's records. The applicant also authorizes the release of any information contained in the application, in supporting documentation, or in USCIS records to other entities or persons "where necessary for the administration and enforcement of U.S. immigration laws."

Part 7—Interpreter's Contact Information, Certification, and Signature

Questions 1-7: The interpreter must sign a certification that he or she is fluent in English and the applicant's language, that the interpreter read every question on the form to the applicant, and that the applicant understood the questions and answers given. The certification must be dated. The interpreter must also provide his or her first and last name, business or organization name, mailing address, and contact information.

Part 8—Preparer's Contact Information, Certification, and Signature

Questions 1–7: The person who prepared the application must list his or her first and last name, business or organization name, mailing address, and contact information. In addition, if the preparer is a BIA-accredited representative or attorney, the preparer may need to include a signed Form G-28, Notice of Appearance. The preparer must declare that the information prepared is based on information obtained from the applicant in response to the questions on the form or based on the preparer's knowledge. The preparer must sign and date the application.

Part 9—Additional Information

Use this section to include any additional information relevant to the application. Indicate to which page, part, and item number the additional information relates. If you plan to include additional information in an attached statement, write "See attached statement" in this section, with the applicant's name and "A" number (if any) at the top of each attached sheet.

Filing Requirements

The regulations and Form I-601A instructions contain specific requirements for the filing of the application. This section will cover the requirements for the submission of the waiver application packet.

The Application and Biometrics Fee

Each application must include a filing fee. Currently, the filing fee is $630. Check the USCIS website to verify that the filing fee has not changed.

All applicants under the age of 79 must include a filing fee for biometrics (fingerprints) in the amount of $85. You should also confirm the amount of the biometrics fee by checking the USCIS website.

The check or money order for the filing and biometrics fees must be payable to the U.S. Department of Homeland Security. Spell out the words "Department of Homeland Security"; do not use initials.

USCIS Address for Filing Waiver Packet

The current USCIS address for all provisional waivers is the USCIS Chicago lockbox. You can confirm that the Chicago lockbox remains the filing address on the USCIS website. If you are using the U.S. Postal Service to mail the waiver packet, the address is:

USCIS
P.O. Box 4599
Chicago, IL 60680

If you are using a courier service such as UPS or FedEx, the address is:

USCIS
Attn: I-601A
131 S. Dearborn, 3rd Floor
Chicago, IL 60603-5517

The Chicago lockbox will transfer the waiver applications to the appropriate Service Center for adjudication.

Copy of the Immigrant Visa Application Fee Bill Receipt

USCIS will not accept the provisional waiver packet unless it includes evidence that the applicant paid the immigrant visa application fee to the Department of State.[23] Place a copy of the receipt of the immigration visa application fee bill issued by the National Visa Center on top of the Form I-601A.[24] The fee receipt should include the National Visa Center case number and show payment of the immigrant visa application fee. If the fee was paid online, a printed receipt from the online payment is acceptable evidence of payment.[25] For a sample copy of a fee receipt, see Appendix 14A.

Name of Applicant and USCIS Receipt Number on Supporting Documents

Every page of each supporting document must contain the applicant's name and the USCIS receipt number. If the applicant has an "A" number, that should be included.[26] The USCIS website also states that you may include pagination for the attached documents. For example, write at the bottom of the page "1 of 11."

Copy of the I-797 Approval Notice

Include a copy of the I-130, I-140, or I-360 approval notice, Form I-797, with the waiver packet.[27]

Copy of Administrative Closure Order

An applicant in removal proceedings that have not resulted in a final order will not be eligible to file a provisional waiver unless the removal proceedings have been administratively closed and not re-calendared.[28] Attach a copy of the EOIR order administratively closing the applicant's removal proceedings with the waiver packet. An applicant in removal proceedings that have resulted in a final order will not be eligible to file a provisional waiver unless USCIS has granted the applicant's Form I-212, Application for Permission to Reapply for Admission into the United States After Deportation or Removal.

Make sure that the applicant's name on the EOIR order is the same as that on the waiver application and supporting documents.

Biometrics Appointment

After USCIS receives the waiver application, the applicant will be scheduled for a biometrics appointment at an Application Support Center. The applicant will receive a notice of the biometrics appointment and must attend the appointment.

Applicant and Qualifying Relative Declarations

The applicant and the qualifying relatives must submit a statement in support of the waiver application. Provide proof of the relationship between the applicant and the qualifying relative, such as a copy of a marriage certificate, a copy of a birth certificate, an adoption decree, etc. In addition, include proof of the qualify-

---

[23] USCIS, Rejection of Provisional Unlawful Presence Waiver Applications (Apr. 25, 2013).

[24] USCIS, Instructions for Application for Provisional Unlawful Presence Waiver, p. 14 (Oct. 20, 2019), http://www.uscis.gov/i-601a.

[25] USCIS, Invitation to Stakeholders Teleconference on Provisional Waivers (May 10, 2013), AILA Doc. No. 13050641.

[26] USCIS, Provisional Unlawful Presence Waivers, (May 6, 2013).

[27] USCIS, Instructions for Application for Provisional Unlawful Presence Waiver, p. 13 (Oct. 20, 2019), http://www.uscis.gov/i-601a.

[28] 8 CFR §212.7(e)(4)(v).

ing relative's U.S. citizenship. Evidence of the U.S. citizenship may include a copy of a birth certificate issued by one of the 50 states or by Guam or Puerto Rico, a copy of a naturalization certificate, a copy of a U.S. passport, or Form FS-240, Report of Birth Abroad.

Documents Proving Extreme Hardship and Supporting Favorable Exercise of Discretion

Submit copies of the documents proving extreme hardship to the qualifying relatives and copies of documents that establish that discretion should be favorably exercised in the case. See Chapters 4 and 7. As noted, the documents should be identified in an index, paginated, and contain the applicant's name and USCIS receipt number.

Practice Tip: After preparing the application and supporting documents, ask a colleague to review the packet to make sure you have complied with all of the filing requirements. A second set of eyes always helps. The application may be rejected or denied if the requirements are not met.

Chapter 9
Requests for Evidence and Denials

After submission of the waiver packet, U.S. Citizenship and Immigration Services (USCIS) may request additional evidence, deny the waiver application, or approve it. In this chapter, we address requests for evidence (RFEs), denials, and possible ways to respond to each. Chapter 10 will discuss what happens after the waiver is approved.

The standard procedures for responding to RFEs and denials are *not* applicable to applications for provisional waivers. The USCIS rationale for not providing the same procedural safeguards available in other immigration applications is that to do so would undermine the "efficiencies USCIS and the Department of State (DOS) will gain through the streamlined provisional unlawful presence waiver process."[1] In deciding whether a provisional waiver is the right procedure for your client's waiver case, make sure that your client understands the limitations on rebutting unfavorable decisions.

RFEs

RFE: Reason to Issue and Form of Request

USCIS may issue RFEs for waiver applications that are missing critical information related to extreme hardship or to whether the applicant merits a favorable exercise of discretion.[2] Although USCIS may also issue an RFE on other issues, it anticipates that most RFEs for provisional waivers will focus on extreme hardship and the exercise of discretion.[3] The RFE will be in writing and will specify the type of evidence required and whether the request is for initial or additional evidence.[4] By providing this information in the RFE, USCIS believes the applicant is being provided with adequate notice and sufficient information to respond.[5] However, practitioners have complained in the past that RFEs did not contain specific information regarding the request for additional evidence.[6] USCIS has listened to that complaint, and "boilerplate" RFEs should be less common.

USCIS is not required to issue an RFE when it finds that the waiver applicant has not submitted sufficient evidence to meet his or her burden of proof. Instead, USCIS may deny an application for a provisional waiver without issuing an RFE.[7] Also, on July 13, 2018, USCIS issued a policy memorandum titled "Issuance of Certain RFEs and NOIDs; Revisions to Adjudicator's Field Manual (AFM) Chapter 10.5(a), Chapter 10.5(b)."[8] That memo expands adjudicators' discretion to deny an immigration application, petition, or request without first issuing an RFE or a Notice of Intent to Deny (NOID) pursuant to 8 CFR §103.2(b)(8). USCIS officials may now issue a denial without sending an RFE in cases filed without sufficient initial evidence. The memo provides two examples, one of which is when a waiver application is submitted with little or no supporting evidence.

---

[1] 78 *Federal Register* (Fed. Reg.) 536 at 553 (Jan. 3, 2013).

[2] 78 Fed. Reg. 536 at 553.

[3] *Id.*

[4] 8 Code of Federal Regulations (CFR) §103.2(b)(8)(iv).

[5] *Id.*

[6] *See* "Practice Pointer: Responding to Boilerplate I-601A Requests for Evidence," AILA I Doc. No. 14111846.

[7] 8 CFR §212.7(e)(8) ("Notwithstanding 8 CFR §103.2(b)(16), USCIS may deny an application for a provisional unlawful presence waiver without prior issuance of a request for evidence or notice of intent to deny.").

[8] AILA Doc. No. 18071380 and also available on the USCIS website.

Time Frame to Respond to RFE

The general rule governing the time frame for a response to an RFE is that if USCIS requests evidence before adjudicating an application or petition, the maximum time to respond to the request is 84 days.[9] This time frame is true for RFEs involving all applications and petitions with the exception of two applications: the provisional waiver and the Form I-539, Application to Extend/Change Nonimmigrant Status. In the case of provisional waivers, the time frame to submit evidence requested by USCIS is limited to 30 days.[10] The agency's justification for the shortened deadline is to "streamline USCIS processing, prevent delays at the National Visa Center (NVC) and at consular posts, and allow applicants to complete immigrant processing in a timelier manner."[11] USCIS measures the 30-day period from the date that the RFE is issued (the date on the RFE), to the date on which the response to the RFE is received by USCIS. The date that the RFE is postmarked by the agency or the applicant is not applicable.

The 30-day deadline applies whether the request is for initial or additional evidence, and whether the evidence is available in the United States or must be requested from outside the country. However, as a matter of discretion, a USCIS adjudicator *may* increase the response time for the receipt of the evidence if a supervisor permits the additional time. The decision to permit additional time to receive the response to an RFE is made on a case-by-case basis in the discretion of the adjudicator and supervisor.[12]

> *Example*: Rosa is applying for a provisional waiver based on health-related hardship to her lawful permanent resident (LPR) husband Tomas. Tomas has suffered from asthma and bronchial conditions since childhood and receives medical treatment from Dr. Jones. Rosa was anxious to file the provisional waiver as soon as possible, and her representative filed the application with a copy of the prescription for Tomas's asthma medicine but without a letter from Dr. Jones. Yesterday, Rosa received an RFE asking for a doctor's letter confirming the asthma diagnosis. Dr. Jones is on vacation and will not return to his office until 10 days after the evidence is due. Rosa will need to request additional time to respond to the RFE and explain the basis for her request. In this case, she should include evidence that the doctor will not be returning until after the 30-day period has expired.

> *Practice Tips*: With only a 30-day time frame within which to obtain the necessary documents and send them to USCIS, it is very important that the initial application be as complete and thorough as possible. Do not submit the waiver application if it lacks critical evidence—especially declarations or documents from a foreign country—needed to satisfy the extreme hardship standard.

Given the short amount of time allowed to supply the required documentation, it will probably be necessary to enlist the support of your client. Consider having your client request the necessary documentation directly and also providing him or her with a cover letter explaining the evidence that is needed. If there is insufficient time to obtain it, seek alternate evidence. For example, if you need a doctor's letter and your client's doctor is on vacation, ask another doctor in the group practice for a letter. Or, submit a copy of a medical record that addresses the concerns raised by the RFE.

Notice of Intent to Deny (NOID)

In many types of applications and petitions, USCIS may issue a notice of intent to deny (NOID) to provide an applicant or a petitioner with an opportunity to address reasons that USCIS is considering denying the case.[13] However, USCIS will not issue NOIDs in the provisional waiver application process.[14] The waiver

---

[9] U.S. Citizenship and Immigration Services (USCIS), Policy Memorandum PM-602-0040, "Change in Standard Timeframes for Applicants or Petitioners to Respond to Requests for Evidence, Revisions to AFM Chapter 105.(b), Chapter 25.2(e)(3), Chapter 38.1(e)(6), and Appendix 10-9, AFM Update AD11-36" (July 7, 2011), AILA Doc. No. 11071334.

[10] USCIS, "Standard Timeframe for Applicants to Respond to Requests for Evidence Issued in Relation to a Request for a Provisional Unlawful Presence Waiver, Form I-601A" (Mar. 1, 2013), Doc. No. 13031842. The RFE time frame for Form I-539 is also 30 days.

[11] *Id.*

[12] *Id.*

[13] 8 CFR §§103.2(b)(8)(iii)–(iv).

[14] 78 Fed. Reg. 536 at 553.

application may be denied without providing the applicant an opportunity to provide additional information or to rebut the negative information that USCIS discovered its background check.[15]

Application Rejected and Returned

The regulations require that the application be rejected and the application packet and fee be returned to the applicant if the applicant:

- Fails to pay the required filing fee or pay the correct filing fee;
- Fails to sign the Form I-601A;
- Fails to provide his or her family name, home address in the United States, and date of birth;
- Is under the age of 17;
- Does not include evidence of an approved I-130 or I-360 visa petition in the immediate relative classification;
- Fails to include a copy of the immigrant visa application fee form to the Department of State indicating payment of the fee, or
- Has indicated that the Department of State scheduled a consular visa interview prior to January 3, 2013.[16]

On April 25, 2013, USCIS issued a reminder to applicants that it cannot accept a waiver application without evidence that the applicant paid the Immigrant Visa Application Fee to the Department of State.[17] If the applicant fails to include a copy of the receipt indicating that the fee has been paid, USCIS will automatically reject and return the application packet and fee to the applicant. USCIS will accept only an official receipt from the NVC containing the NVC case number with the fee status "paid," or if the fee was paid online, a printed receipt from the online payment.[18]

Failure to Attend Biometrics Appointment

An applicant for the provisional waiver must pay the biometrics fee and complete biometrics.[19] After the waiver application is received, USCIS will schedule a biometrics appointment. If the applicant fails to attend the scheduled biometrics appointment, USCIS will deny the waiver application for abandonment.[20] The applicant cannot appeal or request reopening or reconsideration of the denial based on abandonment of the application.

Practice Tip: If the applicant cannot attend the biometrics appointment on the day and time that it is scheduled, he or she can request that the appointment date be rescheduled. Information regarding how to reschedule the biometrics appointment may be found on the back of the biometrics appointment notice. Individuals frequently need to reschedule biometrics appointments, and it is usually easy to do so. If the applicant needs to reschedule the appointment, he or she should make sure that the rescheduling request is not immediately before the appointment.

Denials

Appeals

In the case of most petitions and applications, petitioners and applicants whose cases are denied may appeal that decision to an appellate division of USCIS, the Administrative Appeals Office (AAO), or the Board of Immigration Appeals (BIA). There is no appeal from the denial of a provisional waiver.[21] An applicant

---

[15] 8 CFR §212.7(e)(8).

[16] 8 CFR §§212.7(e)(5)(ii)(A)–(G).

[17] USCIS Press Release, "Rejection of Provisional Unlawful Presence Waiver Applications (Form I-601A)" (Apr. 25, 2013), AILA Doc. No. 13042554.

[18] USCIS, Invitation to Stakeholders Teleconference on Provisional Waivers (May 10, 2013), AILA Doc. No. 13050641.

[19] 8 CFR §212.7(e)(6).

[20] 8 CFR §212.7(e)(6)(ii).

[21] 8 CFR §212.7(e)(11).

may re-file for a provisional waiver and submit additional evidence if the immigrant visa application is still pending with the Department of State (DOS).[22] The applicant must also notify DOS again that he or she intends to file a new Form I-601A, and pay the waiver application and biometrics fees again.

Practice Tip: Unless the applicant missed the biometrics appointment and USCIS denied the application as abandoned, it will usually not be worthwhile to re-file the application with the same evidence that resulted in the prior denial. Make sure that the new I-601A application packet contains information not previously provided that demonstrates that the applicant meets the eligibility criteria for the I-601A waiver and merits the approval of the waiver in the exercise of discretion.

The applicant may also file a Form I-601, Waiver of Grounds of Inadmissibility—the general waiver application—under the centralized waiver process after an interview at the consulate or embassy and a finding of inadmissibility.[23] In this case, the applicant will be eligible to request a waiver for other grounds of inadmissibility. The applicant will also be able to file an appeal to the AAO if the waiver application is denied.[24]

Example: Joan decided to file a provisional waiver, even though she had made a misrepresentation on an application for a visitor's visa two years before she entered the United States without inspection. USCIS denied her waiver in the exercise of discretion. Joan decided to proceed with consular processing, attend her interview, and file a Form I-601 application for waiver for unlawful presence, and if necessary, for the second ground of inadmissibility.

Practice Tip: Evaluate your client's case carefully to determine if there are grounds of inadmissibility that may bar your client from filing for the provisional waiver. Review FBI and state criminal records checks to determine if arrests or convictions render your client inadmissible. If your client has a conviction that falls within the "petty offense" or "youthful offender" exception or is not a crime involving moral turpitude, USCIS will weigh the positive and negative factors in the case to determine whether the applicant warrants a favorable exercise of discretion.

Motion to Reopen or Reconsider

Motions to reopen or reconsider are not available under the provisional waiver process.[25] USCIS expressed concern that allowing motions to reopen or reconsider would eliminate the efficiencies the agency anticipated it would gain through the streamlined provisional waiver process.[26] In addition, USCIS indicated that motions to reopen or reconsider could "significantly interfere with the operational agreements between USCIS and DOS and could substantially delay waiver and immigrant visa processing."[27] Since a motion to reopen or reconsider is not available in the provisional waiver process, an applicant who wanted to show changed circumstances or that he or she was the victim of an ineffective application prepared by a notary would need to re-file a new waiver application following a denial. USCIS, however, may reopen and reconsider its decision at any time.[28]

Consider notifying the Office of the Citizenship and Immigration Services Ombudsman if you believe an I-601A application was wrongly denied. The agency may file a formal inquiry with USCIS and a possible review of the decision. The Ombudsman Office can be contacted at cisombudsman@hq.dhs.gov.

Removal Proceedings Following Denial

If the waiver is denied by the USCIS service center, the applicant will be subject to the current USCIS policy on issuance of a Notice to Appear (NTA), which commences removal proceedings. On June 28, 2018, USCIS formally rescinded its prior policy memorandum on the referral of cases and issuance of

---

[22] 8 CFR §212.7(e)(9).
[23] *Id.*
[24] *Id.*
[25] 8 CFR §212.7(e)(11).
[26] 78 Fed. Reg. 536 at 553.
[27] *Id.*
[28] 8 CFR §212.7(e)(13).

NTAs and replaced it with a stricter one.[29] According to the current memo, USCIS will issue NTAs when a waiver application is denied and the applicant is not lawfully present. Most provisional waiver applicants are not lawfully present in the United States. In a USCIS teleconference on the new policy guidance, the agency confirmed that it "is implementing the memo incrementally to ensure sufficient time for training and attention to logistical detail."[30] At the present time, the USCIS has not publicly announced that it will implement the NTA memo on denied I-601A applications.

If the applicant is lawfully present but removable and the waiver is denied, USCIS will issue an NTA if he or she falls into a specific enforcement category. USCIS may refer a case to ICE before adjudicating the waiver if there is suspected fraud or the applicant has a certain criminal history.

---

[29] USCIS Policy Memorandum PM-602-0050.1, "Updated Guidance for the Referral of Cases and Issuance of Notices to Appear (NTAs) in Cases Involving Inadmissible and Deportable Aliens" (June 28, 2018), AILA Doc. No. 18070539.

[30] USCIS Teleconference on Notice to Appear (NTA), Updated Policy Guidance (Nov. 15, 2018), AILA Doc. No. 18110836.

CHAPTER 10
APPROVALS AND WHAT COMES NEXT

Approval Notices

If the U.S. Citizenship and Immigration Services (USCIS) approves the waiver application, it will send notification to the applicant, the applicant's attorney or representative, and the National Visa Center (NVC). It will notify the applicant by mailing the approval notice to the address listed in response to Question 7 on the Form I-601A. It will send notification electronically to the NVC. The next step for the applicant depends on where he or she is in the immigrant visa application process, which is described below.

Significance of an Approved I-601A

Approval of the Form I-601A does not provide any interim rights or benefits. For example, it does not allow the applicant to obtain employment authorization or advance parole.[1] It does not allow the applicant to be eligible to apply for adjustment of status; the applicant must still depart the United States and appear at the immigrant visa interview. It does not provide a lawful immigration status, so it does not toll or end the running of unlawful presence. It does not extend any authorized period of stay, and it does not provide any protection from being placed into removal proceedings or being removed. Approval of the I-601A application does not guarantee that the immigrant visa will be approved, since that will depend on the outcome of the consular interview. Even if the immigrant visa is approved by the consulate, the applicant must still be granted admission to the United States by U.S. Customs and Border Protection (CBP) before entering as a lawful permanent resident (LPR).[2]

Approval of the Form I-601A is made on a provisional basis. This is because the applicant has not yet triggered the unlawful presence bar by departing the United States. The agency cannot technically approve a waiver for a ground of inadmissibility before a determination has been made that the applicant is inadmissible. That finding is made by the consular officer at the time of the immigrant visa interview.

The waiver approval is also provisional because the consulate retains power to find that the applicant was not entitled to receive it. The consulate will conduct its own review to determine if the applicant is inadmissible based on any other ground. Although the consulate will not go behind the USCIS finding of extreme hardship or that the applicant merits a favorable exercise of discretion, it will make an independent determination of admissibility. USCIS determines eligibility to apply for the provisional waiver based on information in its databases, the biometrics results, and the applicant's self-reporting of a ground of inadmissibility on the Form I-601A, but the Department of State (DOS) relies on different information.

The consulate will review responses to questions on the Form DS-260, Online Immigrant Visa Application. It will check its databases and the results of its biometric screening. It will also question the applicant in person during the consular interview. Some of the more common grounds of inadmissibility that may appear at the consular interview stage, but that did not arise at the USCIS adjudication stage, include the following:

- Fraud or misrepresentation when applying for a nonimmigrant visa or when seeking admission to the United States;
- False claim of citizenship;
- Public charge;
- Other immigration violations;
- Smuggling;
- Health-related ground, such as prior use of a controlled substance (drug abuser or drug addict);

---

[1] 8 Code of Federal Regulations (CFR) §212.7(e)(2)(ii).

[2] U.S. Citizenship and Immigration Services (USCIS), *Instructions for Application for Provisional Unlawful Presence Waiver*, p. 11 (Oct. 20, 2019), http://www.uscis.gov/i-601a.

- Health-related ground, such as driving while impaired or intoxicated (mental disorder with associated harmful behavior); and
- Criminal conviction that was not identified by USCIS or was entered after adjudication of the I-601A waiver application.

If the consulate determines at the time of the immigrant visa interview that the client is inadmissible under any ground other than unlawful presence, then the approved provisional waiver is automatically revoked.[3] (All of these grounds of inadmissibility are covered in Chapter 3.) If the approved provisional waiver is revoked, the immigrant visa applicant has the right to apply for a waiver on Form I-601, Application for Waiver of Grounds of Inadmissibility, which would be adjudicated by the Nebraska Service Center. USCIS has indicated that the finding of extreme hardship that was made for the I-601A waiver application will not carry any weight in the adjudication of a subsequent I-601 waiver application. It stated that "the extreme hardship and discretionary determination is based on a careful consideration of the evidence of record at the time of decision. … USCIS will consider the DOS consular officer's findings when reviewing the Form I-601 and assessing whether the applicant warrants a favorable exercise of discretion."[4]

Advising the Client

Review the points described above with the client after the I-601A application is approved and explain what the approval does and does not provide. Emphasize that this does not guarantee that the client will be granted the immigrant visa at the consulate. The client must still establish eligibility for the immigrant visa (*e.g.*, bona fide marriage to a U.S. citizen or legal parent-child relationship). Discuss the possible grounds of inadmissibility that the consulate might discover during the interview, and make sure that none of them apply in his or her case.

Inform the client of the consequences of leaving the country and then returning or attempting to return illegally. The approved I-601A application will be automatically revoked if the client at any time before or after approval of the waiver or before issuance of the immigrant visa reenters or attempts to reenter the country without being inspected and admitted or paroled.[5] In addition to revoking the waiver, illegal reentry or attempted illegal reentry after accruing one year or more of unlawful presence triggers the "permanent" bar, as discussed in Chapter 3.[6]

The approved waiver will also be automatically revoked should the I-130 petitioner withdraw the approved petition before the immigrant visa is issued.[7] Should the petitioner die before issuance of the visa, the petition itself will automatically be revoked, thus revoking the approved waiver.[8] But in cases in which the U.S. citizen spouse dies, the approved I-130 petition converts to an approved I-360 petition, and the widow or widower, as well as any derivative children, should be able to proceed under special provisions described in Chapter 1. Finally, should the I-130 petition and immigrant visa application be terminated based on Immigration and Nationality Act (INA) §203(g) because of the client's failure to attend the consular interview or respond to notices from the NVC, the waiver approval will also be revoked.[9]

Some practitioners may want the client to sign an advisal that incorporates all of these issues. This puts the client on written notice of the limitations of the approved waiver and the consequences of certain action or inaction. A sample advisal in English and Spanish is included in Appendix 15.

If the client is still in removal proceedings that were administratively closed, he or she should have those proceedings terminated or dismissed without prejudice by the Executive Office for Immigration Review be-

---

[3] 8 CFR §212.7(e)(14)(i).

[4] USCIS, "Questions and Answers, USCIS—American Immigration Lawyers Association (AILA) Meeting" (Apr. 11, 2013), AILA Doc. No. 13041143, at 2.

[5] 8 CFR §212.7(e)(14)(iv).

[6] Immigration and Nationality Act (INA) §212(a)(9)(C)(i)(I).

[7] 8 CFR §212.7(e)(14)(ii).

[8] *Id.*

[9] 8 CFR §212.7(e)(14)(iii).

fore departing for the consular interview. This will require the involvement, if not the cooperation, of the Immigration and Customs Enforcement (ICE) trial attorney. Practitioners have reported that local ICE attorneys have opposed such motions and that immigration judges are insisting that the respondents accept voluntary departure. This has resulted in difficulties coordinating the client's departure and appearance at the immigrant visa interview.

If formal termination of the proceedings is not accomplished before departing, it theoretically could result in the immigrant visa's issuance being delayed or the applicant's being found ineligible because of inadmissibility based on a separate ground of inadmissibility. This could be the ground for failure to attend a removal proceeding without reasonable cause,[10] or having been ordered removed, or having departed the United States while an order of removal was outstanding.[11] However, there is no clear authority indicating that departure while immigration proceedings are still pending automatically triggers an order of deportation or removal. The U.S. consulate in Cd. Juarez recently confirmed that it would grant an immigrant visa to an applicant whose removal proceedings were administratively closed but not terminated.

Preparing the Client for Consular Processing

The client has already begun the immigrant visa process by, at a minimum, paying the DOS immigrant visa fee bill. USCIS has reassured provisional waiver applicants that the pending I-601A application will not affect the validity of the DOS immigrant visa fee.[12] In other words, the client will not be required to pay the fee again because of Form I-601A processing, provided the applicant has complied with all DOS processing requirements.

USCIS will notify DOS electronically of the I-601A approval. The NVC, upon receipt of the notice, will record the approval in its system, which will allow the consular officer to verify the approval. If the applicant is "documentarily qualified"—*i.e.*, has paid all remaining fees and submitted all necessary documents—the NVC will then schedule the applicant for the consular interview.[13] The timing of the interview will depend on the backlog at the particular consular post. The NVC will notify the applicant of the interview date and then forward the case with a cover sheet noting the Form I-601A approval to the consular post.

If the applicant has not completed all the steps necessary for the NVC to schedule the interview, the following is an overview of what will take place.

Immigrant Visa Application and Document Submission

After the immigrant visa and affidavit of support fees have been paid, all applicants must complete and submit the DS-260, Online Immigrant Visa and Alien Registration Application. The form is completed and submitted through the Consular Electronic Application Center (CEAC). To log on to CEAC the applicant or preparer must use the NVC case number and invoice ID number provided in the initial case creation notice from NVC. All of the information entered online is accessible by the NVC and consular officers and the applicant is not required to bring a copy to the visa interview. Once the form is completed and electronically submitted, the applicant will be instructed to print a confirmation page. At the interview, the applicant will be required to swear under oath that the information entered into the form is true and correct and will provide a biometric signature.

The petitioner must complete and submit Form I-864, Affidavit of Support, and supporting documentation to the NVC for a technical review. Additionally, the applicant must submit civil documents and police certificates (unless the applicant is from a country where those are not available) to the NVC. Most applicants will upload and submit the required documents through CEAC. CEAC creates a list of the required documents for each applicant based on information provided on the DS-260. For older cases, the applicant will not upload the documents, but will send photocopies of them to the NVC. For these older cases, it is important to send

---

[10] INA §212(a)(6)(B).

[11] INA §212(a)(9)(A)(i).

[12] Provisional Unlawful Presence Waivers of Inadmissibility for Certain Immediate Relatives, 78 *Federal Register* (Fed. Reg.) 535–578 at 549 (Jan. 3, 2013).

[13] *Id.* at 552.

the documents with the NVC cover sheet that contains the case number and barcode. In all cases, the applicant must present the original documents, plus a photocopy of each at the immigrant visa interview.

Documents not in English or in the native language of the jurisdiction where the consular post is located will have to be translated into English. The translations should bear a certificate of accuracy in which the translator swears that he or she is familiar with both languages, has translated the document into English, and that it is a true and complete translation.

The documents that are required include the following:

- a photocopy of the biographic data page of the applicant's valid, unexpired passport[14];
- applicant's birth certificate;
- marriage certificate (if applicable);
- evidence of the termination of each prior marriage, such as a final divorce decree, death certificate, or annulment papers;
- if the applicant has served in the military forces of any country, a copy of his or her military record;
- if the applicant has been convicted of a crime, a certified copy of each court disposition; and
- if the applicant is age 16 or older, a police certificate, if available, from that country.

Primary documentation, such as of birth or marriage, would be a certificate from a government agency that maintains official records. If such a document is unavailable in the issuing country, the applicant may submit secondary evidence, which may consist of such documents as baptismal or other church records.[15] If these are also unavailable, then an affidavit from a person who has personal knowledge of the event in question may be accepted. For more information on acceptable documents, see 8 CFR §204.1(g). For information on the availability of documents in foreign countries, see the U.S. Visa Reciprocity and Civil Documents by Country page on the travel.state.gov website.

Appointment Letter for Immigrant Visa Applicants

Approximately four to six weeks before the scheduled immigrant visa interview, the applicant will receive an appointment letter or e-mail that contains the date, time, and location of the visa interview.16 . The appointment letter instructs applicants to visit the DOS website for interview preparation instructions and to review consulate-specific instructions. A sample appointment packet is included as part of Appendix 14C. The website provides information to the visa applicant on preparing for the medical examination and reminds the applicant of the documents that he or she must bring to the visa interview including the interview appointment notice from the NVC, a passport valid for at least six months beyond the intended date of entry into the U.S, a copy of the biographic page of the passport, the original required civil documents and the confirmation page from the DS-260 that was submitted on CEAC.

Once the NVC has completed the administrative processing and scheduled the visa interview, it will send the case file along with electronic data to the appropriate U.S. consulate abroad.

For information on the status of a case still pending at the NVC, one may call the automated voice center at (603) 334-0700. Telephone operators are available to answer questions Monday through Friday from 7:00 a.m. to midnight (Eastern Time). Lately, however, the telephonic system has proved ineffective due to the volume of callers and the limited number of operators. The mailing address is 31 Rochester Avenue, Suite 200, Portsmouth, NH 03801-2915. Case inquiries may also be made through the Ask NVC Public Inquiry form on the travel.state.gov website. The form asks for the NVC case number or USCIS receipt number, the principal applicant's name and date of birth, the petitioner's name and an e-mail address. The form requires the inquirer to identify him or herself as the petitioner, principal applicant, attorney of record or other.

---

[14] The original passport should not be sent to the NVC.

[15] 22 CFR §42.65(d).

[16] 22 CFR §42.62(b).

The Medical Examination

All applicants for an immigrant visa must undergo a medical examination.[17] The examination must be conducted by a designated doctor, called a panel physician, located in the country where the interview takes place.[18] Medical examinations are conducted according to regulations published by the Department of Health and Human Services (HHS) and procedures established by the Centers for Disease Control and Prevention, an agency of HHS.[19] The medical examination is not a complete examination but is designed to screen for certain medical conditions that are relevant to the applicant's admissibility to the United States.

The U.S. embassy and consulate websites provide a listing of the panel physicians authorized to conduct the medical examination in the location where the consulate is located Applicants are instructed to contact one of the physicians to schedule a medical examination and to obtain information on the cost of the examination and necessary testing. In addition to the list of panel physicians, some consulates provide specific instructions on scheduling the medical examination and the documents needed for the appointment. A sample Instructions for Medical Examination is included as Appendix 14D. In all cases, the applicant must bring the visa appointment letter, his or her passport, and vaccination records, if available. The vaccination requirements constitute an important part of the medical examination. A discussion of the vaccination requirements and other health-related grounds of inadmissibility can be found in Chapter 3.

Following the medical examination, the panel physician either will forward the results directly to the consulate or will provide the applicant with the result in a sealed envelope for the applicant to bring to the interview.

Consular Interview

During the interview, the consular official will confirm the information contained in the DS-260 application, screen for any applicable ground of inadmissibility, review the supporting documents, confirm that the medical examination does not reveal any health-related problem that could prevent approval or require a waiver, and determine whether the applicant is likely to become a public charge. The consular officer has the right to inquire into the validity of the marriage or the relationship that forms the basis of the immigrant petition.[20]

When an immigrant visa is issued, it can be valid for up to six months.[21] To obtain permanent resident status, the immigrant visa holder must travel to the United States with an immigrant visa packet and be admitted within the visa validity period. Additionally, in order to obtain a visa, the applicant must present a passport that is valid for at least 60 days beyond the validity of the immigrant visa.[22]

If an immigrant visa is refused, the consular officer will inform the applicant of the reasons for the denial, including the provision of law or regulation on which the refusal is based.[23] If the reason for the refusal may be overcome with the submission of additional documents and the applicant indicates an intention to submit the additional evidence, the file will remain open for up to one year.[24] Once the applicant has obtained the necessary documentation, the interview should be rescheduled. However, if no action is taken on the case for one year after the interview, registration—*i.e.*, eligibility to apply for an immigrant visa—will be terminated.[25] The consular officer at the post should notify the applicant of the termination and the right to have the

---

[17] INA §221(d); 22 CFR §42.66(a).

[18] 22 CFR §42.66(b).

[19] 42 CFR §34.3; Centers for Disease Control and Prevention, Technical Instructions for the Medical Examination of Aliens [panel physicians], http://www.cdc.gov/panelphysicians/index.html.

[20] 22 CFR §42.62(b).

[21] 22 CFR §42.72(a).

[22] 22 CFR §42.64(b).

[23] 22 CFR §42.81(b).

[24] *Id.*

[25] 9 *Foreign Affairs Manual* (FAM) 504.13-2(A)(2).

registration reinstated within one year by demonstrating that the failure to act was because of circumstances beyond his or her control.[26]

If the consular officer is requesting information or documentation that the applicant or representative believes is inappropriate or unnecessary, it is advisable to communicate directly with the consular post.. Put concerns in writing with cites to the appropriate regulations, FAM section, or DOS cables that support your position. If attempts to persuade the consular official who is handling the case are unsuccessful, the applicant or representative may seek review from the principal consular officer at that post.[27] In most instances, there is no judicial review of a visa denial.[28] Representatives also may seek intervention from officials at the DOS Visa Office in Washington, D.C. For such intervention, or to request an advisory opinion on a specific legal issue, send an email to legalnet@state.gov.

USCIS Immigrant Fee

An immigrant visa holder must pay a USCIS immigrant fee (currently $220) after he or she receives the visa packets from the consulate or embassy.[29] This fee is separate from the immigrant visa fee paid to DOS. The fee covers the cost of producing and delivering the permanent resident card once the visa holder is admitted to the United States. The fee must be paid online through the USCIS website with a debit or credit card or a checking account from a U.S. financial institution. Once the fee is paid, the payer should print a receipt and keep it for his or her records. The applicant need not pay the fee himself or herself; any other person may pay on the applicant's behalf.

If the USCIS immigrant fee is not paid, the visa holder will still be admitted to the United States and will receive a passport stamp valid for one year evidencing lawful permanent residence status. However, the new resident will not receive a Form I-551 Permanent Resident Card until the required fee is paid. Adopted children who immigrate under the inter-country adoption program and K visa holders are exempt from paying this fee.

Termination of Registration

Under INA §203(g), DOS is authorized to terminate the registration of anyone who fails to apply for an immigrant visa within one year of notification of the availability of the visa. This provision applies if the applicant fails to contact the NVC after being notified of visa availability, or if the applicant fails to appear for a scheduled interview and does not contact the consulate within one year of the missed appointment.[30] Registration is also terminated if an alien fails to submit evidence to overcome the basis for a visa denial within one year after visa refusal.[31]

The regulations require that the consulate notify the registrant of the termination of registration and the right to seek reinstatement within one year of notification by establishing that the failure to apply for an immigrant visa within one year was because of circumstances beyond the applicant's control.[32] Such circumstances include illness preventing the alien from traveling and inability to obtain travel documents.[33]

---

[26] 22 CFR §42.83(d).

[27] 22 CFR §42.82(c).

[28] *Kleindienst v. Mandel*, 408 U.S. 753 (1972) (judicial review when the government denies a visa if no facially legitimate and bona fide reason).

[29] Always confirm fee amount, as fees change regularly.

[30] 22 CFR §42.83(a).

[31] 22 CFR §42.83(b).

[32] 22 CFR §42.83(c).

[33] 22 CFR §42.83(e).

APPENDICES

Appendix 1: Provisional Waiver Regulations	117
Appendix 2: I-601A Comparison Chart	121
Appendix 3: General Immigration Law Intake Form	123
Appendix 4: Extreme Hardship Intake Sheet – Questions for Practitioners	127
Appendix 5A: Extreme Hardship Intake Sheet – Questions for Clients	137
Appendix 5B: Extreme Hardship Intate Sheet – Questions for Qualifying Relative	139
Appendix 6: Sample List of Documents	149
Appendix 7: Expert Reports and Other Resources	153
Appendix 8: Guidelines for Writing Declarations	157
Appendix 9: Sample Letters for Doctors, Employers, Teachers, and Others in Preparing Declarations	159
Appendix 10A: Sample Declaration of Qualifying Relative	163
Appendix 10B: Sample Declaration of Qualifying Relative	167
Appendix 10C: Sample Declaration of Waiver Applicant	169
Appendix 11: Sample Financial Statement	171
Appendix 12A: Sample Cover Letters and Index of Exhibits	173
Appendix 12B: Sample Cover Letter and Index of Exhibits	177
Appendix 13: Sample Legal Brief	181
Appendix 14A: Sample IV Fee Receipt	191
Appendix 14B: Sample NVC Instruction Packet	193
Appendix 14C: Sample NVC Interview Appointment Packet	195
Appendix 14D: Sample NVC Medical Exam Letter	197
Appendix 15: Sample Advisal	201

APPENDIX 1
PROVISIONAL WAIVER REGULATIONS
Regulations on Provisional Unlawful Presence Waivers, 8 CFR §212(e)

(e) Provisional unlawful presence waivers of inadmissibility. The provisions of this paragraph (e) apply to certain aliens who are pursuing consular immigrant visa processing.

(1) Jurisdiction. USCIS has exclusive jurisdiction to grant a provisional unlawful presence waiver under this paragraph (e). An alien applying for a provisional unlawful presence waiver must file with USCIS the form designated by USCIS, with the fees prescribed in 8 CFR 103.7(b), and in accordance with the form instructions.

(2) Provisional unlawful presence waiver; in general. (i) USCIS may adjudicate applications for a provisional unlawful presence waiver of inadmissibility based on section 212(a)(9)(B)(v) of the Act filed by eligible aliens described in paragraph (e)(3) of this section. USCIS will only approve such provisional unlawful presence waiver applications in accordance with the conditions outlined in paragraph (e) of this section. Consistent with section 212(a)(9)(B)(v) of the Act, the decision whether to approve a provisional unlawful presence waiver application is discretionary. A pending or approved provisional unlawful presence waiver does not constitute a grant of a lawful immigration status or a period of stay authorized by the Secretary.

(ii) A pending or an approved provisional unlawful presence waiver does not support the filing of any application for interim immigration benefits, such as employment authorization or an advance parole document. Any application for an advance parole document or employment authorization that is submitted in connection with a provisional unlawful presence waiver application will be rejected.

(3) Eligible aliens. Except as provided in paragraph (e)(4) of this section, an alien may be eligible to apply for and receive a provisional unlawful presence waiver for the grounds of inadmissibility under section 212(a)(9)(B)(i)(I) or (II) of the Act if he or she meets the requirements in this paragraph. An alien may be eligible to apply for and receive a waiver if he or she:

(i) Is present in the United States at the time of filing the application for a provisional unlawful presence waiver;

(ii) Provides biometrics to USCIS at a location in the United States designated by USCIS;

(iii) Upon departure, would be inadmissible only under section 212(a)(9)(B)(i) of the Act at the time of the immigrant visa interview;

(iv) Has a case pending with the Department of State, based on:

(A) An approved immigrant visa petition, for which the Department of State immigrant visa processing fee has been paid; or

(B) Selection by the Department of State to participate in the Diversity Visa Program under section 203(c) of the Act for the fiscal year for which the alien registered;

(v) Will depart from the United States to obtain the immigrant visa; and

(vi) Meets the requirements for a waiver provided in section 212(a)(9)(B)(v) of the Act.

(4) Ineligible aliens. Notwithstanding paragraph (e)(3) of this section, an alien is ineligible for a provisional unlawful presence waiver under paragraph (e) of this section if:

(i) The alien is under the age of 17;

(ii) The alien does not have a case pending with the Department of State, based on:

(A) An approved immigrant visa petition, for which the Department of State immigrant visa processing fee has been paid; or

(B) Selection by the Department of State to participate in the Diversity Visa program under section 203(c) of the Act for the fiscal year for which the alien registered;

(iii) The alien is in removal proceedings, in which no final order has been entered, unless the removal proceedings are administratively closed and have not been recalendared at the time of filing the application for a provisional unlawful presence waiver;

(iv) The alien is subject to an administratively final order of removal, deportation, or exclusion under any provision of law (including an in absentia order under section 240(b)(5) of the Act), unless the alien has already filed and USCIS has already granted, before the alien applies for a provisional unlawful presence waiver under 8 CFR 212.7(e), an application for consent to reapply for admission under section 212(a)(9)(A)(iii) of the Act and 8 CFR 212.2(j);

(v) CBP or ICE, after service of notice under 8 CFR 241.8, has reinstated a prior order of removal under section 241(a)(5) of the Act, either before the filing of the provisional unlawful presence waiver application or while the provisional unlawful presence waiver application is pending; or

(vi) The alien has a pending application with USCIS for lawful permanent resident status.

(5) Filing. (i) An alien must file an application for a provisional unlawful presence waiver of the unlawful presence inadmissibility bars under section 212(a)(9)(B)(i)(I) or (II) of the Act on the form designated by USCIS, in accordance with the form instructions, with the fee prescribed in 8 CFR 103.7(b), and with the evidence required by the form instructions.

(ii) An application for a provisional unlawful presence waiver will be rejected and the fee and package returned to the alien if the alien:

(A) Fails to pay the required filing fee or correct filing fee for the provisional unlawful presence waiver application;

(B) Fails to sign the provisional unlawful presence waiver application;

(C) Fails to provide his or her family name, domestic home address, and date of birth;

(D) Is under the age of 17;

(E) Does not include evidence of:

(1) An approved immigrant visa petition;

(2) Selection by the Department of State to participate in the Diversity Visa Program under section 203(c) of the Act for the fiscal year for which the alien registered; or

(3) Eligibility as a derivative beneficiary of an approved immigrant visa petition or of an alien selected for participation in the Diversity Visa Program as provided in this section and outlined in section 203(d) of the Act.

(F) Fails to include documentation evidencing:

(1) That the alien has paid the immigrant visa processing fee to the Department of State for the immigrant visa application upon which the alien's approved immigrant visa petition is based; or

(2) In the case of a diversity immigrant, that the Department of State selected the alien to participate in the Diversity Visa Program for the fiscal year for which the alien registered.

(6) Biometrics. (i) All aliens who apply for a provisional unlawful presence waiver under this section will be required to provide biometrics in accordance with 8 CFR 103.16 and 103.17, as specified on the form instructions.

(ii) Failure to appear for biometric services. If an alien fails to appear for a biometric services appointment or fails to provide biometrics in the United States as directed by USCIS, a provisional unlawful presence waiver application will be considered abandoned and denied under 8 CFR 103.2(b)(13). The alien may not appeal or file a motion to reopen or reconsider an abandonment denial under 8 CFR 103.5.

(7) Burden and standard of proof. The alien has the burden to establish, by a preponderance of the evidence, eligibility for a provisional unlawful presence waiver as described in this paragraph, and under section 212(a)(9)(B)(v) of the Act, including that the alien merits a favorable exercise of discretion.

(8) Adjudication. USCIS will adjudicate a provisional unlawful presence waiver application in accordance with this paragraph and section 212(a)(9)(B)(v) of the Act. If USCIS finds that the alien is not eligible for a provisional unlawful presence waiver, or if USCIS determines in its discretion that a waiver is not warranted, USCIS will deny the waiver application. Notwithstanding 8 CFR 103.2(b)(16), USCIS may deny an application for a provisional unlawful presence waiver without prior issuance of a request for evidence or notice of intent to deny.

(9) Notice of decision. (i) USCIS will notify the alien and the alien's attorney of record or accredited representative of the decision in accordance with 8 CFR 103.2(b)(19). USCIS may notify the Department of State of the denial of an application for a provisional unlawful presence waiver. A denial is without prejudice to the alien's filing another provisional unlawful presence waiver application under this paragraph (e), provided the alien meets all of the requirements in this part, including that the alien's case must be pending with the Department of State. An alien also may elect to file a waiver application under paragraph (a)(1) of this section after departing the United States, appearing for his or her immigrant visa interview at the U.S. Embassy or consulate abroad, and after the Department of State determines the alien's admissibility and eligibility for an immigrant visa.

(ii) Denial of an application for a provisional unlawful presence waiver is not a final agency action for purposes of section 10(c) of the Administrative Procedure Act, 5 U.S.C. 704.

(10) Withdrawal of waiver applications. An alien may withdraw his or her application for a provisional unlawful presence waiver at any time before USCIS makes a final decision. Once the case is withdrawn, USCIS will close the case and notify the alien and his or her attorney or accredited representative. The alien may file a new application for a provisional unlawful presence waiver, in accordance with the form instructions and required fees, provided that the alien meets all of the requirements included in this paragraph (e).

(11) Appeals and motions to reopen. There is no administrative appeal from a denial of a request for a provisional unlawful presence waiver under this section. The alien may not file, pursuant to 8 CFR 103.5, a motion to reopen or reconsider a denial of a provisional unlawful presence waiver application under this section.

(12) Approval and conditions. A provisional unlawful presence waiver granted under this section:

(i) Does not take effect unless, and until, the alien who applied for and obtained the provisional unlawful presence waiver:

(A) Departs from the United States;

(B) Appears for an immigrant visa interview at a U.S. Embassy or consulate; and

(C) Is determined to be otherwise eligible for an immigrant visa by the Department of State in light of the approved provisional unlawful presence waiver.

(ii) Waives, upon satisfaction of the conditions described in paragraph (e)(12)(i), the alien's inadmissibility under section 212(a)(9)(B) of the Act only for purposes of the application for an immigrant visa and admission to the United States as an immigrant based on the approved immigrant visa petition upon which a provisional unlawful presence waiver application is based or selection by the Department of State to participate in the Diversity Visa Program under section 203(c) of the Act for the fiscal year for which the alien registered, with such selection being the basis for the alien's provisional unlawful presence waiver application;

(iii) Does not waive any ground of inadmissibility other than, upon satisfaction of the conditions described in paragraph (e)(12)(i), the grounds of inadmissibility under section 212(a)(9)(B)(i)(I) or (II) of the Act.

(13) Validity. Until the provisional unlawful presence waiver takes full effect as provided in paragraph (e)(12) of this section, USCIS may reopen and reconsider its decision at any time. Once a provisional unlawful presence waiver takes full effect as defined in paragraph (e)(12) of this section, the period of unlawful presence for which the provisional unlawful presence waiver is granted is waived indefinitely, in accordance with and subject to paragraph (a)(4) of this section.

(14) Automatic revocation. The approval of a provisional unlawful presence waiver is revoked automatically if:

(i) The Department of State denies the immigrant visa application after completion of the immigrant visa interview based on a finding that the alien is ineligible to receive an immigrant visa for any reason other than inadmissibility under section 212(a)(9)(B)(i)(I) or (II) of the Act. This automatic revocation does not prevent the alien from applying for a waiver of inadmissibility for unlawful presence under section 212(a)(9)(B)(v) of the Act and 8 CFR 212.7(a) or for any other relief from inadmissibility on any other ground for which a waiver is available and for which the alien may be eligible;

(ii) The immigrant visa petition approval associated with the provisional unlawful presence waiver is at any time revoked, withdrawn, or rendered invalid but not otherwise reinstated for humanitarian reasons or converted to a widow or widower petition;

(iii) The immigrant visa registration is terminated in accordance with section 203(g) of the Act, and has not been reinstated in accordance with section 203(g) of the Act; or

(iv) The alien enters or attempts to reenter the United States without inspection and admission or parole at any time after the alien files the provisional unlawful presence waiver application and before the approval of the provisional unlawful presence waiver takes effect in accordance with paragraph (e)(12) of this section.

APPENDIX 2
I-601A COMPARISON CHART

I-601A Before and After	78 Federal Register (Fed. Reg.) 536 (Jan. 3, 2013)	81 Federal Register (Fed. Reg.) 50243 (July 29, 2016)
Effective date	March 4, 2013	August 29, 2016 (requires new I-601A 9-page form updated on 07/29/2016)
Qualifying relative for extreme hardship	U.S. citizen spouse or parent	U.S. citizen or LPR spouse or parent
Qualifying approved petitions	Form I-130, Petition for Alien Relative, for immediate relative (spouse, child, or parent of U.S. citizen)	Form I-130, Petition for Alien Relative, for any beneficiary; Form I-360, Petition for Amerasian, Widow(er), or Special Immigrant; Form I-140, Immigrant Petition for Alien Worker); proof that selected to participate in the Diversity Visa Program
Effect, if any, of prior scheduling of consular processing interview?	Applicants who were scheduled for an interview before January 3, 2013 are precluded, even if they failed to appear for the interview, the interview was cancelled, or the interview was rescheduled on or after January 3, 2013. These applicants had to file a new I-130.	None.
Pending removal proceedings **NO CHANGE**	Ineligible to file if currently in removal proceedings. Must obtain admin closure or termination of proceedings.	Ineligible to file if currently in removal proceedings. Must obtain admin closure or termination of proceedings.
Final orders	Ineligible if have final order of removal, exclusion, or deportation.	If have final order of removal, exclusion, or deportation, must file Form I-212, Application for Permission to Reapply for Admission into the United States After Deportation or Removal, and receive approval from USCIS. File approval notice with Form I-601A.

"Reason to believe"	USCIS can deny I-601 if there is "reason to believe" applicant is inadmissible on grounds other than unlawful presence. This is to help prevent applicant from being found inadmissible by consulate and having approved I-601A revoked.	USCIS can no longer deny based on "reason to believe" applicant will be found inadmissible on separate ground. Prior acts that could form basis for inadmissibility finding will only be considered as possible adverse discretionary factor. Counsel must screen for possible inadmissibility ground and advise applicant.
Process **NO CHANGE**	Once provisional waiver is approved, it will take effect after: 1. Depart the United States and appear for immigrant visa interview; and 2. Consular officer determines that applicant is otherwise admissible to the United States and eligible to receive an immigrant visa.	Once provisional waiver is approved, it will take effect after: 1. Depart the United States and appear for immigrant visa interview; and 2. Consular officer determines that applicant is otherwise admissible to the United States and eligible to receive an immigrant visa.

APPENDIX 3

GENERAL IMMIGRATION LAW INTAKE FORM

Catholic Charities *of the East Bay*

CASE TYPE U-VISA ☐ VAWA ☐ I-601A ☐ DACA ☐ AOS ☐ UAC ☐ I-130 ☐ NATZ ☐ TPS ☐ OTHER ☐

Paid (✓) _____ **PREFERRED LANGUAGE:** _____ **TODAY'S DATE:** _____

PERSONAL/DEMOGRAPHIC INFORMATION

NAME (First, Middle, Last): _____

ADDRESS: _____ **CITY:** _____

ZIP CODE: _____ **TEL#: (___)** _____ **CELL#: (___)** _____

EMAIL ADDRES: _____

DATE OF BIRTH: ___/___/___ (month)/(day)/(year) **COUNTRY OF BIRTH:** _____

EMERGENCY CONTACT NAME/RELATION: _____ **TEL#: (___)** _____

SEX: ☐Male ☐Female ☐Transgender   **MARITAL STATUS:** ☐Single ☐Married ☐Divorced ☐Widow(er) ☐Legally Separated

RACE: ☐ White ☐ Black or African American ☐ Asian ☐ Native American or Native Alaskan ☐ Pacific Islander or Native Hawaiian ☐ Other: _____ ☐ Declined to state

ARE YOU HISPANIC/LATINO? ☐ YES ☐NO   **ARE YOU SINGLE HEAD OF HOUSEHOLD?** ☐ YES ☐NO

NUMBER OF CHILDREN (IN US & OVERSEAS): _____ **AGES:** _____ (Circle the ones born in the US)

HOW MANY ADULTS (25-54) LIVE IN HOUSEHOLD? _____ **CHILDREN (0-18)?** _____ **YOUTH (19-24)?** _____ **SENIORS (55+)?** _____

HOUSEHOLD ANNUAL INCOME: ☐$0-$12,000 ☐$12,001-$18,000 ☐$18,001-$24,000 ☐$24,001-$28,000 ☐$28,001-$32,000 ☐$32,001-$36,000 ☐$36,001-$40,000 ☐$40,001-$44,000 ☐$44,001-$52,000 ☐$52,001-$60,000 ☐$52,001-$60,000 ☐$60,001 or more

HOW DID YOU LEARN ABOUT OUR SERVICES: ☐Flyer or Brochure ☐Website ☐Radio or TV ☐Friend or Family ☐Fair or Event (please specify) _____ ☐Shelter (please name) _____ ☐Church (name below) ☐Social Worker (which agency?) _____ ☐Other (please specify) _____

LEGAL INFORMATION (please answer all questions)

IS THIS YOUR FIRST LEGAL CONSULTATION WITH OUR OFFICE? ☐ YES ☐NO **STATE REASON FOR YOUR VISIT BELOW:**

_____
_____

DID YOU ENTER THE U.S. WITHOUT LEGAL DOCUMENTATION? ☐ YES ☐NO
IF YES, HOW MANY TIMES? _____ DATE OF LAST ENTRY: _____ PLACE OF ENTRY: _____ AGE AT ENTRY: _____

DID YOU PRESENT ANY FALSE DOCUMENTS TO ENTER? (Passport, Green Card, Birth Certificates) ☐ YES ☐NO

HAVE YOU EVER CLAIMED TO BE A U.S. CITIZEN OR UNLAWFULLY VOTED IN AN ELECTION? ☐ YES ☐NO

HAVE YOU EVER BEEN DETAINED BY IMMIGRATION SERVICES OR BEEN TO IMMIGRATION COURT? ☐ YES ☐NO
DATE(S) of detainment or court hearing: _____

HAVE YOU EVER BEEN ARRESTED OR DETAINED BY THE POLICE IN THE US? ☐ YES ☐NO
REASON for detainment: _____ DATE(S): _____

HAVE YOU EVER HELPED, SUPPORTED, OR PAID FOR ANOTHER PERSON TO ENTER U.S. UNLAWFULLY? ☐ YES ☐NO

HAVE YOU FACED PERSECUTION IN YOUR COUNTRY? ☐ YES ☐NO
Harm as a result of your race, nationality, religion, political opinion, social group (such as sexual orientation, family status, or domestic violence), please explain: _____

DO YOU HAVE A PARENT SPOUSE OR CHILD IN ACTIVE DUTY OR VETERAN OF ARMED FORCES? ☐ YES ☐NO

HAS A US CITIZEN OR RESIDENT EVER FILED A FAMILY-BASED VISA PETITION FOR YOU? ☐ YES ☐NO

HAS A FAMILY-BASED VISA PETITION FOR YOUR PARENTS WHEN YOU WERE UNDER 21 YEARS OF AGE? ☐ YES ☐NO
If YES to either above, please state WHEN: _____ WHO SUBMITTED THE PETITION: _____

HAVE YOU, YOUR SPOUSE, CHILD OR PARENT BEEN VICTIM(S) OF A VIOLENT CRIME WITHIN THE U.S? ☐ YES ☐NO
If YES, was a police report filed? ☐ YES ☐NO   Do you have a copy of the police report? ☐ YES ☐NO

HAVE YOU BEEN A VICTIM OF DOMESTIC VIOLENCE? ☐ YES ☐NO
If YES, INDICATE THE LEGAL STATUS OF YOUR SPOUSE OR FORMER SPOUSE: ☐ US Citizen ☐ Legal Resident ☐ Not Legally Married ☐ Other: _____

Catholic Charities of the East Bay

CASE TYPE: U-VISA ☐ VAWA ☐ I-601A ☐ DACA ☐ AOS ☐ UAC ☐ I-130 ☐ NATZ ☐ TPS ☐ OTHER ☐

Pagado (✓)_____ LENGUAJE PREFERIDO:_____ FECHA DE HOY:_____

DATOS BIOGRÁFICOS Y PERSONALES

NOMBRE (Primero, Segundo, Apellido(s)): _____
DIRECCIÓN: _____ **CIUDAD:** _____
CÓDIGO POSTAL: _____ **TEL#:** (____) _____ **CEL/OTRO#:** (____) _____
CORREO ELECTRÓNICO: _____
FECHA DE NACIMIENTO: ___/___/___ **PAÍS DE ORIGEN:** _____
(mes) / (día) / (año)
CONTACTO DE EMERGENCIA Y RELACION _____ **TEL#:** (____) _____

SEXO: ☐ Masculino ☐ Femenino ☐ Transgénero **ESTADO CIVIL:** ☐ Soltero ☐ Casado ☐ Divorciado ☐ Viudo ☐ Separado Legalmente

RAZA: ☐ Blanco ☐ Moreno o de origen Africano ☐ Asiático ☐ Indio Americano o Nativo de Alaska
☐ Nativo de Hawái o Isleño del Pacifico ☐ Otro: _____ ☐ Rehusó a declarar

¿ES USTED HISPANO/LATINO? ☐ SÍ ☐ NO **¿ES USTED CABEZA DE FAMILIA?** ☐ SÍ ☐ NO
(Un círculo alrededor de los nacidos en los EE.UU.)
NUMERO DE HIJOS (EN LOS EEUU Y EL EXTRANJERO): _____ **EDADES:** _____

¿CUANTOS ADULTOS (25-54) VIVEN EL EN HOGAR? ___ **NIÑOS (0-18)?** ___ **JOVENES (19-24)?** ___ **ADULTOS MAYORES (55+)?** ___

INGRESO ANUAL DEL HOGAR: ☐ $0-$12,000 ☐ $12,001-$18,000 ☐ $18,001-$24,000 ☐ $24,001-$28,000 ☐ $28,001-$32,000 ☐ $32,001-$36,000 ☐ $36,001-$40,000 ☐ $40,001-$44,000 ☐ $44,001-$52,000 ☐ $52,001-$60,000 ☐ $52,001-$60,000 ☐ $60,001 o más

¿COMO SE ENTERO DE NUESTROS SERVICIOS?: ☐ Folleto o volante ☐ Sitio Web ☐ Radio o TV ☐ Amigo o familia ☐ Feria o evento (especifique)_____ ☐ Refugio (nombre) _____ ☐ Iglesia (nombre abajo) ☐ Trabajador social (¿de qué agencia?)_____ ☐ Otro (explique por favor) _____

INFORMACIÓN LEGAL (CONTESTE TODOS LAS PREGUNTAS POR FAVOR)

¿ESTA ES SU PRIMER CONSULTA LEGAL CON NUESTRA OFICINA? ☐ SI ☐ NO **ESCRIBA EL MOTIVO DE SU VISITA:**
_____
_____

¿COMO ENTRO AL PAÍS? ☐ CON VISA ☐ SIN VISA
¿CUÁNTAS ENTRADAS? ____ **¿CUÁNDO ENTRO?:** _____ **¿POR DÓNDE?:** _____ **EDAD AL ENTRADA:** ____

¿CUÁNDO ENTRÓ, PRESENTÓ DOCUMENTOS FALSOS? (Pasaporte, Mica, Acta de nacimiento) ☐ SÍ ☐ NO

¿HA DECLARADO SER CIUDADANO DE LOS EE.UU. O HA VOTADO ILEGALMENTE EN UNA ELECCIÓN? ☐ SÍ ☐ NO

¿HA SIDO DETENIDO POR EL SERVICIO DE INMIGRACIÓN O IDO A LA CORTE DE INMIGRACION? ☐ SÍ ☐ NO
Si la respuesta es sí, ¿CUÁNDO?:_____ ¿DONDE?_____

¿ALGUNA VEZ HA SIDO ARRESTADO O DETENIDO POR LA POLICÍA EN LOS EEUU? ☐ SÍ ☐ NO
Si la respuesta es sí, ¿CUÁNDO?:_____ ¿DONDE?_____

¿HA AYUDADO, APÓYADO O PAGADO PARA QUE OTRA PERSONA ENTRE LOS EE.UU. ILEGALMENTE? ☐ SÍ ☐ NO

¿TIENE MIEDO DE REGRESAR A SU PAÍS DE ORIGEN (HA SUFRIDO PERSECUCIÓN)? ☐ SÍ ☐ NO
Si ha sufrido persecución como consecuencia de su orientación sexual, raza, nacionalidad, religión, opinión política, grupo social o víctima de violencia doméstica, por favor explique: _____

¿TIENE ALGUN PARIENTE EN SERVICIO ACTIVO O VETERANO DE LAS FUERZAS ARMADAS? ☐ SÍ ☐ NO
Si la respuesta es sí, ¿QUIÉN?_____

¿ALGUNA VEZ SE HA SOMETIDO UNA PETICIÓN POR UD.? ☐ SÍ ☐ NO
¿O POR SUS PADRES CUÁNDO USTED ERA MENOR DE 21 AÑOS DE EDAD? ☐ SÍ ☐ NO
Si la respuesta es sí, ¿CUÁNDO?:_____ ¿QUIÉN?_____

¿USTED, PAREJA O HIJOS HAN SIDO VÍCTIMAS DE UN CRIMEN EN EEUU? ☐ SÍ ☐ NO
Si la respuesta es sí, ¿Se hizo un reporte de policía? ☐ SÍ ☐ NO ¿Usted tiene una copia del reporte de policía? ☐ SÍ ☐ NO

¿HA SIDO USTED VÍCTIMA DE VIOLENCIA DOMÉSTICA? ☐ SÍ ☐ NO
Si la respuesta es sí, ¿CUÁL ES EL ESTATUS LEGAL DE SU ESPOSO(A) O PAREJA O EX-ESPOSO(A)?: ☐ Ciudadano ☐ Residente Permanente ☐ No estaban casados ☐ Otro: _____

Copyright © 2020. American Immigration Lawyers Association.

APPENDIX 3: GENERAL IMMIGRATION LAW INTAKE FORM

CASE TYPE U-VISA ☐ VAWA ☐ I-601A ☐ DACA ☐ AOS ☐ UAC ☐ I-130 ☐ NATZ ☐ TPS ☐ OTHER ☐

OFFICE USE ONLY, DO NOT WRITE IN THIS SPACE

Information about entries

Date of Entry	Place of Entry	Status at Entry

Criminal History

Date	Reason	Location	Outcome or Disposition

NOTES: _____
_____
_____
_____
_____
_____
_____
_____
_____
_____

Copyright © 2020. American Immigration Lawyers Association.

APPENDIX 4
EXTREME HARDSHIP INTAKE SHEET – QUESTIONS FOR PRACTITIONERS

INTERVIEWS TO ELICIT EXTREME HARDSHIP INFORMATION

A detailed interview with the waiver applicant and qualifying relative is essential to elicit information concerning the hardship requirement necessary to demonstrate eligibility for a waiver of inadmissibility or deportability. The following questions are designed to obtain information about extreme hardship and other positive equities relevant to establishing extreme hardship.

Sample Questions Related to Employment and Economic Prospects:

How many years of formal education have you had?

Describe your job skills and experience?

Are you working now?

What special skills does your job require, if any?

How do you feel about your job and your co-workers?

Will you be able to find employment with these skills upon relocating? If not, why?

Will you be able to obtain any employment upon relocating? If yes, what type of employment will you be able to obtain?

Will this employment be available year-round? If not, for how many months out of the year will you be able to find work?

What will be your income from this employment?

Will you have medical or other employment-related benefits?

Describe in detail the consequences of this reduced income on your family's health and welfare.

If you will be unable to obtain employment, explain why.

Describe in detail the consequences to your family's health and welfare if you are unable to find work in your home country.

Do you know of others with your job skills who are unable to find work in your home country?

What have been the consequences for them?

Have you ever tried to find work in your home country by making inquiries in the town to which you will be retuning? If so, what were the results of your inquiries? What specific inquiries did you make?

Questions Related to Business Owners:

What type of business do you own?

What will you do with your business if you are forced to return to your home country?

How much loss will you suffer if you sell or liquidate your business?

Will you be able to use the money from the sale of your business to start a new life in your home country? If not, why not?

Will you be able to start a new business in your home country? If not, why?

Questions Related to Applicants Who Will Return to Rural Areas:

Do you own land?

If yes, is the land owned by you as an individual or by your family?

How much land do you own?

Do you plan to farm?

If yes, what problems will you face?

If you do not own land, will you be able to buy land?

Is the land you own or plan to purchase sufficient to support your family?

What problems are faced by small farmers in the region you will be relocating to?

If you cannot farm land of your own do you plan to do agricultural work? If so, will you be able to find such work?

If you are able to find such work, how many months a year will you be able to work?

What conditions will you face as an agricultural worker?

How much will you earn?

What will be the consequences of such work to you and your family?

Questions Relating to Violence and Country Conditions in Home Country:

Is there drug cartel violence in the area to which you will be relocating?

How do you know about the violence (from family, friends, newspapers, etc. - or personal knowledge)?

Do you know the names of the drug cartels operating in the area?

Do you know anyone who has been affected in your home area by such violence - if so, who are they?

What happened to the people you know who suffered violence at the hands of the drug cartels?

If the people you know were injured by drug cartel violence, do you have any proof of such injury (newspaper clippings, police reports, death certificates, photos of injured people, photos of damaged property)?

Are there problems with gangs in the country you will relocate to?

What are those problems?

Have you or anyone you know had problems with the gangs in your home country?

If so, what were the problems?

What would you do to keep yourself and your family safe from gang violence?

Is there anything you could do to be safe?

Is there ongoing political violence in your home country between different political groups? If so, what are the groups?

What effect has political violence had on the place that you will relocate to? Economic, safety, etc.?

Does the violence prevent you from traveling, working, going out at night?

Has anyone in your family suffered harm due to the political violence? If so, who? What happened?

Have any of your friends or former co-workers suffered harm due to the political violence? If so, who? What happened?

Questions Relating to Education:

Will your children be able to attend school if you return to your home country - if not, why?

Is there a primary school in the city to which you will relocate?

Is there a secondary school in there?

How far will your children have to travel to attend school?

Will there be any transportation available to get them to school?

Will you have to pay to send your children to school?

What will be your costs?

Will you be able to afford it?

What problems will your children have in adjusting to the educational system in your home country?

Do your children speak the language?

Are they able to read and write in the language?

How are they doing in school in the US?

Do they have any learning disabilities?

Do they receive special services for their disabilities?

Are they in special classes for children with disabilities?

Do your children receive speech therapy in school?

Are your children especially academically talented?

Are they in special classes for gifted children?

What are their future educational goals?

What are their career goals?

Has anyone in your family abroad ever gone to college?

Is anyone in your family abroad a professional?

How is the US educational system different than the one your children will encounter abroad?

What consequences would your children face if uprooted at this time in terms of education (any special study in which they are engaged)?

If your children are US citizens, will they go with you abroad or will you keep them in the US with someone else?

What will happen to them if they do not go with you abroad?

Who will they stay with if you leave them in the US?

Who will pay for their expenses in the US?

Questions Relating to Health:

Do you know of anyone who has had TB in your town?

Do you have any relatives who died as children?

Have you known any women who died in your home community?

Do you know any men who died in your home community?

Do you or anyone in your family suffer from a medical condition?

If so, what is it called?

What type of treatment are you or someone in your family receiving?

How often are you or the person in your family being treated?

What type of treatment is being received?

How often is the treatment received?

What will be the consequences of interrupting the treatment?

Will you be able to obtain the same treatment in your home country?

If not, explain.

Do you or any family member receive psychological counseling?

Do you worry about your own or your family members' psychological health if you return?

Has a psychological evaluation been done on you or any member of your family?

Will there be changes in your family's diet if you return to your home country?

Will you be able to buy sufficient food for your family?

How many doctors are there in your town?

How many days a week are they available?

If there is no doctor in your town, how far will you have to travel to see a doctor?

Will you have access to maternity care?

Will you be able to afford it?

Does your family have health insurance in the US? If so, what is the name?

If you are forced to return to your home country will your family be covered by health insurance?

Will you be able to afford adequate medical services in your home country? If not, why not?

Questions Relating to Housing:

Do you own or rent your home?

How long have you lived at your current address?

Will you be able to afford housing in your home country?

If yes, describe what your housing conditions will be like?

Will your home have indoor plumbing?

Will your home have electricity?

Will your home have drainage?

How many rooms will your home have?

How will your housing compare with your home in the US?

How many people will have to live in your house abroad?

If you will not be able to afford housing, what will you do? Do you have friends or relatives with whom you could live?

Questions Related to Women:

In the US, women commonly work outside the home. Is that true in the country you will relocate to?

Would you be able to work in your home to support your family?

What obstacles would you face in finding work?

How have your daughters adjusted to life in the US?

Would your daughters face unique problems as females in the country to which you will relocate?

Are the educational opportunities for girls in your home country similar to those in the US? If not, how are they different?

Have you or any member of your family ever suffered domestic violence in the US or abroad? If so, please describe.

Where does the abuser live?

Questions Related to Being Victim of a Crime:

Have you or any member of your family ever been the victim of a crime in the US?

If so, please describe?

Are you receiving any services based on having been the victim of a crime?

Are you assisting in the prosecution of the perpetrator?

Have you or any member of your family ever been the victim of a crime in your home country?

If so, please describe.

How do you feel about returning to a place where you or your family member was the victim of a crime?

Do you believe you would be in danger if you return?

Questions Related to Family and Community Ties in the United States:

Do you know your neighbors?

How much time do you spend with them?

Do you have friends in the US?

Do you have many relatives in the US?

What is your relationship with each of them and where do they live?

What is their immigration status?

What kinds of activities do you do with your friends and relatives?

How often do you see them?

Please describe your daily routine during the work week, including what you do after work?

Please describe what your activities are during the weekend and other free time?

Are you involved in any community organization (church groups, sorts teams, counseling groups, school groups, labor unions)?

Are you active with such groups - how much time do you spend with such groups?

Are you in a leadership position with such groups?

If you are a member of a church, how often do you attend?

Do you know the priest or minister?

Would he be willing to write a letter on your behalf?

Do you have many close relatives in your home country - where do they live?

Do you have man y friends in your home country-have you maintained contact with them?

Would your friends or relatives be able to assist you in locating housing and employment abroad? Why not?

If not, would the lack of personal contacts make it difficult for you to obtain adequate housing and employment?

APPENDIX 5A

EXTREME HARDSHIP INTAKE SHEET – QUESTIONS FOR CLIENTS

Catholic Charities
Immigration Consultation Services
249 W. Thornhill Dr.
Fort Worth, TX 76115
(817) 534-0814

> These questions are to be answered form the point of view of the petitioner

This series of questions is designed to help you think through all the aspects that could help to establish your "extreme hardship" case due to the separation from your spouse. Please, review them and think about them carefully. Discuss them with your spouse. The next time you meet with your immigration counselor to work on your case, you should have considered these questions and should be ready to talk about them specifically and in detail. You do not have to write out your answers to these questions, but jotting down some notes might help you to have on hand the specific details that could make a world of difference for your case.

In General
Would you be willing to live outside of the United States for 10 years? Why or why not?

Health
How is your health? Are you under some kind of medical treatment? How is your spouse's health? How is your children's health?

Finances
Do you have a job? Does your spouse have a job? If you do not have a job, have you ever had one? What would keep you from getting a job if you needed to? What kind of job could you get? Do you have a lot of debt? Do you have a house payment, car payment, etc.?

Personal/Emotional
What are your emotions toward your spouse? What are you like as a couple? What makes your marriage strong? Do you spend a lot of time together? Have you ever been apart for a long time? How did you feel about that time? What kind of relationship does each of the children have with each one of you? Do you have a history of depression, anxiety or other emotional distress? Have you ever been in therapy or spoken with a professional counselor?

Education/Professional
Are you in school? Do you plan to continue with a course of study or training? Is your ability to work right now dependent on your spouse's schedule? If your spouse has to leave, would you have to change jobs or quit school?

Changes in your lifestyle
If your spouse could not return for 10 years, how would your lifestyle change? Would you have to move? Would you have to quit any family activities: sports, arts, volunteering, etc.?

Children/other relatives
How would your children be affected if your spouse could not return for 10 years? Have the kids been separated from him/her before? How did they feel? Have the children been in therapy or counseling? Are there other relatives (U.S. citizens or legal permanent residents) that depend somehow on your spouse?

Special circumstances
It is undeniable that any family would suffer if one of the members had to leave. What make your family's case special? In what ways would you experience hardship beyond what other families would experience?

Last revision 06/2011

Immigration Consultation Services
249 W. Thornhill Dr.
Fort Worth, TX 76115
(817) 534-0814

Catholic Charities

> Estas preguntas son para ser respondidas desde el punto de vista del peticionario

Esta serie de preguntas están diseñadas para ayudarle a pensar en todos los aspectos que pueden contribuir a establecer su caso de "dificultad extrema" producto de la separación de su esposo/a. Por favor, revíselas y piense en ellas con detenimiento. Discútalas con su esposo/a. Cuando se reúna con su consultor de inmigración para trabajar en su caso él/ella va estar esperando que Ud. haya considerado estas preguntas y esté listo para hablar al respecto concreta y detalladamente. No tiene que escribir sus repuestas, pero quizás tomar algunas notas le ayudará a tener a mano los detalles específicos que pueden hacer la diferencia en el caso.

En general
¿Estaría Ud. dispuesto/a a fijar residencia fuera de los Estados Unidos por 10 años? ¿Por qué?

Salud
¿Cómo es su salud? ¿Tiene que seguir algún tratamiento especial? ¿Cómo es la salud de su esposo/a? ¿La de sus hijos?

Finanzas
¿Trabaja Ud.? ¿Y su esposo/a? Si no, ¿ha trabajado alguna vez? ¿Hay algún impedimento para que lo haga en el futuro? ¿Qué tipos de trabajo pudiera realizar? ¿Hay muchas deudas en el hogar? ¿Están comprando casa, vehículos, etc?

Personal/Emocional
¿Cómo se sienten Uds. emocionalmente? ¿Son una pareja muy unida? ¿Pasan tiempos juntos? ¿Han estado separados antes? ¿Cómo se sintieron? ¿Cómo es la relación de los niños con cada uno de Uds.? ¿Tiene algún historial de depresión o alguna otra situación de esta naturaleza? ¿Ha recibido terapia o hablado con un consejero?

Educación/Profesión
¿Están estudiando? ¿Tiene planes de estudiar? ¿Su trabajo depende de que su esposo/a esté disponible en un horario en particular? Si su esposo/a no estuviese con Ud., ¿Tendría que cambiar su trabajo o abandonar la escuela?

Cambios en su estilo de vida
¿Cómo cambiaría su estilo de vida si su esposo/a tuviese que irse por 10 años? ¿Tendría que mudarse? ¿Tendría que abandonar ciertas actividades: deportes, artes, actividades voluntarias, etc.?

Hijos/otros familiares
¿Cómo les afectaría a sus hijos el que su esposo/a se fuese por 10 años? ¿Han alguna vez han estado separados los niños de su padre/madre; cómo se sintieron? ¿Han estado sus niños en terapia o consejería? ¿Hay otros familiares (Residentes Legales o ciudadanos de los EE.UU.) que dependen de su esposo/a?

Circunstancias especiales
Es indudable que toda familia sufre si uno de los esposos tiene que irse, ¿Qué cree Ud. que hace su caso especial; en qué manera sufriría Ud. que sería más difícil que para otras personas?

Last revision 06/2011

APPENDIX 5B
EXTREME HARDSHIP INTAKE SHEET—QUESTIONS FOR QUALIFYING RELATIVE

QUESTIONS TO ASK QUALIFYING RELATIVE TO ESTABLISH HARDSHIP (ENGLISH)

LPR OR USC?
1) Are you a U.S. citizen or an LPR?
2) If an LPR, when and how did you immigrate to the U.S.?
3) If a USC, by birth, derivation, or naturalization?
4) When were you naturalized?
5) Did you gain LPR status through asylum or as a refugee?

SEPARATION OR RELOCATION HARDSHIP?
1) If the applicant is denied the provisional waiver and must remain outside the U.S. for ten years, have you decided whether you will remain here or accompany him/her?
2) If so, why have you decided that?

HISTORY OF RELATIONSHIP:
1) Where did you meet your spouse?
2) How old were you when you met your spouse?
3) When was your first date? What happened after?
4) When did you move in together?
5) When did you get married?
6) What was your relationship like at the beginning of the marriage?
7) What is relationship like now?
8) Do you have children? Ages?
9) Explain you and your spouse's relationship with your children.
10) Explain you and your spouse's relationship with your and your spouse's parents.
11) Do you or spouse take care of you or your spouse's parents?
12) If your spouse were to return to his/her native country and separate from you, what would the hardship be to you?

SAMPLE QUESTIONS RELATED TO EMPLOYMENT AND ECONOMIC PROSPECTS:
1) How many years of formal education have you had?
2) Describe your job skills and experience?
3) Are you working now? What is your current income?
4) What special skills does your job require, if any?

5) How do you feel about your job and your co-workers?

6) Is it likely you will be able to find employment with these skills in your spouse's country -- if not, why not?

7) Will you be able to obtain any employment in spouse's country?

8) What will be your income from this employment?

9) Will you have medical or other employment–related benefits?

10) Describe in detail the consequences of this reduced income on your family's health and welfare?

11) If you will not be able to obtain employment, why not?

12) Describe in detail the consequences to your family's health and welfare of your being unable to find work in your home country?

13) What does your spouse do? What is his/her income?

14) What would the impact be to you without your spouse's income?

QUESTIONS RELATING TO EDUCATION

1) Will your children be able to attend school if move to your relative's country – if not, why not?

2) What is the quality of education in your relative's country?

3) How would you feel if your children were not educated in the US?

4) Is there a primary school in the city to which you will be returning?

5) Is there a secondary school in this location?

6) How far will your children have to travel to attend school?

7) Will there be any transportation available to them to get to school?

8) Will you have to pay to send your children to school?

9) What will be your costs?

10) Will you be able to afford it?

11) What problems will your children have in adjusting to the educational system in your home country?

12) Do your children speak the language?

13) Are they able to read and write in the language?

14) How are they doing in school in the US?

15) Do they have any learning disabilities?

16) Do they receive special services for their disabilities?

17) Are they in special classes for children with disabilities?

18) Are your children especially academically talented?

19) Are they in special classes for gifted children?

20) What are their future educational goals?

21) What are their career goals?

22) How is the U.S. educational system different than the one your children will encounter abroad?

23) What consequences would your children face if uprooted at this time in terms of education (any special study in which they are engaged)?

24) If your children are U.S. citizens, will they go with you abroad or will you keep them in the US with someone else?

25) What will happen to them if they do not go with you abroad?

26) Who will they stay with if you leave them in the U.S.?
27) Who will pay for their expenses in the U.S.?

QUESTIONS RELATED TO HEALTH
1) How are the health conditions in the area where you will return?
2) Do you or anyone in your family suffer from a medical condition?
3) What type of treatment are you or someone in your family receiving?
4) How often are you or the person in your family being treated?
5) What type of treatment is being received?
6) How often is the treatment received?
12) What will be the consequences of your treatment being interrupted?
13) Will you be able to obtain the same treatment in your home country?
14) If yes, explain?
15) Do you or any family member receive psychological counseling for any problems?
16) Do you worry about your own or your family members' psychological situation if you return?
17) Has a psychological evaluation been done on you or any member of your family?
18) Will there be changes in your family's diet if you return to your home country?
19) Will you be able to buy sufficient food for your family?
20) If there is no doctor in your town, how far will you have to travel to see a doctor?
21) Will you have access to maternity care?
22) Will you be able to afford it?
23) Does your family have health insurance in the U.S. – if so, what is the name?
24) If you are forced to return to your home country will your family be covered by health insurance?
25) Will you be able to afford adequate medical services in your home country – if not, why not?

QUESTIONS RELATED TO HOUSING
1) Do you own or rent your home?
2) How long have you lived at your current address?
3) Will you be able to afford housing in your home country?
4) If yes, describe what your housing conditions will be like?
5) Will your home have indoor plumbing?
6) Will your home have electricity?
7) Will your home have drainage?
8) How many rooms will your home have?
9) How will your housing compare with your home in the U.S.?
10) How many people will have to live in your house abroad?
11) If you will not be able to afford housing, what will you do? Do you have friends or relatives with whom you could live?

QUESTIONS RELATING TO VIOLENCE AND COUNTRY CONDITIONS

1) Is there drug cartel violence in the area to which you will be returning?

2) How do you know about the violence (from family, friends, newspapers, or personal knowledge)?

3) Do you know the names of the drug cartels operating in the area?

4) Do you know anyone who has been affected in your home area by such violence? If so, who are they?

5) What happened to the people you know who suffered violence at the hands of the drug cartels?

6) If the people you know were injured by drug cartel violence, do you have any proof of such injury (newspaper clippings, police reports, death certificates, photos of injured people, photos of damaged property)?

7) Are there problems with gangs in the country to which you will be returning?

8) What are those problems?

9) Have you or anyone you know had problems with the gangs in your home country?

10) If so, what were the problems?

11) What would you do to keep yourself and your family safe from gang violence?

13) Is there ongoing political violence in your home country between different political groups? If so, what are the groups?

14) What effect has the political violence had on the place that you will be returning to – economic, safety, etc.?

15) Does the violence prevent you from traveling, working, going out at night?

16) Has anyone in your family suffered harm due to the political violence? If so, who, what happened?

17) Have any of your friends or former fellow workers suffered harm due to the political violence? If so, who, what happened?

QUESTIONS RELATED TO WOMEN

1) In the US, women commonly work outside the home. Is that true in the country to which you will be moving/returning?

2) Would you be able to work in your home support your family?

3) What obstacles would you face in finding work?

4) How have your daughters adjusted to life in the U.S.?

5) Would your daughters face unique problems as females in the country to which you will be retuning?

6) Are the educational opportunities for girls in your home country similar to those in the U.S.? If not, how?

QUESTIONS RELATED TO FAIMLY AND COMMUNITY TIES IN THE US

1) Are you involved in your community? If so, how?

2) Do you frequently spend time with family members?

4) What is your relationship with each of them and where do they live?

5) What is their immigration status?

6) What kinds of activities do you do with your friends and relatives?

7) How often do you see them?

8) Please describe your daily routine, during the work week, including what you do after work?

9) Please describe what your activities are during the weekend and other free time?

Copyright © 2020. American Immigration Lawyers Association.

10) Are you involved in any community organization (church groups, sports teams, counseling groups, school groups, labor unions)?

11) Are you active with such groups? How much time do you spend with such groups?

12) Are you in a leadership position with such groups?

13) If you are a member of a church, what is the name of it? How often do you attend?

14) Do you have many close relatives in your home country? If so, where do they live?

15) Do you have many friends in your home country? Have you maintained contact with them?

16) Would your friends or relatives be able to assist you in locating housing and employment abroad? If not, why not?

17) If not, would the lack of personal contacts make it difficult for you to obtain adequate housing and employment?

OTHER CULTURAL FACTORS IN RELATIVE'S HOME COUNTRY

If you or the waiver applicant were to relocate to foreign country, would you face persecution or discrimination due to your sexual orientation, religion, ethnicity, gender or other factors?

QUESTIONS TO ASK QUALIFYING RELATIVE TO ESTABLISH HARDSHIP (SPANISH)

¿CIUDADANO O RESIDENTE PERMANENTE?

1) ¿Es usted un ciudadano Americano? ¿Por nacimiento o por naturalización?

2) ¿Cuándo fue naturalizado?

3) ¿Es usted un residente permanente?

4) ¿Cuándo y como emigró a los Estados Unidos?

5) ¿Recibio residente permanente estatus por asilo o como un refugiado?

¿DIFICULTAD SOBRE SEPARACIÓN O TRASLADO?

1) Si la solicitacion para un perdon es negado y su esposo necesita regrasar a su pais, va a accompanarle o quedar aqui?

2) Cómo pudo hacer este decision?

HISTORIA DE LA RELACIÓN:

1) ¿Adónde conoció a su pareja?

2) ¿Qué edad tenía cuando conoció a su pareja?

3) ¿Cuándo tuvo su primera cita? Como siguió la relación?

4) ¿Cuándo se mudaron juntos?

5) ¿Cuándo se casaron?

6) Describa su relación al principio de su matrimonio.

7) ¿Cómo es su relación ahora?

8) ¿Tiene niños? ¿Edades?

9) ¿Cómo es la relación que usted y su pareja tienen con sus hijos?

10) ¿Cómo es la relación que usted y su pareja tienen con sus padres y los padres de su pareja?

11) ¿Usted o su pareja estan a cargo de sus padres, o de los padres de su pareja?

12) ¿Si su esposo/a se viera obligado/a a vivir en su país natal, cuáles serían las dificultades para ustedes?

EJEMPLOS DE PREGUNTAS RELACIONADAS CON EL EMPLEO Y PERSPECTIVAS DE LA ECONOMÍA:

1) ¿Cuántos años de educación formal ha tenido?

2) Describa sus habilidades de trabajo y experiencia.

3) ¿Está trabajando ahora? ¿Cuál es su ingreso actual?

4) ¿Qué habilidades especiales requiere su trabajo?

5) ¿Cómo se siente acerca de su trabajo y de sus compañeros de trabajo?

6) ¿Usted sería capaz de encontrar un empleo que utilice sus habilidades laborales en el país de su cónyuge? Si no, ¿por qué?

7) ¿Sería capaz de obtener cualquier empleo en el país de su cónyuge?

8) ¿Cuáles serian sus ingresos de este empleo?

9) ¿Obtendría usted algún beneficio medico u otro beneficio relacionado con su empleo?

10) Describa con detalle las consecuencias de una reducción de los ingresos en la salud y el bienestar de su familia.

11) Si no va a ser capaz de obtener empleo, ¿por qué no?

12) Describa con detalle las consecuencias para la salud y el bienestar de su familia si usted es incapaz de encontrar trabajo en su país de origen.

13) ¿Qué hace su pareja? ¿Cuál es su ingreso?

14) ¿Cuál sería el impacto para usted sin el ingreso de su pareja?

PREGUNTAS RELACIONADAS A LA EDUCACIÓN:

1) ¿Sus hijos podrían asistir a la escuela si se movieran a otro país - si no, ¿por qué?

2) ¿Cuál es la calidad de la educación en el país de su familiar?

3) ¿Cómo se sentiría si sus hijos no fueran educados en los Estados Unidos? ¿Hay una escuela primaria en la ciudad a la que va a regresar?

4) ¿Hay una escuela secundaria en esa ubicación?

5) ¿Habrá transporte a su alcance para llegar a la escuela?

6) ¿Tendrá que pagar para enviar a sus hijos a la escuela?

7) ¿Cuáles serian sus costos?

8) ¿Sería capaz de pagarlos?

9) ¿Qué problemas tendrían sus hijos en el ajuste al sistema educativo en su país de origen?

10) ¿Sus hijos hablan el idioma de su país de origen?

11) ¿Son capaces de leer y escribir en la lengua de su país de origen?

12) ¿Cómo les va en la escuela en los Estados Unidos?

13) ¿Tienen problemas de aprendizaje?

14) ¿Reciben servicios especiales si tienen discapacidades?

15) ¿Están en clases especiales para niños con discapacidades?

16) ¿Sus hijos tienen talentos académicos especiales?

17) ¿Están en clases especiales para niños superdotados?

18) ¿Cuáles son sus futuras metas educativas?

19) ¿Cuáles son los objetivos profesionales de sus hijos?

20) ¿Cómo se compara el sistema educativo de Estados Unidos al de su país natal?

21) ¿En cuanto a la educación de sus hijos, qué consecuencias los afectaría si fueran desarraigados en este momento (¿están involucrados en algún programa educativo especial?)

22) ¿Si sus hijos son ciudadanos estadounidenses, se irían con usted al extranjero o se quedarían en los Estados Unidos con otra persona?

23) ¿Qué pasaría con ellos si ellos no fueran con usted al extranjero?

24) ¿Con quién se quedarían sus hijos, si los dejara en los Estados Unidos?

25) ¿Quién pagaría por los gastos de sus hijos en los Estados Unidos?

CUESTIONES RELACIONADAS CON LA SALUD:

1) ¿Cómo son las condiciones de salud en el área adonde va a regresar?

2) ¿Usted o alguien en su familia sufre de una condición médica?

3) ¿Qué tipo de tratamiento está recibiendo usted o alguien en su familia?

4) ¿Con qué frecuencia usted o la persona en su familia está recibiendo tratamiento?

5) ¿Qué tipo de tratamiento se está recibiendo?

6) ¿Con qué frecuencia se recibe el tratamiento?

7) ¿Cuáles serian las consecuencias si su tratamiento fuera interrumpido?

8) ¿Sería capaz de obtener el mismo tratamiento en su país de origen? Por favor, explique.

9) ¿Usted o algún miembro de la familia recibe asesoramiento psicológico para cualquier problema?

10) ¿Usted se preocuparia por su estado psicológico o el estado psicológico de su familia si usted se tuviera que ir al exterior?

11) ¿Se ha hecho una evaluación psicológica para usted o algún miembro de su familia?

12) ¿Habrá cambios en la dieta de su familia si regresa a su país de origen?

13) ¿Sería capaz de comprar suficientes alimentos para su familia?

14) Si no hay un médico en su ciudad, ¿hasta dónde tendría que viajar a ver a un médico?

15) ¿Va a tener acceso a la atención de la maternidad?

16) ¿Sería capaz de pagarlo?

17) ¿Su familia tiene seguro de salud en los Estados Unidos? Si es así, ¿cuál es el nombre?

18) Si se ve obligado a regresar a su país de origen su familia estaría cubierta por un seguro de salud?

19) ¿Sería capaz de pagar los servicios médicos adecuados en su país de origen - si no, ¿por qué no?

PREGUNTAS RELACIONADAS A LA VIVIENDA

1) ¿Es usted el propietario o alquila su casa?

2) ¿Cuánto tiempo ha vivido en su dirección actual?

3) ¿Sería capaz de acceder a una vivienda en su país de origen?

4) ¿Si es así, describa cuáles serian las condiciones de su vivienda?

5) ¿Su casa tendría agua corriente?

6) ¿Su casa tendría electricidad?

7) ¿Su casa tendría drenaje?

8) ¿Cuantas habitaciones tendría su casa?

9) ¿Cómo compararía su vivienda con su hogar en los Estados Unidos?

10) ¿Cuántas personas vivirían en su casa en el extranjero?

11) Si usted no sería capaz de acceder a una vivienda, ¿con quien viviría? ¿Tiene amigos o familiares con los que usted podría vivir?

CUESTIONES RELATIVAS A LA VIOLENCIA Y CONDICIONES DEL PAÍS EN EL PAÍS DE ORIGEN

1) ¿Hay violencia de los cárteles de drogas en el área a la que va a regresar?

2) ¿Cómo sabe usted acerca de la violencia (por medio de su familia, amigos, periódicos, etc. - o conocimiento personal?

3) ¿Conoce los nombres de los cárteles de la droga que operan en la zona?

4) ¿Conoce a alguien que ha sido afectado en su área principal de este tipo de violencia - si es así, ¿quiénes son?

5) ¿Qué pasó con la gente que conoce que sufrieron la violencia a manos de los cárteles de la droga?

6) Si la gente que conoce resultaron heridos por violencia de los cárteles de drogas, ¿tiene alguna prueba de tal lesión? (recortes de prensa, informes de la policía, los certificados de defunción, fotos de personas heridas, fotos de la propiedad dañada).

7) ¿Hay problemas con las pandillas en el país al que va a volver?

8) ¿Cuáles son esos problemas?

9) ¿Usted o alguien que usted conoce ha tenido problemas con las pandillas en su país de origen?

10) Si ese es el caso, que tipos de problemas han tenido?

11) ¿Qué haría usted para que usted y su familia estén a salvo de la violencia de pandillas?

13) ¿Hay violencia política en su país de origen entre los diferentes grupos políticos? - si es así, ¿cuáles son los grupos?

14) ¿Qué efecto ha tenido la violencia política en el lugar al que usted tendría que regresar, a niveles económico y de seguridad?

15) ¿La violencia le impediría viajar, trabajar, salir por la noche?

16) ¿Alguien de su familia ha sufrido daños debido a la violencia política - si es así, quién, qué sucedió?

17) ¿Alguno de tus amigos o ex compañeros de trabajo han sufrido daños debido a la violencia política - si es así, quién, qué sucedió?

CUESTIONES RELACIONADAS CON LA MUJER

1) En los Estados Unidos las mujeres suelen trabajar fuera de casa, ¿sucede lo mismo en el país al que regresarían?

2) ¿Sería usted capaz de trabajar en su casa y mantener a su familia?

3) ¿Qué obstáculos enfrentaría en la búsqueda de trabajo?

4) ¿Cómo se han adaptado sus hijas a la vida en los Estados Unidos?

5) ¿Qué problemas tendrían sus hijas por ser mujeres en el país al que se mudarían?

6) Son las oportunidades educativas para las niñas en su país de origen similares a las de los Estados Unidos. Si no, ¿cómo son?

CUESTIONES RELACIONADAS CON LA COMUNIDAD Y LAZOS FAMILIARES EN LOS ESTADOS UNIDOS

1) ¿Está involucrado en su comunidad?

2) ¿Con que frecuencia pasa tiempo con miembros de la familia?

4) ¿Cuál es su relación con cada uno de ellos y dónde viven?

5) ¿Cuál es su estatus migratorio?

6) ¿Qué tipo de actividades hace usted con sus amigos y familiares?

7) ¿Con qué frecuencia se les ve?

8) Por favor describa su rutina diaria durante la semana de trabajo, incluyendo lo que se hace después del trabajo

9) Por favor describa sus actividades durante el fin de semana y otro tiempo libre.

10) ¿Está involucrado con alguna organización comunitaria (grupos de la iglesia, equipos, grupos de asesoramiento, grupos escolares, sindicatos)?

11) ¿Se mantiene activo en esos grupos - cuánto tiempo pasa con dichos grupos?

12) ¿Está usted en una posición de liderazgo con dichos grupos?

13) Si usted es miembro de una iglesia, ¿con qué frecuencia asiste usted?

14) ¿Tiene muchos parientes cercanos en su país de origen - ¿Dónde viven?

15) ¿Tiene muchos amigos en su país natal? Usted mantuvo contacto con ellos?

16) ¿Sus amigos o familiares podrían ayudarle a encontrar una vivienda y empleo en el extranjero? - ¿por qué no?

17) Si no, ¿usted cree que la falta de contactos personales le haría difícil obtener una vivienda adecuada y empleo?

Otros Factores Culturales En Su País Natal. ¿Usted enfrentaría persecución en su país natal debido a su género sexual, religión, ideas políticas, u otros factores?

APPENDIX 6
SAMPLE LIST OF DOCUMENTS

SUPPORTING DOCUMENTS LIST FOR PROVISIONAL WAIVERS

ENGLISH:

Proof of ties to the country through property/benefits
- Contract of Property Deed, or lease contract
- Car titles
- Auto registration
- Insurance polices: home, car, life, and health for you and your family
- Driver's license

Proof of ties to the US through family/friends

- Copies of birth certificates from the United States, passports from the United States, naturalization certificates or legal permanent resident cards for ALL family members. Include spouse, children, parents, siblings, grandparents, aunts and uncles, cousins, parents-in-law, etc.
- Photos of you with your family
- Children's school registrations
- Letter from teachers at school explaining how it will affect your children if separated from you
- Letters from family and friends who are citizens or legal permanent residents (15 minimum)

Proof of ties to the country through education/profession
- School registration in the United States, certificates, diplomas from schools and universities in the United States
- Letter from employer and evidence of history of employment

Proof of good faith marriage
- Birth Certificate of applicant and qualifying relative spouse
- Marriage Certificate
- Photos of your wedding

Proof of financial difficulty
- Bills or correspondence that has your name or your spouse's name for the last 4 months (electricity, water, telephone, gas, etc.)
- Bank statement of checking or savings for the last 4 months

Proof of medical/emotional condition
- Medical receipts for you or an immediate family member that suffers a medical condition
- Report from counselor or psychologist explaining your emotional hardship

Proof of good moral character
- Proof you registered for Selective Service
- Clearance Police letter showing clean record of applicant
- Proof of community service
- Letter from your church

Proof of country of origin's condition
- Photos or newspaper clippings that indicate the condition of the place where the family would relocate if waiver not approved

Most importantly
- Letter from you asking for forgiveness and asking that waiver be approved. Mention everything you own here in the United States and explain in detail how you and your family will suffer emotionally, mentally and economically. (Applicant)
- Letter from Qualifying Relative explaining how he or she would be affected if the Applicant were deported from the United States

SPANISH:

<u>**Lista de Documentos Para el Perdón**</u>

Pruebas de lazes al pais por medic de propiedad/beneficios
- Contratos de Propiedad o contrato de renta
- Titulos de autos
- Registro de auto
- Segura de Casa, de auto, de vida o de salud para usted y su familia
- Licencia de manejo del Peticionario

Pruebas de lazes al pais por media.de familia/amigos
- Copias de certificados de nacimiento de los Estados Unidos, pasaportes de los Estados Unidos, certificados de naturalizaci6n o copias de tarjetas de residencia permanente legal de TODOS los miembros de la familia. Incluyendo esposos, hijos, padres, hermanos, abuelos, Uos, primos, suegros, etc.
- Fotos de usted y su familia
- Registro de la escuela de los nirios
- Cartas de maestros de la escuela explicando coma afectara a sus hijos si es separado de ellos
- Cartas de familiares y amigos que son ciudadanos o residentes permanentes legales (un minima de 15 cartas)

Pruebas de lazes al pais por medio de educación/profesión
- Registro de escuela en las Estados Unidos, certificados, diplomas de escuelas en los Estados Unidos del Peticionario o Beneficiario
- Carta de empleador y evidencia de historia de empleo del Peticionario o Beneficiario

Pruebas de matrimonio de buena fe
- Certificado de Nacimiento de Peticionario y Beneficiario
- Certificado de Matrimonio
- Fotos de su boda

Pruebas de dificultad financiera
- Recibos con el nombre de alguno de las conyugues de los ultimas 4 meses (electricidad, agua, telefono, gas, etc.)
- Copia de cuentas de banco de cheques o ahorros de los ultimas 4 meses

Prueba de condición medica/emocional
- Reporte medico de usted o de algun miembro cercano de su familia que sufre de alguna condición medica
- Reporte de consejero o psicólogo explicando su dificultad extrema (Peticionario)

Pruebas de buen caracter moral
- Prueba que se registro con el Servicio Selective
- Reporte policial que muestre el record del beneficiario
- Prueba de servicio a la comunidad del Beneficiario
- Cartas de su iglesia

Pruebas de condición del pais de origen
- Fotografias o recortes de papel periódico que indiquen la condición del lugar donde se mudaria la familia en caso de que el perdón no sea aprobado

Lo mas importante
- Carta de usted pidiendo perdón par su familiar y pidiendo que su perdón sea aprobado. Mencione todo lo que tiene aqul en los Estados Unidos y explique en detalle coma usted y su familia sufrira emocionalmente, mentalmente, y económicamente. (Peticionario)
- Carta de esposo/a explicando coma le afectara al Peticionario si es deportado de las Estados Unidos (Beneficiario)

APPENDIX 7

EXPERT REPORTS AND OTHER RESOURCES

Expert reports are available from various sources, including governmental and nongovernmental organizations; academic institutions and research centers; think tanks; and human rights groups. This list is a non-exhaustive selection of resources that may be helpful for locating hardship evidence that will help demonstrate the facts concerning conditions in the home country. Although website information is subject to change, you may be able to use the information below to find similar and timely reports and articles.

Experts on Health Care and Conditions

Resources Regarding Healthcare and Medical Conditions

A number of websites include information on medical conditions and diseases, as well as the effects of failure to provide treatment. It is useful to include general, basic information about the disease affecting an applicant or family member and the impact of untreated conditions.

The following websites may be useful:

- The Mayo Clinic: *www.mayoclinic.com/health/DiseasesIndex/DiseasesIndex*
- The Centers for Disease Control (CDC): *www.cdc.gov/diseasesconditions*
- The National Institutes of Health (NIH): *www.health.nih.gov*
- State departments of public health, such as the California Department of Public Health: *www.cdph.ca.gov*
- Disease-specific associations, such as the American Diabetes Association: *www.diabetes.org*

Reports on access to medical treatment in other countries are available on U.S. government, U.S. nonprofit, and international nongovernmental organizations' websites. Academic studies and other articles may also have helpful information. Reports may examine the incidence of specific diseases and conditions, the availability of health services, the availability of healthcare by gender, the prevalence of health conditions in the elderly, and other particularized health factors. Information about the cost of medical treatment and access to health insurance by the waiver applicant, as well as U.S. citizen and LPR family members, is available on international nongovernmental organizations' websites, government websites, and the websites of private companies. Environmental conditions, including clean drinking water sources, sanitation, and pollution, may have a significant impact on health.

- U.S. Department of Health and Human Services, National Institute of Health. Includes biomedical research on health conditions around the world. www.nih.gov
- World Health Organization. The WHO coordinates the international response to humanitarian health emergencies. The maintain statistics and publish information assessing health trends worldwide. www.who.int/en
- Pan American Health Organization. The PAHO is an international health organization with resources on health in the Americas, including publications, news releases and country reports. www.paho.org/hq/
- UNICEF. UNICEF advocates for the protection of children's rights worldwide. They publish reports and statistics regarding health, education and safety issues impacting children. www.unicef.org

Experts on Economic Issues and Financial Concerns

- The Migration Policy Institute (MPI) is an independent, nonprofit think tank that studies migration worldwide. The MPI website includes a list of experts on Latin America. *www.migrationpolicy.org*.
- Organization for Economic Co-operation and Development. OCED is a nonprofit that helps governments foster prosperity and fight poverty through economic growth and financial stability. They publish reports on global economic development. *www.oced.org*

- The Hass School of Business at the University of California, Berkeley has a list of experts on global financial issues. *www.haas.berkeley.edu/news/mediaexperts.html* .
- Center for Comparative Immigration Studies, University of California, San Diego conducts research on migration from Mexico and around the world. The Center has staff with expertise on Mexico, including the well-known Wayne Cornelius. *http://ccis.ucsd.edu/people/wayne-cornelius/*.
- The Woodrow Wilson International Center for Scholars, or the Wilson Center, is a research institution on U.S. and international issues. The Wilson Center website includes a list of experts on Mexico. *http://www.wilsoncenter.org/expert-list/Mexico.*

Experts on Social and Cultural Issues

Education

- The Brookings Institution is a nonprofit research institute. They publish reports on issues such as global development, economies, health concerns and more. Their website allows one to search a list of experts on many different countries and issues. *www.brookings.edu*
- Center for Latin American Studies, U.C. Berkeley. The Center for Latin American studies website includes a list of faculty divided by area of expertise. The website contains e-mail addresses for the faculty. *clas.berkeley.edu/affiliated-faculty-clas*
- Stanford University Center for Latin American Studies. The Center website maintains a list of affiliated faculty, including faculty in the Department of Education. Clicking on the faculty member's name will provide an e-mail address. *las.stanford.edu/people/clas-affiliated-faculty*
- Center for Latin American Studies, School of Foreign Service, Georgetown University. The Center website includes a list of faculty and the faculty member's area of concentration. *clas.georgetown.edu/faculty/*
- Center for Latin American Studies, University of Florida. The Center website lists the faculty by name, area of interest, and e-mail: *www.latam.ufl.edu/people*

Country Conditions: Crime, violence, public safety, human rights, social and cultural issues,

- U.S. Department of State (DOS). DOS publishes annual human rights reports and issues alerts and warnings against travel to certain countries or regions when safety issues arise.
  - Human Rights Reports: *www.state.gov/j/drl/rls/hrrpt/*
  - Travel Alerts and Warnings: *www.travel.state.gov/content/passports/en/alertswarnings.html*
- UNHCR. The UN's refugee agency publishes reports and statistics regarding country conditions and refugees. www.unhcr.org/en-us
- Center for Gender and Refugee Studies. CGRS conducts legal trainings and engages in impact litigation, policy development, research, and in-country fact-finding. Resources include publications on gender based violence, violence against children, and gang based violence. *www.cgrs.uchastings.edu*
- Human Rights Watch. HRW is a nonprofit organization that publishes fact-finding and human rights reports and briefings on conditions in countries around the world. *www.hrw.org*
- The Council on Foreign Relations. The Council on Foreign Relations, a non-profit think tank and membership organization, publishes reports and articles on policy issues and developing crises around the world. Publications include reports on violence in Mexico and Central America. *www.cfr.org*
- InSight Crime in America. InSight Crime in America is a non-profit foundation dedicated to the study of organized crime in Latin America and the Caribbean. Resources include investigations, reports, and other articles. *www.insightcrime.org*

- WOLA. WOLA is a research and advocacy organization focused on human rights in the Americas. They publish reports and analysis regarding conditions in Latin America. *www.wola.org*
- Amnesty International. Amnesty International investigates and reports on human rights abuses worldwide. *www.amnestyinternational.org*
- Universities, think tanks, and other organizations may have departments focusing on various social and cultural issues in different countries

Recommendations by Practitioners

Other practitioners may be a good source of identifying and locating individuals who can provide expert affidavits. In addition to following up with colleagues to identify experts, you can use list serves to ask practitioners around the country about potential experts. For example, you can join the following list serves:

- CLINIC's list serve on waivers: *http://groups.yahoo.com/group/CLINIC_Waivers/join*
- Detention Watch Network list serve: *http://www.detentionwatchnetwork.org/listserve*
- American Immigration Council list serve: *http://wfc2.wiredforchange.com/o/8531/signup_page/signup*
- National Immigration Project of the National Lawyers Guild list serve: *http://www.nationalimmigrationproject.org/memberlistserv.htm*
- Clients may also know of individuals who have particular expertise or familiarity in an area related to the hardship claim.

APPENDIX 8

GUIDELINES FOR WRITING DECLARATIONS

Guide to Help You Write a Supporting Letter
I-601A Provisional Unlawful Presence Waiver

Qualifying Relative: _____
Waiver Applicant: _____

Your written statement in support of this case is vitally important. The legal protections this family seeks are difficult to obtain, and a supporting letter will provide helpful documentation of the claim. This guide will explain the basics of the law and give you some guidelines. Your written statement should contain several specific elements, which are mentioned below. Immigration issues affect the entire family, but your letter should focus especially on hardship faced by the Qualifying Relative named above.

Your written statement should demonstrate the following:
- You personally know the Waiver Applicant, the Qualifying Relative, or both
- The Waiver Applicant has a good moral character
- Forcing these relatives to **separate** from each other or **relocate** to the Waiver Applicant's home country would cause **extreme hardship to the Qualifying Relative**

The following questions may be used to guide your written statement:
- What is your relationship to the persons named above? (spouse, family, friend, neighbor, teacher, colleague, etc.)
- When and how did you meet?
- Where and how often have you seen each other? (every day at work, twice a week at church)
- What is your immigration status in the U.S.? (citizen, legal permanent resident, other)
- Is the Waiver Applicant a responsible individual? Is he or she a hard worker? Give examples of positive character traits he or she demonstrates.
- Is the family involved in their church, school, or community in any way?
- What type of hardships would the Qualifying Relative face if he or she chose to relocate to the Waiver Applicant's home country?
- What type of hardships would the Qualifying Relative face if he or she chose to separate from the Waiver Applicant and remain here?
- Does the Qualifying Relative have any physical or psychological health conditions that would make separation or relocation to another country particularly difficult?
- How would the family be financially affected by separation? How would they be financially affected by relocation?
- What other challenges would the family face due to separation or relocation?

Your letter should be written clearly and concisely. It should be **signed** by you and include your **name**, **address** and **telephone number**. It should also include a statement that everything you wrote is true, such as "I swear under penalty of perjury that the above is true and accurate."

APPENDIX 9

SAMPLE LETTERS FOR DOCTORS, EMPLOYERS, TEACHERS AND OTHERS IN PREPARING DECLARATIONS

Date:

Dear Dr._____,

We represent **[Applicant]** in an immigration matter. He has been living in the United States for many years, and is applying for permanent residence through his father, **[Qualifying Relative]**, whom you have treated for diabetes. In order for **[Applicant]** to immigrate to the United States, we need to present evidence showing that it would create an extreme hardship to **[Qualifying Relative]** if **[Applicant]** were unable to become a legal resident of the United States.

[Applicant] plays an important role in the support of his family. **[Applicant]** helps to take care of his father, who is very ill with diabetes and vision problems. **[Applicant]** supports the family financially since his father is often unable to work. **[Applicant]** is studying to be an emergency medical technician and has almost finished the program.

It would be helpful if you could assist us by writing a letter or declaration on behalf of **[Qualifying Relative]**. Please begin your letter by explaining who you are, address the letter to the "Immigration Service" and write it on your letterhead if possible. We encourage you to write a descriptive letter regarding **[Qualifying Relative's]** health issues. A letter using laymen's terms will be helpful to the officer in understanding the impact of his medical conditions. Also, if you have reason to be aware of it, please describe the personal hardship **[Qualifying Relative]** would face if **[Applicant]** were forced to live in Mexico, separated from his father and his family.

We understand that writing a letter of this type can be a very time-consuming task. To help you, we have listed some specific things you might want to mention in your letter. You are not limited by this list; if you have additional helpful information, please include it. Please remember that you are writing a letter recommending this person for permanent residence.

1. Describe how you came to know **[Qualifying Relative]** (and his family, if you know them), how well you know them, and for how long.
2. What medical problems does **[Qualifying Relative]** have? What is the diagnosis? What medications is the patient currently taking? What care does he need? What is the short-term and long-term prognosis? Do you believe he would receive the same quality medical care in a small town in Mexico?
3. What hardships would he suffer if he was separated from his son?

Thank you in advance for your kindness and assistance in this matter. Please feel free to call us if you have any questions or concerns.

Sincerely,

Date:

Dear _____ (employer):

We represent **[Qualifying Relative]** in an immigration matter. She has lived in the United States for many years, and is applying for permanent residence for her husband **[Applicant]**. In order for her spouse to immigrate to the U.S., we must show that **[Qualifying Relative]** would suffer extreme hardship if she were forced to relocate abroad to avoid separation from her husband. The hardship she would face include being forced to leave her current employment, the difficulty of finding work in Mexico, and the loss of income.

It would be very helpful if you could assist us by writing a letter on behalf of **[Qualifying Relative]**. Please begin your letter by explaining who you are and your role at **[Employer]**. Please address the letter to the "Immigration Officer" and put it on your letterhead.

We encourage you to write a descriptive letter about **[Qualifying Relative]** since this type of letter will be more helpful to the officer. Please describe the length of time **[Qualifying Relative]** has been employed, her job title, hours and salary, an explanation of her duties and responsibilities, the quality of her performance, interaction with coworkers, trustworthiness, work ethic, friendliness, and reliability. What opportunities will she lose if she is forced to leave the U.S. to avoid separation from her husband? If you have seen **[Qualifying Relative]** progress and learn any new skills on the job, please mention this.

Thank you in advance for your kindness and assistance in this matter. Please feel free to call us if you have any questions or concerns.

Sincerely,

Representative

Date:

Dear _____ (teacher),

We represent [**Applicant**], [**Student's**] mother, in her immigration matter. She has been living in the United States for many years and is now in the final stages of immigrating.

In order for [**Applicant**] to obtain legal status, she needs to present evidence showing that it would create an extreme hardship for her and her family if she was unable to immigrate and the family was to be separated.

It would be very helpful if you could assist [**Applicant**] by writing a letter or declaration on her behalf. Please address the letter to the "Immigration Officer" and put it on your letterhead. We encourage you to write a descriptive letter since this type of letter will be more helpful to the officer. Below you will find a list of suggestions to include in your letter; please address only those items you feel comfortable with and include any other helpful information that reflects positively on [**Applicant**] or her family:

1. State who you are, where you work, and for how long you have been a teacher.
2. Indicate how long you have known _____ and her child, _____. How long have you been the child's teacher?
3. Describe the student's scholastic strengths and weaknesses. How doe the student interact with his/her peers? What are the student's positives qualities (be specific and include such characteristics like intelligence, charm, friendliness, dedication, cooperativeness). Give specific examples of where he/she has displayed these qualities.
4. Is there a particular subject that the student likes or excels in? Does the student have any special needs that are being addressed? Are there any educational goals that have been set for him/her?
5. Give specific examples of activities or events that the family has attended and how they interact with each other. Do they help each other? To your knowledge, are they a close family?
6. Does _____ attend parent/teacher meetings, evidence an active interest in the scholastic performance of the child, or attend school activities?

Thank you in advance for your assistance in this matter. We understand that writing this type of letter can be time-consuming, and we would not ask if it were not so important. Please let us know if there are any other educational professionals who have had contact with the child and who might be willing to write a letter.

Sincerely,

Representative

Date:

Dear_____,

We are representing _____ in his/her immigration matter. He/she has been living in the United States for many years, and is applying for permanent residence for his/her spouse_____.

In order for his/her spouse to remain in the United States, we need to present evidence showing that it would create an extreme hardship to him/her and the family if his/her spouse were unable to immigrate.

It would be very helpful if you could assist us by writing a letter on behalf of _____. Please begin your letter by explaining who you are. Your letter does not have to be typed out, but it would help. Please address the letter to the "Immigration Officer," and please put it on your letterhead. We encourage you to write a descriptive letter since it will be more helpful to the officer.

We understand that writing a letter of this type can be a time-consuming task. Below you will find a list of some specific things you might want to mention in your letter. You are not limited by this list; if you have additional helpful information, please include it. Please remember that you are writing a letter regarding the hardship the family would suffer should his/her spouse not obtain legal status.

1. Describe how you came to know_____ (and his family, if you know them), how well you know them, and for how long.
2. Describe his/her positive characteristics (think of specific characteristics, such as intelligence, sense of humor, hardworking, sincerity, etc.) Give specific examples of where he/she has displayed these qualities.
3. Does_____ have a close family? Give specific examples of activities or events that the family has attended and how they help each other.
4. Is he/she integrated into life in the United States and his community? What activities does he/she do? Has he/she done any volunteer work with the church or any other group? Does he/she speak English? Does he/she have friends? Do you feel he/she is a positive addition to this country? Why?
5. If you know, please comment on the personal hardship the family would suffer if they were required to live apart or relocate to Mexico.

Thank you in advance for your kindness and assistance in this matter. Please feel free to call us if you have any questions or concerns.

Sincerely,

Representative

APPENDIX 10A
SAMPLE DECLARATION OF QUALIFYING RELATIVE

I swear that under penalty of perjury that the following is true and correct:

My name is Joe Moreno and I was born on September 15, 1985. I am a naturalized citizen of the United States. My wife is Juanita Moreno, a citizen of Mexico. After dating for a year and a half, we got married on August 25, 2014.

If my wife's application for a provisional waiver is denied, our lives will be devastated. We have decided that I will relocate to Mexico with her since I depend on her for my physical and emotional well-being. A move to Mexico means that I will be separated from my family here in the United States. I would lack access to the health care treatment that I need and to quality master's degree programs and job opportunities. I will also be uprooted from my hometown and be dropped into a dangerous place and a culture I am not familiar with.

Even though I was born in Mexico, it feels like I have lived my whole life in the United States. I came here when I was three years old, so my Spanish isn't very good and I speak with an accent. Some other Mexicans make fun of my accent and wonder why I don't speak Spanish very well even though I am Mexican.

I am not familiar with Mexico because I have only been back to Mexico to visit some family for three short visits. The last time I went back to Mexico was ten years ago because many areas in the country are dangerous and hard to navigate in, especially because my Spanish isn't very good. I also do not have many relatives that have remained in Mexico. Most of my family has migrated to the United States. My family comes from the Mexican state of Guerrero, which is not safe, so they fled the gang violence and came to the United States to live their lives without fear. Because my family has been in the United States for many generations, we have lost some of our Mexican customs.

My wife's family would not be able to offer us a safe place to live in Mexico. Juanita comes from Sinaloa, where her parents still live and where there are many gangs committing brutal murders and robbing people.

I have been very anxious about the possibility that I may have to move to Mexico because of the stories of violence in Mexico that my family tells. They say that people get killed without any cause, sometimes just for looking at someone the wrong way. If I have to move back to Mexico, I fear that I may be targeted by gangs due to my lack of Spanish language skills or that I will be taken advantage of due to my poor knowledge of local customs or that I will be seen as having wealth due to my living in the United States.

I suffer from anxiety, panic attacks, and insomnia. I also have a history of depression and suicidal thoughts. Moving to Mexico would worsen these conditions due to the constant danger I would face as well as the adjustment to a new culture.

In the past, when I have experienced major changes in my life, I have not reacted very well. When my best friend died in my 20's, I became an alcoholic and was convicted for DUIs. My time in jail was very difficult and I suffered from depression and had many suicidal thoughts. I also developed insomnia, anxiety, and began to have panic attacks. I believe these conditions stem from the constant fear I was in while I was in jail. There was a lot of violence there and I was beat up a lot.

It took about two and a half years for me to stabilize a little bit, not feel like taking my own life, and start seeking the help I needed for alcoholism and depression. Juanita played a huge role in my recovery.

Juanita and I met while we were both taking classes at our local community college. She was very kind to me and offered to help me with my homework. As we got to know each other more, we learned about each other's lives. I learned about her difficult childhood in Mexico and she learned about my struggles with alcoholism and depression. She encouraged me to go to Alcoholics Anonymous meetings a few times per week and she held me accountable. She also helped me find a therapist that takes my health insurance. Since we started living together, Juanita has taken care of me even more. She makes sure that I take my medicines for my conditions every morning. She also makes sure that I am relaxed and feel loved and comfortable.

Since we initiated the process of changing Juanita's status in this country, I have not been doing as well with my recovery because I fear that her application will be denied and we will have to move back to Mexico and face violence. I have had a much harder time sleeping because I have nightmares about living in Mexico. I feel very anxious so I start grinding my teeth at night which I am afraid will lead to issues with my teeth. I have more panic attacks that don't let me do my work, and I have been having more depressing thoughts.

Juanita and I are very close and love each other. We spend extra time together every day since she drives me to work every morning because my license is still suspended for another year. My job is about 15 miles from our home and there is no public transportation available to take me there, so Juanita as taken on this effort.

It would be a great sacrifice to leave my loving parents, as well as my supportive brothers, all of whom have lived close to me for all my life. My parents are legal permanent residents and by brothers are U.S. citizens. My family has supported me through the death of my best friend, my incarceration, and my recovery. They have provided emotional and financial support when I have needed it the most. Juanita and I visit my parents every weekend and we visit my brothers and their families at least once a month. We also spend all our holidays with my family since Juanita's family is either in Mexico or far from us in the United States. I would really miss my family if I had to leave them to move to Mexico.

It would be difficult to visit my family in the United States if I lived in Mexico because I do not have much in savings and it does not seem like I will be able to make a decent living. It doesn't look like I will have many employment opportunities available to me in Mexico because in Guerrero and Sinaloa, the gang violence is damaging the economy. Since I finished college, I have always worked as a forest ranger. The gang activity in these areas of Mexico have basically shut down the national park system.

There is a lot of poverty in both areas. I also don't speak Spanish very well, so I would not be able to find employment until my Spanish language skills can improve, which would take at least a few months.

I have my bachelor's degree and have been seriously considering getting a master's degree in engineering to obtain better employment. However, a move to Mexico would preclude me from obtaining my master's degree because there aren't any reputable master's programs in engineering in Guerrero or Sinaloa.

Moving to Mexico would drastically change every aspect of my life. I feel that I have to be with Juanita for my well-being. I also love her so much that I could not be without her. I hope that her application for a provisional waiver is approved so that we do not have to face the extremely difficult hardship of having to move to Mexico.

_____   _____
Joe Moreno   Date

APPENDIX 10B

SAMPLE DECLARATION OF QUALIFYING RELATIVE

I declare under penalty of perjury that the following is true and correct:

My name is Maria Menendez. I am a U.S. citizen. My husband is Enrique Menendez and he is applying for a waiver of the unlawful presence bar. Our four-year-old son is Aaron Menendez.

I am writing to ask you give my husband the opportunity to reside here with me and our son. We love him and need him here with us. Enrique and my son are my world, my everything. Enrique is the best father and husband in the world and we are the happiest when we are together.

If Enrique had to reside in Michoacán, Mexico, my son and I would be devastated. We cannot go there to live with him because it is not safe there. Last year my husband's uncle was kidnapped, and they found his burned body months later. We would have to separate because we cannot put our son's life at risk like that. I cannot even imagine how hard that would be for me.

My anxiety and depression would be so much worse, and I could not work or care for my son. About 10 years ago, my nephew went into a coma and he has not come out still after all these years. When that happened, I started feeling sad and worried all the time. I went for help and was prescribed medicine, but I never took it because I did not want to depend on it.

Not long after that, I met my husband and we started going out. He was such a gentleman and we loved spending time together. He helped me when I was feeling depressed. Eventually, we decided to get serious and we were so happy to find out I was pregnant. We got married soon after that and then the light of our lives was born: Aaron Menendez. My husband has taken care of us ever since. He is the best dad and husband.

I kept experiencing times when I was depressed and anxious, but my husband helped me through them. For that reason, I stopped going back to the therapist or taking the medicine. I signed up for classes to become a medical assistant and took out a student loan. But then my brother landed in the hospital last year and we watched him suffer terribly until he died. My husband supported me through it all. I had to drop out of my classes because my depression and anxiety got too bad.

Now I am trying to manage with the thought that I will be left here without my husband. He was coming home from work with his boss and they were stopped by Border Patrol. He has been given a period of voluntary departure, after which he will have to return to Mexico. We are in the last stages of preparing for his immigrant visa appointment and filing for this waiver. My son is having a really hard time and I do not know how much more pressure I can stand before I break.

I work the night shift while my husband takes care of Aaron and puts him to bed at night. I am worried because my husband is usually the one who gives my son his medication since he has asthma. I know I can count on him. My son already notices that his father may not be here much longer. I am worried that he will be traumatized if he is separated from his father for too long. He does not understand why his daddy must leave.

We have a lot of debts and I cannot afford even half the payments on my own. We depend on both our incomes to pay our bills. I do not earn as much as him and I have not been working very long. I would not be able to finish my school program and get a better job and I would never be able to continue school without my husband's financial and physical support.

_____   _____
Maria Menendez   Date

APPENDIX 10C
SAMPLE DECLARATION OF WAIVER APPLICANT

I declare under penalty of perjury that the following is true and correct:

My name is Graciela Munoz and I am applying for a waiver of the unlawful presence ground of inadmissibility. I believe my application should be approved because otherwise my husband Anthony would be devastated. We have decided based on everything that he would stay in the United States with our children if I were forced to return and live in Mexico for ten years.

My husband is a U.S. citizen. If I were to leave, he would become not only the principal wage earner but also the sole financial provider in our family. I now stay at home and oversee the care for our six children. They were all born here. I take them to school, help them with their homework, and take them to their doctor's appointments. Separating us would upset the balance we have achieved to care for each other and our family.

My husband currently works Monday to Saturday for at least eight hours per day. His only days off are Sundays, which he dedicates to spending time with our family and attending church. If I were not here, he would have to hire someone to look after our children. He would also probably have to cut back his hours at work to be with our children. Both situations would would have a negative effect on his finances. It would also affect our children to be without me to support them, which I know would affect him as well.

My husband cannot come with me to Oaxaca, Mexico because of the high unemployment rate and the low wages there. He does not speak very good Spanish and would not be able to find a job. Plus, we have heard reports of crimes and kidnappings related to organized crime. We would not take the risk of endangering our children, since they are already established in schools and programs here. We have chosen for them to stay in their country where they can have a bright future.

It would be extremely devastating for him since we have never been separated from each other. I have been in the United States for 18 years and have never had any troubles with the law. I admit that I entered the United States illegally, but that was only once, and I was a teenager at the time. I am sorry for that action. Since then I have worked to maintain a healthy family and bring them up to respect the great opportunities they have here.

_____   _____

Graciela Munoz   Date

APPENDIX 11

SAMPLE FINANCIAL STATEMENT

Home Loan Payment	$781.74
Truck Payment	$596.00
Insurance Payments	$173.03
Water Bill Payment	$ 80.89
Electricity Bill Payment	$ 48.78
Gas Bill Payment	$ 53.19
Mobile Phone Service Payments	$102.11
Credit Card Payment	$303.74
Medical Services Payments	$179.81
Food and Groceries	$504.78
Gasoline	$154.29
TOTAL	**$ 2978.36**

RENE AND ALEXANDRA POSADA

- Rene makes an average of $2,160.00 per month
- Alexandra makes an average of $1,440.00 per month
- With combined incomes, the couple is able to meet all monthly expenses
- If Alexandra is denied the waiver and is required to live in Mexico, Rene will not be able to cover all expenses with only his income
- Rene would have to look for childcare for his son, which will increase expenses of about $600 per month
- Rene would have to look for an additional part-time job in order to make ends meet, thereby not being able to spend any quality time with his young son
- Rene will not be able to send money to Alexandra in Mexico, since he will hardly have enough to sustain the household here
- If Alexandra is able to become an LPR, she will be able to continue to contribute to household expenses and the couple will eventually be able to reach their goal of buying a home.

Appendix 12A
Sample Cover Letters and Index of Exhibits

USCIS
P.O. Box 4599
Chicago, IL 60680

Re: Form I-601A unlawful presence waiver for Edgar Mendez

Dear Sir/Madam:

I am submitting the enclosed I-601A waiver for the unlawful presence bar on behalf of the applicant, Edgar Mendez. His U.S. citizen wife, Esmeralda Montaldo, would suffer extreme hardship if the waiver were not granted. In support of this application please find detailed declarations from the applicant and his qualifying relative, as well as other supporting documents.

The couple has decided that the qualifying relative will remain in the United States. This waiver application is therefore based on the separation hardship she will suffer if forced to remain apart from her husband for ten years. Ms. Montaldo is unable to accompany and reside with her husband in Mexico for the following reasons. She was born in Chicago where she has lived all her life, surrounded by her parents and other close family members. The only time she traveled abroad, to Central America, she suffered severe culture shock. Both of her children have serious medical problems. Her son has been diagnosed with ureteral reflux and hydronephrosis and is in the care of a pediatric nephrologist. Her daughter was also born with the same problem, given that it is a hereditary affliction. Ms. Montaldo is currently 15 weeks pregnant and in the care of specialists who are ready to treat their third child. This medical treatment is unavailable in that part of northern Mexico where Mr. Mendez would reside.

Ms. Montaldo also is the primary care provider for her parents, who each have serious medical problems. Her mother has been receiving treatment for lung cancer, while her father is recovering from a stroke and hepatitis C, in addition to having diabetes and high blood pressure. Her son also receives special education due to developmental delay. Ms. Montaldo is currently in school pursuing a bachelor's degree in Criminal Justice, and a move to Mexico would interrupt both her education and career.

Ms. Montaldo is dependent on her husband for both emotional and financial support. She would experience two "significant hardship factors," since she is caring for a disabled family members and she would become both the sole child care provider and wage earner should the waiver be denied.

Finally, as supported by the attached documents, the drug-related violence in the province of Sinaloa, where her husband would reside, is a significant factor in her inability to live in Mexico.

Please see the attached documentation that supports her claim of extreme hardship due to health factors, family and social factors, financial factors, and conditions in the applicant's home country.

Mr. Mendez has also submitted evidence of his good moral character and positive discretionary factors. He has no criminal record or immigration violations other than the one illegal entry into the United States many years ago. If Mr. Mendez must wait in Mexico for ten years, the family would be devastated emotionally and financially.

Sincerely,

USCIS
P.O. Box 4599
Chicago, IL 60680

Re: Form I-601A unlawful presence waiver for Edgar Mendez

Dear Sir/Madam:

I am submitting the enclosed I-601A waiver for the unlawful presence bar on behalf of the applicant, Edgar Mendez. He and his U.S. citizen wife, Esmeralda Montaldo, would relocate to Mexico and suffer extreme hardship if the waiver were not granted. The combination of the particularly significant hardships in this case, coupled with the other hardship factors, support a finding of extreme hardship. Please find detailed declarations from the applicant and his qualifying relative, as well as other supporting documents.

Esmeralda Montaldo would suffer the following relocation hardship should she accompany and reside with her husband in Mexico. First, the state of Sinaloa, where the applicant is from and where the family would reside, is subject to a Department of State "Do Not Travel" Warning. The drug- and gang-related violence there is a particularly significant hardship factor. Second, Ms. Montaldo is the primary care provider for her parents, who have serious medical problems and should be considered disabled. Her mother has been receiving treatment for lung cancer, while her father is recovering from a stroke and hepatitis C, in addition to having diabetes and high blood pressure. Third, Ms. Montaldo would experience serious family and social/cultural hardships. She was born in Chicago where she has lived all her life, surrounded by her parents and other close family members. The only time she traveled abroad, to Central America, she suffered culture shock. Fourth, both of her children have serious medical problems. Her son has been diagnosed with ureteral reflux and hydroneephrosis and is in the care of a pediatric nephrologist. Her daughter was also born with the same problem, given that it is a hereditary affliction.

Ms. Montaldo is currently 24 weeks pregnant and in the care of specialists who are ready to treat their third child. This medical treatment is unavailable in Sinaloa. Her son also receives special education due to developmental delays. Ms. Montaldo is in school pursuing a Bachelor's degree in Criminal Justice, and a move to Mexico would interrupt both her education and career. Finally, the couple would suffer financial hardship since she would be unable to get a job in Mexico with her inability to speak Spanish. The applicant would also have difficulty getting anything other than a subsistence-level job. The couple has amassed significant debt, which is supported by documentary evidence.

Mr. Mendez has also submitted evidence of his good moral character: and positive discretionary factors. He has no criminal record or immigration violations other than the one illegal entry into the United States many years ago. If Mr. Mendez must wait in Mexico for ten years, the family would be devastated emotionally and financially.

Sincerely,

INDEX OF EXHIBITS

Exhibit 1: Declaration from qualifying relative, Esmeralda Montaldo
Exhibit 2: Declaration from applicant, Edgar Mendez

Evidence of Unsafe Conditions in Sinaloa, Mexico

Exhibit 3: State Department Travel Warning for the State of Sinaloa, Mexico
Exhibit 4: Article from LA Times on drug-related violence in Sinaloa, Mexico
Exhibit 5: Amnesty International report on drug violence in Mexico

Health-Related and Disability Evidence of Parents

Exhibit 6: Medical records for Olga Montaldo from Mercy Hospital, Chicago, IL, for cancer surgery
Exhibit 7: Medical records for Jaime Montaldo from Mercy Hospital, Chicago, IL, for treatment for stroke

Evidence of Family and Social/Cultural Factors

Exhibit 8: Letter from Chicago Public School system, confirming employment of Esmeralda Montaldo
Exhibit 9: Application for teaching certification of Esmeralda Montaldo
Exhibit 10: Transcript from the University of Illinois at Chicago for Esmeralda Montaldo, showing that she is one class away from completing a Bachelor's degree in Criminal Justice

Health-Related Evidence for Children

Exhibit 11: Letter from Dr. Robert Harris, detailing hydronephrosis (chronic kidney illness) of Tomas Mendez
Exhibit 12: Records from Dr. Elsa Garcia-Perez, showing pregnancy of Esmeralda Montaldo

Education-Related Evidence for son Tomas

Exhibit 13: Letter from occupational therapist detailing developmental delays and speech difficulties of Tomas Mendez

Evidence of Financial Hardship

Exhibit 14: Documents showing car loan to Esmeralda Montaldo and Edgar Mendez for 2010 Nissan Quest
Exhibit 15: Documents showing car loan to Esmeralda Montaldo and Edgar Mendez for 2009 Honda Civic
Exhibit 16: IRS payment plan for Edgar Mendez, for payment of 2015 taxes
Exhibit 17: Documents showing student loan to Esmeralda Montaldo through Loyola University, Chicago
Exhibit 18: Statement from Chase for MasterCard account of Esmeralda Montaldo and Edgar Mendez, showing outstanding balance of $1907.29
Exhibit 19: Statement from Chase for Visa account of Esmeralda Montaldo and Edgar Mendez, showing outstanding balance of $831.06.
Exhibit 20: Statement from Citifinancial for loan account of Esmeralda Montaldo and Edgar Mendez, showing outstanding balance of $5,000.00

Evidence of Relationship to US Citizen Spouse and Children

Exhibit 21: Birth certificate of Tomas Mendez, son of Esmeralda Montaldo and Edgar Mendez, born in Chicago on March 20, 2015

Exhibit 22: Birth certificate of Teresa Mendez, daughter of Esmeralda Montaldo and Edgar Mendez, born in Chicago, IL on September 4, 2016
Exhibit 23: Birth certificate of Esmeralda Montaldo, showing birth in Chicago, IL on September 14, 1986.
Exhibit 24: Marriage certificate between Esmeralda Montaldo and Edgar Mendez

APPENDIX 12B
SAMPLE COVER LETTER AND INDEX OF EXHIBITS

USCIS
PO Box 4599
Chicago, IL 60680
RE: I-601A Application for Graciela Munoz

Dear USCIS officer:

Please find the attached application for a waiver pursuant to INA § 212(a)(9)(B)(i)(II). The applicant, Graciela Munoz, is the spouse of a U.S. citizen. She has been unlawfully present in the United States since 2001, when she came from Oaxaca, Mexico. Her husband, Anthony Munoz, is the qualifying relative. The couple has discussed the issue if the waiver were to be denied and they have decided that Anthony will remain here with their six children. Therefore, the waiver application is based on the separation hardship he would suffer.

If this waiver petition is not granted Anthony would be devastated. Graciela and her husband have six children together: Israel, Mia, Maritza, Marco, Miguel and Andrew. The youngest of their children are only 4, 6, and 8 years old. Graciela's husband works full-time while she takes care of their home and children.

Graciela is from the state of Oaxaca, which is under a level 2 U.S. Department of State travel warning due to ongoing crime. The couple would separate rather than move their children to Mexico due to the lack of safety, as well as the poverty, lack of employment opportunity, inadequate healthcare, low quality education, and limited possibilities for advancement. Anthony would continue living and working in the United States, providing for their children, meeting all their financial and social obligations here, and send money to support his wife in Mexico. He would struggle with the overwhelming dual role of sole financial provider and lone caretaker after depending on his wife to share half of the load. As such, he would suffer a a particularly significant hardship.

He would suffer emotionally to lose his life partner after all their years together and to witness the trauma to his children of losing their mother. The chronic stress of his new role, together with the daily fear of knowing Graciela is living in such conditions, would cause extreme hardship. His financial stability would also be endangered because of the increased expenses he would have to take on.

We respectfully request you consider the positive discretionary factors in this case and how they outweigh one unfavorable one. Graciela entered the United States illegally when she was 17 years old. She has demonstrated exemplary character over the 18 years she has lived in the United States. She is a devoted wife and mother and is respected and loved by family and friends. She has never been arrested or had any legal problems. The totality of circumstances merits granting this waiver. Thank you so much for your time and attention.

Sincerely,

INDEX OF EXHIBITS

ITEM	DESCRIPTION	PAGE
1	Declaration from qualifying relative, Anthony, Graciela's U.S. citizen husband.	1
	EVIDENCE OF RELATIONSHIP TO QUALIFYING RELATIVE	
2	Birth certificate with translation for Graciela, who was born in Oaxaca, Mexico	3
3	Qualifying relative Anthony's U.S. passport	5
4	Graciela and Anthony's marriage certificate	6
	EVIDENCE OF PERSONAL HARDSHIP FACTORS	
5	Birth Certificate for the couple's 4-year-old son, Israel, born 10/09/2015	8
6	Birth Certificate for the couple's 6-year-old daughter, Mia, born 09/12/2013	9
7	Student Demographics report for Mia who was in Kindergarten last year	10
8	Birth Certificate for the couple's 8-year-old daughter, Maritza, born 10/03/2011	11
9	Student Demographics report for Maritza who was in 2nd grade at Sierra Vista Elementary.	12
10	Birth Certificate for 11-year-old son, Marco	13
11	Student ID and letter of support from Marco who is in 5th grade this year. He shares how devastating it would be if Graciela had to leave her family.	15
12	Birth Certificate for 13-year-old son, Miguel	18
13	Birth Certificate for 14-year-old son, Andrew	19
14	Student Data Printout, School ID and letter of support from Andrew. He is in 9th grade this year and says the family would miss his mother tremendously since she cares for them all while the father works.	21
15	Letter from Graciela's brother, Noe Vasquez, stating that Graciela is a great mother not only to her and Marco Antonio's children but to Noe's kids as well. Noe describes how Graciela has become an important mother-figure for his children and as a single father he states how important it is that she stays for their entire family. Attached is his Certificate of Naturalization and his California Driver License.	24

	EVIDENCE OF HEALTH HARDSHIP FACTORS	
16	Articles from American Psychological Association and The Hormone Foundation regarding the serious long-term effects of chronic stress which Graciela's husband, Anthony, would be under if they are separated from her and he is left as the sole financial provider and must also assume caretaking of their children by himself. Chronic stress can cause serious problems with the digestive, immune, nervous and cardiovascular systems.	28
	EVIDENCE OF FINANCIAL HARDSHIP FACTORS	
17	Family budget showing that Anthony would be spending over $700 more per month than his anticipated income should his wife have to leave him to return to Mexico due to the added expenses of maintaining her abroad and managing his household alone, including paying for childcare. He does not anticipate being able to take off work to visit her due to the cost and lost income.	32
18	2018 and 2017 Income Tax Returns for Anthony and Graciela. He is their sole financial provider while she cares for their children and home. He earned $73,485 in wages for 2018 and $70,323 in 2017.	33
19	Employment verification letter for Anthony stating that he has worked for Quality First Woodworks since 2014 as a Finish Carpenter/Cabinet Installer.	38
20	Paystubs for Marco Antonio's employment from recent months. He had earned over $40,000 for the year as of August 22, 2019 including overtime hours each pay period. Working such long hours would make it difficult to manage childcare on his own.	39
21	Anthony and Graciela's rental agreement with recent rent receipts. They pay $1,400 per month for their apartment.	42
22	Household bills for utilities and insurance.	45
23	Various credit card statements including Citibank with a $5,344 balance in Anthony's name. Their electricity bill was paid by credit card in October last month.	50
24	Wells Fargo Joint Checking Account Statements for the couple showing recent payments for household and family expenses including auto loan payments. Their combined checking and savings account balance was only $1,498 as of July 2019.	59
25	Airplane quote from Google flights to travel from LAX to Oaxaca. The round-trip cost is about $341 per person plus shuttles, baggage fees and taxes for Anthony to visit his wife if she must leave the family. This would be too much for him and his six children to afford, especially since he would have to take off work to travel.	63

	EVIDENCE OF SPECIAL CONSIDERATIONS CONTRIBUTING TO HARDSHIP	
26	US Department of State Travel Advisory excerpt advising caution to travelers to Mexico in general and the state of Oaxaca, where Graciela was born. Oaxaca is under a Level 2 Travel Warning and, per our government, people like Marco Antonio and their children should exercise caution throughout this region due to safety concerns. Crime, including kidnapping, homicide and carjacking, are serious enough problems to mention for the country as a whole.	65
27	Current table of payroll hardship allowances for US Government employees working in the Mexico City Consular District, which includes the state of Oaxaca. This is a factor when considering hardship, per USCIS policy manual.	68
28	Excerpt of US Department of State report "Mexico 2018 Crime & Safety Report: Mexico City" including the state of Oaxaca. Per the report, violent crime (kidnapping, extortion, homicide, sexual assault, personal robbery, residential break-ins) continue to be serious concerns for those living in this consular district.	69
29	US Department of State "Mexico 2018 Human Rights Report" excerpt. The most significant human rights issues include government and law enforcement corruption leading to low rates of prosecution for all crimes. Employment human rights issues include the extremely low rate of pay – minimum wage is now $5.26 US dollars per day – less than the official poverty level of $5.67 US dollars per day. Long work hours, unjustified dismissals and unsafe workplaces are other issues highlighted in the report.	77
30	U.S. Congressional Research Service report excerpt entitled "Mexico: Organized Crime and Drug Trafficking Organizations" dated 7/3/2018. Drug trafficking organizations are "parasitic" for local populations in Mexico, per the report. Forced disappearances are a growing concern. Police corruption is extensive.	92
31	Articles on causes of violence in Mexico, as well as the growing threats of extortion and kidnapping for innocent people throughout the country due to the breaking up of large criminal organizations.	104
32	*Wall Street Journal and Business Insider* articles regarding Mexico's daily minimum wage of 102.68 pesos ($5.10 US dollars) for 2019. Per the OECD, Mexicans work longer hours than those in other countries, but wages are among the lowest of the OECD countries.	130
	EVIDENCE OF FAVORABLE DISCRETIONARY FACTORS	
33	Graciela's California Driver's License	141
34	Letters from church, family and friends attesting to the applicant's excellent character as a responsible, hardworking and loving wife and mother, and the difficulty for Anthony and their children should they be separated.	142
35	Photos of this loving family over the years.	179

APPENDIX 13

SAMPLE LEGAL BRIEF

JAN AUSTERLITZ
ATTORNEY AT LAW
2000 Hearst Ave. #401
Berkeley, CA 94709
(510) 540-0987
(510) 849-0749

Attorney for Applicant

DEPARTMENT OF HOMELAND SECURITY
UNITED STATES CITIZENSHIP AND IMMIGRATION SERVICES
CIUDAD JUAREZ, MEXICO

In the Matter of:)
)
)
███████████,) CDJ███████
)
Applicant.) BRIEF IN SUPPORT OF
) INA § 212(a)(9)(B)(v) WAIVER

The Applicant, ███████████, through his legal representative, Jan Austerlitz, hereby requests a waiver of inadmissibility under INA § 212(a)(9)(B)(v) due to the fact that his United States citizen wife already is suffering **extreme hardship** in his absence and will continue to suffer extreme hardship if he does not return to the United States as soon as possible.

FACTS

The Applicant's wife, ███████████, is 26 years old and was born and raised in the U.S. Her parents have lived in the U.S. for at least 40 years and are U.S. citizens. All of her siblings were born and raised in the U.S. ██████ and ███████ have a two year-old daughter and ██████ is currently pregnant and due in October. Her pregnancy has caused her health problems such as migraine headaches and nausea and has recently been told that she might need to go on bed rest for the remainder of her pregnancy.

Soon after ▓▓▓ left for Mexico, ▓▓▓ lost her job. At this point her only source of income is her husband's vacation pay, which expires on July 2. She applied for unemployment insurance, which will be approximately $800/mo., but has not yet received any checks. If she is placed on bed rest through to October, when she is due to give birth, she will need her husband in the U.S. even more than ever to take care of their daughter, take care of the household, and work. Ms. ▓▓▓ is now suffering extreme hardship in her husband's absence and will continue to do so if he does not return immediately to help her financially and emotionally through the pregnancy and beyond.

ARGUMENT

I. ORDINARY HARDSHIPS MUST BE CONSIDERED IN THE AGGREGATE IN DETERMINING WHETHER EXTREME HARDSHIP EXISTS

The Applicant is eligible to seek a waiver of inadmissibility pursuant to INA Sec. 212(a)(9)(B)(v) in that the refusal of admission would result in extreme hardship to his U.S. citizen spouse.

The standard for extreme hardship should not be confused with the much higher standard of outstanding and unusual hardship now required for cancellation of removal. The District Director must consider the entire range of relevant factors concerning hardship in their totality and determine whether the combination of factors results in hardships greater than those ordinarily associated with deportation. *Matter of O-J-O*, Int. Dec. 3280 (BIA 1996). In *Jara-Navarrete v. INS*, 813 F.2d 1340, 1343 (9th Cir. 1986), the Ninth Circuit stressed that each relevant factor presented in a case, particularly harm to U.S. citizens, must be carefully and individually considered.

In *Matter of Chumpitzai*, 16 I&N 629 (BIA 1978), the Board recognized relevant factors in determining extreme hardship to a qualifying relative,

> …[P]resence of lawful permanent resident or United States citizen family ties to the country; the qualifying relative's family ties outside the United States; the conditions in the country or countries to which the qualifying relative would relocate and the extent of the qualifying relative's ties to such countries; the financial impact of departure from this country; and finally, significant conditions of health…

The Board made it clear in that case that not all of these factors would be present in any given case. Id.

The BIA in *Matter of Cervantes-Gonzalez*, 22 I&N 560 (BIA 1999), set out the following factors as relevant in determining whether or not extreme hardship exists: **presence of a lawful permanent resident or U.S. citizen spouse or parent in the U.S.; the qualifying relatives' family ties in the United States and abroad; length of residence in the United States; conditions of health; conditions in the country where the qualifying relative would live; and the financial impact of leaving the U.S.** What is unclear from the BIA's holding in that case, however, is whether these factors should be viewed as positive or negative factors and how much weight they should be given. For example, in that case, the U.S. citizen spouse had come to the U.S. as a small child and her entire immediate family lived in the U.S. as LPRs or U.S. citizens. She and her husband lived with her parents and were financially dependent on them. The BIA, in applying the factors listed above, chose to find that a large documented family in the U.S. was a negative factor, in that the hardship to the qualifying relative was minimized by being able to rely on the family's support if she remained in the U.S. without her husband. It also viewed her poor financial status in the U.S. as a negative factor, finding that since the qualifying relative had no means of support in the U.S., she would not be losing anything by moving to Mexico and would be in a comparable financial situation there.

In Ms. ▓▓▓▓ case, however, she does not and cannot rely on her parents or siblings in the U.S. for financial support since her father recently was laid off from his job and her siblings lack the financial resources.

We argue that _Cervantes-Gonzales_ is an anomaly and that years of precedent decisions have viewed a large documented family in the U.S. as a **favorable** factor in assessing hardship, ie., that **the hardship to the qualifying relative is more extreme when forced to separate from other members of her family in the U.S.** The Ninth Circuit, in _U.S. v. Arrieta_, 224 F.3d 1076, 1079 (9th Cir. 2000), held that **the most important factor in evaluating hardship is the family ties in the U.S.** In addition, a qualifying relative's poor financial status in the U.S. is not the same as poor financial status in Mexico when the qualifying relative is able to live with and rely on parents in the U.S. but has no one on whom to rely in Mexico. To equate the two in order to minimize the hardship to the qualifying relative renders irrelevant the §212(i) waiver. Therefore, it seems unclear how the factors set out in Cervantes are to be viewed or what weight they should be given.

The BIA in _Matter of Cervantes-Gonzales_, _supra,_ also chose to define extreme hardship narrowly in support of its position. However, in _Watkins v. INS_, _supra_, at 848, the Ninth Circuit made quite clear that although the Board may choose to interpret 'extreme hardship' narrowly, as it did in _INS v. Wang_, 450 U.S. 139, 145, 101 S. Ct. 1027, 1031, 67 L. Ed. 2d 123 (1981) (per curiam), it must consider all factors relevant to the hardship determination.

II. **DENIAL OF APPLICANT'S APPLICATION FOR PERMANENT RESIDENCE WOULD RESULT IN EXTREME HARDSHIP TO HIS U.S. CITIZEN SPOUSE**

Applying the factors set out in years of precedent decisions, and *U.S. v. Arrieta, supra*, and considering them cumulatively and with the appropriate weight, it is clear that Ms. ▇ meets the standard for showing that she would suffer extreme hardship if her husband's I-601 waiver is denied.

Ms. ▇ was born and raised in the U.S. She has never lived in Mexico. Her parents are U.S. citizens who have lived in the U.S. for 40 years. Ms. Solano recently lost her job and she is supporting herself and her daughter on her husband's vacation pay from Pacific BioLabs while she waits to start receiving her $800/mo. unemployment checks. On July 2, 2010, her husband's vacation pay ends, leaving Ms. ▇ to support herself, her husband, and her daughter on her unemployment payments. There also is a possibility that Ms. ▇ will be placed on bed rest for the remainder of her pregnancy, which will create an even greater hardship for her if her husband has not returned from Mexico.

Congress did not intend to separate U.S. citizens from their spouses when it imposed this ground of inadmissibility. Instead, it provided for a waiver that would allow families to remain intact. See *Delmundo v. INS*, 43 F.3d 436, 442-43 (9th Cir. 1994), citing *Casem v. INS*, 8 F.3d 703 (9th Cir. 1993). The Ninth Circuit pointed out:

> We have held consistently that the "most important single hardship factor may be the separation of the alien from family living in the U.S." Contreras-Buenfil v. INS, 712 F.2d 401, 403 (9th Cir.)

Cases such as *Matter of Pilch*, 21 I&N Dec. 627 (BIA 1996), are often cited by CIS to support its argument that "emotional hardship caused by severing family... ties" is a common result of deportation and that "economic detriment alone is insufficient to support a finding of extreme hardship." We have no argument with the reliance on this case or this language, however, in citing this case, CIS often ignores the fact that the Board referred to economic detriment "*alone*," ie., when there are no other factors in support of hardship, and fails to consider the specific facts in that case in comparison to those being presented. The facts in *Pilch* are so distinguishable from the instant case that it renders *Pilch* irrelevant to the instant case.

In *Pilch*, the Board noted that in Poland, the country to which the Respondents would be removed, <u>the Respondents would not face difficult economic conditions, **and they would be reuniting with one of their sons, their mothers, the female Respondent's father, and their siblings**</u>. The Board found that the numerous family members in Poland could provide an emotional base during the time of readjustment. For these reasons, the Board found that the severing of community ties and economic detriment were insufficient <u>in that case</u> to rise to the level of extreme hardship. The Board's language must be viewed in context of the facts of that specific case and cannot be cited as a rule of thumb upon which to measure all cases.

In the case at issue, Ms. ▮▮▮ faces a very different situation. If her husband is not permitted to immigrate to the U.S., she faces a serious dilemma. If she chooses to keep her family intact, she will be forced to move to Mexico with her husband and young daughter. **Since she currently is pregnant and having a difficult pregnancy, she must choose whether to stay in the U.S. throughout her pregnancy or reunite with her husband in Mexico and risk losing the baby.** She has never lived in Mexico and does not have any close family relatives remaining there. <u>Ms. ▮▮▮ parents and siblings live in the U.S. as citizens.</u> She will face <u>critical</u> economic conditions in Mexico which may endanger her pregnancy.

As a mother of two young children, she will not be able to work in Mexico and the Applicant most likely will be unable to find employment or other job opportunities there due to his age and lack of skills. Age discrimination in employment is a well-known and accepted reality in Mexico, leaving adults over 25 years of age with few opportunities for employment.

Currently, the Applicant provides all of the financial support for the family. In this regard, the Ninth Circuit reasoned:

> "Although economic detriment is not sufficient to establish extreme hardship, this factor should not be entirely eliminated from consideration. Certainly this can be considered along with other factors. **Economic loss is not the same as economic hardship.** An alien who is forced to sell property because he is being deported, whether he shows a financial loss or a profit, might nonetheless suffer hardship." Wang v. INS, 622 F.2d 1341, 1349 (9th Cir. 1980).

Conditions in the country to which the alien is returnable also must be taken into consideration. *Matter of Anderson*, *supra*; *Matter of Cervantes*, 22 I&N 560; *Cervantes-Gonzales v. INS*, 244 F.3d 1001; *Matter of Kao & Lin*, 23 I&N Dec. 627. **Employability in the country of relocation is a significant consideration in this regard.** *See Matter of Cervantes*, at 583 (Rosenberg, *concurring*). The situation in Mexico is extremely critical. The unemployment rate has been estimated to be around 40%. A large part of the population is employed in the informal sector. The average salary for people doing manual labor is around $10 per day. Such salary is completely inadequate to feed a family of six and to cope with the other living expenses.

In *Pilch*, the BIA found that the aliens would not face difficult economic conditions and their extended family in Poland would help them during their readjustment period. **This is not the case here**, however. As documented, the economic situation in Mexico is critical and was the reason that Ms. ▓▓▓▓ parents and the Applicant came to the U.S. in the first place. Ms. ▓▓▓▓ faces extremely serious economic hardship if she moves to Mexico. Her entire immediate family lives in the U.S. in lawful status. **She has never lived in Mexico and has no desire to. Although she speaks Spanish she does not read or write the language. She sees herself as an American only and has no desire to live in Mexico.** Denying an immigrant visa to her husband and forcing her to abandon the U.S., the only country in which she has lived and where she has just begun to pursue a career, in order to keep her family together makes her give up her larger family of parents, siblings, in-laws and nieces and nephews, and her desire for a career. **This IS extreme hardship.**

As a U.S. citizen, Ms. ▇▇▇ should not be forced to choose between remaining in her native country or moving to a country where she has never lived and has no remaining relatives except her husband. She married her husband with the intention of living with him in the U.S., and not moving with him abroad. She has no interest in living abroad and has never done so in the past. Congress did not intend for these types of choices to have to be made when the facts are as they are in this case.

CIS often argues that it is the qualifying relative's *choice* to accompany her spouse and that she is not the one being forced to leave the U.S. That assertion is ludicrous. What kind of a choice is it when she is forced to decide between losing her husband and the desire for her children to know their father or losing the only life she has known and separating from her parents and siblings. It certainly isn't a free choice. **Is it a choice that Congress intended a U.S. citizen spouse to have to make?**

Ms. ▇▇▇ <u>had no idea when she married her husband that the time he had spent in the U.S. would be held against him when he tried to immigrate, since she has no prior experience with the immigration laws.</u> She assumed that since she was a U.S. citizen and her husband was a hard working man with no criminal record, he would not have any problems becoming a permanent resident. Unfortunately, she and her husband met after the deadline for INA Sec. 245(i) eligibility. <u>**Should the timing of the marriage determine whether or not she, her husband, and children will be able to live together in the U.S?**</u> Did Congress intend for such a drastic distinction?

Other precedent decisions emphasize the often determinative weight given to family ties and, particularly, to marriage to a United States citizen. For example, the Board held in *Matter of Arai*, 13 I&N Dec. 494, 495-96 (BIA 1970) that "[g]enerally, favorable factors such as family ties, hardship, length of residence in the United States, etc., will be considered as countervailing factors meriting **favorable exercise of administrative discretion.**". It cannot be denied that in *Matter of Ibrahim*, 18 I&N Dec. 55 (BIA 1981),10 the Board clarified and reaffirmed its decision in *Matter of Cavazos*, 17 I&N Dec. 215 (BIA 1980), as standing for the rule that, in the absence of other adverse factors, an **application for adjustment of status as an immediate relative should generally be granted in the exercise of discretion** notwithstanding the fact that the applicant entered the United States as a nonimmigrant with a preconceived intention to remain. **In addition, subsequent Board decisions found the fact of marriage and family relationships to override the adverse factor of a criminal conviction.** *See, e.g., Matter of Batista*, 19 I&N Dec. 484 (BIA 1987)

Ms. ▇▇ relies on a history of precedent decisions that set out the precise factors to be considered in determining whether extreme hardship exists, and argues that her case possesses all of the pertinent factors.

IV. CONCLUSION

In determining whether Ms. ▇▇ would suffer extreme hardship if her husband is not permitted to immigrate to the U.S., USCIS must undertake the proper review of the evidence and give appropriate weight to the favorable factors *as a whole*, and not individually, as required by controlling precedent. What is the U.S. government's interest in tearing apart a hardworking and supportive family unit based solely on the date of their marriage?

Ms. ▇▇ is a 26 year old, native born citizen of the U.S. who has never lived in Mexico or anywhere else outside of the U.S. She has no family left in Mexico. The Applicant no doubt will be unable to find employment in Mexico sufficient to provide for the family whether they are in the U.S. or in Mexico. Therefore, it makes little sense for the family to move to Mexico where there is no family on which they can rely, just to live in poverty. On the other hand, if Ms. ▇▇▇ remains in the U.S. without her husband, she will have to struggle through her current pregnancy alone while caring for her young daughter and struggling financially.

Ms. Solano faces a no-win situation since both alternatives create extreme hardships for her. **The only option that does not create extreme hardship for her is for the Applicant to return immediately to his life in the U.S.** Therefore, she requests that her husband's waiver be granted.

Dated: _____

                                                                               Jan Austerlitz
                                                                               Attorney at Law

APPENDIX 14A
SAMPLE IV FEE RECEIPT

Payment Receipts for IV Case RDJ
IV Fee Payment Receipt Details

Principal Applicant
Payment of Services Initiated 17-OCT-2019 14:23:24
Payment Processed Date 18-OCT-2019
Payment Amount $325.00
Payer
Payer Email
Transaction ID

Applicant	IV Fee Payment Status	Fee Amount
	PAID	$325.00

Next Steps

If your payment status shows that it is IN PROCESS, wait two to three business days for the payment to clear. Then sign into the system again to check for a status update.

If your payment status shows a status other than IN PROCESS or PAID, sign in to the Immigrant Visa Invoice Payment Center page https://ceac.state.gov/CTRAC/Invoice/Signon.aspx and click on Get Help.

If you receive a notice that your case has entered termination, **do not attempt to pay any fees**. You must contact the National Visa Center (NVC). You can find NVC contact information at nvc.state.gov/inquiry.

When the IV fee payment status is PAID, visit nvc.state.gov/260 for instructions on continuing the processing of your immigrant visa petition.

IMPORTANT NOTES:

- If you decide to file Form I-601A, Application for Provisional Unlawful Presence Waiver with USCIS, you must include a copy of this fee payment receipt or USCIS will reject your Form I-601A.
- Please keep this receipt for your records. If you can't print the receipt now, return to the Receipt Screen and email a copy to an address where you can print it later.
- Do not let more than one-year pass from the date your visa becomes available per the Final Action Date for your visa without contacting the NVC about your immigrant visa petition or login to the CEAC

portal. If a period of one-year passes from the last date of contact, all submitted forms and fees will expire and you must resubmit them to resume processing.

APPENDIX 14B

SAMPLE NVC INSTRUCTION PACKET

From:	National_Visa_Center@state.gov
Sent:	Thursday, November 7, 2019 10:55 AM
To:	
Subject:	Notice of Immigrant Visa Case Creation

Dear

Thank you for your interest in immigrating to the United States of America. The Department of State's National Visa Center (NVC) received your approved immigrant visa petition from U.S. Citizenship and Immigration Services (USCIS). NVC's role is to ensure you are prepared for your immigrant visa interview at a U.S. Embassy/Consulate General, and to schedule your interview appointment.

NVC is responsible for collecting any applicable fees, the Immigrant Visa Application, supporting civil documents, police certificate(s), Affidavits of Support, and financial documents, if applicable, prior to your visa interview at a U.S. Embassy/Consulate General. **Do not mail documents to NVC, even if you received instructions to mail documents to NVC in the past.**

You will need to log on to the Department of State's Consular Electronic Application Center (CEAC) at https://ceac.state.gov/IV to check your case status, pay any necessary fees, upload and submit documents, and read messages from NVC.

If you are logging into CEAC for the first time, please be aware that it can take up to three days (72 hours) from receipt of this notice for your account to be activated. Once activated, you can log into CEAC using the following unique NVC case number and Invoice Identification Number.

NVC Case Number: HCM2007
Invoice ID Number: IVSCA00000

You should keep this information available in a safe place as you will need it every time you log on to CEAC. Please keep in mind that you **must** use CEAC to provide NVC with the fees and documents that are required prior to your immigrant visa interview. We do not accept these by mail.

Please Note: You must bring the exact original of any scanned document you upload to CEAC that NVC accepts to your immigrant visa interview. Failure to bring the exact original you uploaded to CEAC may delay the processing of your case.

You can find detailed instructions and frequently asked questions at https://nvc.state.gov/ceac. After you complete the steps above, we will review the forms and documents you submit. If something is missing or incorrect, we will tell you how to fix it. Otherwise, we will schedule your case for a visa interview at the U.S. Embassy or Consulate in HO CHI MINH CITY, VTNM.

If you need to contact NVC, please follow the instructions at https://nvc.state.gov/inquiry. NVC may send questions, instructions, and status updates to your CEAC account. If we do this you will receive an email asking you to log into your CEAC account to review a message from NVC.

IMPORTANT: *If you do not log into CEAC or communicate with NVC regarding this immigrant visa case for a period of one year, by law the Department of State must terminate your visa application.*

FINANCIAL SPONSORSHIP RESPONSIBILITIES: Financial sponsors, joint sponsors, and applicants should be aware of the responsibilities arising from a sponsor signing an I-864 and the consequences of a sponsored immigrant's acceptance of federal means-tested public benefits. For more information, visit https://nvc.state.gov/aos.

PRESIDENTIAL PROCLAMATION ON HEALTH CARE: On October 4, 2019, the President issued Presidential Proclamation 9945 on the "Suspension of Entry of Immigrants Who Will Financially Burden the United States Healthcare System." For the most up to date information on how PP 9945 might affect your case, please visit https://travel.state.gov/healthcare.

Regards,
National Visa Center,
U.S. Department of State
https://nvc.state.gov/ask

NOTE: Please do not reply to this email. This is not a monitored account. If you have questions or need to get in touch with NVC, please follow the instructions at https://nvc.state.gov/ask to call or email us.

APPENDIX 14C

SAMPLE NVC INTERVIEW APPOINTMENT PACKET

From: National_Visa_Center@state.gov
Sent: Thursday, October 24, 2019 2:36 AM
To:
Subject: Immigrant Visa Interview Appointment

OCTOBER 24, 2019

Case Number: HCM2007

Invoice ID: IVSCA0000

:

The National Visa Center (NVC) completed its processing of your immigrant visa application and forwarded it to the U.S. Embassy/Consulate General, where an immigrant visa interview has been scheduled. Appointment information is located at the bottom of this email.

Important Information:
You submitted forms and supporting documents to the NVC in electronic form. You must present the original forms and documents for review by the consular officer during your interview.

Please promptly read and follow all Interview Preparation Instructions located on the Department of State's web site at: https://nvc.state.gov/interview.

Important information regarding the required medical appointment is also listed on this site. Failure to promptly follow all instructions provided on this site will result in your immigrant visa being refused at the initial interview.

You should present this letter upon arrival at the Embassy/Consulate General.

Those members of your family, named below, must appear at the Embassy/Consulate General on the appointment date.

PRESIDENTIAL PROCLAMATION ON HEALTH CARE: You must be able to demonstrate to the consular officer at the time of interview you will be covered by approved health insurance within 30 days of entry into the United States or have the financial resources to pay for reasonably foreseeable medical costs. Inability to meet this requirement will result in the denial of the visa application. For complete requirements and/or exemptions, visit https://travel.state.gov/healthcare.

What To Do if You Cannot Keep the Appointment:
Some Embassies/Consulates General reschedule interview appointments themselves; others utilize an outside service provider to reschedule appointments. To determine the proper procedure for rescheduling your interview appointment, please go to the Department of State's web site at: https://nvc.state.gov/interview, under "Step 2", select your interview location from the dropdown and click "Download PDF" and follow your Embassy/Consulate General's instructions listed under "Contact Information" on the right.

Reminders:

- Read and follow all interview instructions located at https://nvc.state.gov/interview.
- Bring this letter to your medical examination because the panel physician may need to review it before performing the examination.
- If a sponsor filed an I-864 (Affidavit of Support) AND provided the NVC with proof of an IRS Federal Income Tax Extension in lieu of a Federal Income Tax Return, you must upload this to CEAC or bring the sponsor's most recent Federal Income Tax Return to the visa interview.

- Failure to present all necessary documents to the Consular Officer will result in your immigrant visa being refused at the initial interview.

Questions:
The National Visa Center has completed its processing of this case and any further inquiries should be addressed to the U.S. Embassy, Consulate General, or Diplomatic Mission listed below. When communicating with the Embassy/Consulate General by e-mail, letter, or fax, always refer to your name and case number exactly as they appear.

Immigrant Visa Interview Details:

Interview Date/Time: NOVEMBER 21, 2019 at 08:30 AM
Interview Location: THANH PHO HO CHI MINH, VIETNAM
NVC Case Number: HCM2007█████
Invoice ID: IVSCA00000█████
Principal Applicant: ████████████████

HO CHI MINH CITY
VIETNAM

Preference Category: F31-Married Son/Daughter of U.S. Citizen
A #: ████████

Additional Applicants:

Name	A#	Appointment Date/Time
██████	██████	NOVEMBER 21, 2019 at 08:30 AM
██████	██████	NOVEMBER 21, 2019 at 08:30 AM
██████	██████	NOVEMBER 21, 2019 at 08:30 AM
██████	██████	NOVEMBER 21, 2019 at 08:30 AM

APPENDIX 14D
SAMPLE NVC MEDICAL EXAM LETTER

CONSULATE GENERAL OF THE UNITED STATES
CIUDAD JUAREZ, MEXICO
IMMIGRANT VISA UNIT
P.O. BOX 17000, EL PASO, TX 79917
PASEO DE LA VICTORIA # 3650, CIUDAD JUAREZ, CHIH. 32543
https://mx.usembassy.gov/embassy-consulates/ciudad-juarez/
IMMIGRANT VISA INFORMATION https://ais.usvisa-info.com/en-mx/iv

INSTRUCTIONS FOR THE MEDICAL EXAMINATION

The date of your visa interview appointment is indicated in the letter that you received from the National Visa Center or from the Consulate General of the United States in Ciudad Juarez. Please be aware that it is your responsibility to complete the medical examination with one of the authorized medical clinics before the interview date. We suggest that you make arrangements for your medical examination at least two days prior to your appointment date. Complete details about medical exams can be found at
https://travel.state.gov/content/travel/en/us-visas/immigrate/the-immigrant-visa-process/interview/interview-prepare/medical-examination.html

All immigrant visa applicants, regardless of age, must have a medical examination. The only medical clinics authorized by this Consulate to perform such medical examinations are:

*CLINICA MEDICA INTERNACIONAL	*SERVICIOS MEDICOS DE LA FRONTERA
Ave. Ramon Rivera Lara # 9020	Prol. Ramon Rivera Lara # 8950
Fracc. Las Lunas	Col. Partido Senecu
Cd. Juarez, Chih., Mexico C.P.32543	Cd. Juarez, Chih., Mexico C.P.32540
Tel: (011-52-656) 227-2800	Tel: (011-52-656) 688-2700
Fax: (011-52-656) 227-2808	Fax: (011-52-656) 688-2701
Toll Free from US 1 844-624-9447	Toll Free from US 1 844 847-5340
Toll Free from Mexico 01800-801-8585	Toll Free from Mexico 01 800 201-8472
http://www.clinicamedicainternacional.com.mx/	www.smf.com.mx

Immigrant visa applicants are received between 6:00 a.m. and 11:00 a.m. Monday through Friday. It is not a requirement to schedule an appointment for your medical examination. Medical clinics are located next to the Consulate.

NOTE: Only applicants residing in the **State of Mexico and Mexico, D.F must** go to the following authorized clinic:

*MEDICOS ESPECIALIZADOS INTERNACIONALES

Hamburgo 206, Interior 204, 2nd Floor,
Colonia Juarez, Delegación Cuauhtémoc,
Ciudad de Mexico 06600
Phone (55)2624-0630 and (55)5207-3794 ext. 101
www.mei-mexico.com

Applicants may make appointments or request information by phone from 8:00 a.m. to 2:00 p.m. The medical examinations in Mexico City are from 7:30 a.m. to 12:00 p.m., Monday through Friday.

Each applicant must present the appointment letter and passport at the time of their medical appointment. If you have a chronic medical condition, if you have been treated for any venereal disease or you have been under psychiatric care, you must bring a medical summary with you at the time of your medical appointment or have it forwarded to the doctor prior to your medical examination.

Applicants who show signs or symptoms of tuberculosis or who are HIV/AIDS positive must complete a further medical process in order to comply with the regulations of the Centers for Disease Control (CDC). This process is designed to detect and treat tuberculosis in order to reduce the risk of spreading tuberculosis within the population of

Mexwide 202 SEP2018

CONSULATE GENERAL OF THE UNITED STATES
CIUDAD JUAREZ, MEXICO
IMMIGRANT VISA UNIT
P.O. BOX 17000, EL PASO, TX 79917
PASEO DE LA VICTORIA # 3650, CIUDAD JUAREZ, CHIH. 32543
https://mx.usembassy.gov/embassy-consulates/ciudad-juarez/
IMMIGRANT VISA INFORMATION https://ais.usvisa-info.com/en-mx/iv

the United States. It may take between three and six months before the clinic will be able to complete the final medical exam for these applicants.

All applicants must undergo a medical examination at least two business days prior to the scheduled appointment at the Consulate. Failure to do so may result in delays or rescheduling of the initial appointment date. It is also recommended that children within this age range not receive immunizations within four weeks prior to the medical examination.

As directed by the Centers for Disease Control and Prevention of the United States of America, beginning on October 1, 2018 all immigrant visa applicants whose age is between 2 – 14 years must provide a blood test for tuberculosis screening. All applicants whose age is 15 years or older must provide a urine sample for gonorrhea screening.

The costs of the medical examinations at any of the clinics are:

A. Applicants ages 15 and over: USD $220.00
B. Applicants between ages 2 and 14: USD $178.00
C. Applicants younger than 2: USD$135.00
D. A tax of 16% (I.V.A.) will be added to the cost of any medical examination.

The medical examination fees cover only the general medical examination. DNA tests have an additional cost when it is required. It will be necessary for the petitioner / applicant to cover the cost of additional examinations required at the time of their examination. The vaccination fee is not included in the cost of the medical examination.
Payment can be made in cash or charged to Visa and / or MasterCard credit cards.

NOTE: Fiancé (e) visa applicants must present the letter confirming their visa interview appointment.

Mexwide 202 SEP2018

CONSULATE GENERAL OF THE UNITED STATES
CIUDAD JUAREZ, MEXICO
IMMIGRANT VISA UNIT
P.O. BOX 17000, EL PASO, TX 79917
PASEO DE LA VICTORIA #3650, CIUDAD JUAREZ, CHIH. 32543
https://mx.usembassy.gov/embassy-consulates/ciudad-juarez/
IMMIGRANT VISA INFORMATION https://ais.usvisa-info.com/en-mx/iv

VACCINATION REQUIREMENTS

The United States immigration law requires immigrant visa applicants obtain certain immunizations prior to the issuance of their visa. The clinics authorized to perform medical examinations are responsible for verifying that all immigrant visa applicants meet the vaccination requirements.

All applicants must submit their available vaccination records during their medical examination. If you do not have the vaccination record, the panel physician will determine which vaccines are medically appropriate for you, according to age, medical history and current medical condition.

The cost of the vaccine(s) will depend on the type of vaccine(s) you need to meet the vaccination requirement. This charge is not included in the cost of your medical examination.

The information on the vaccines you will need to complete the vaccination requirement should be consulted directly with the clinics authorized to perform the medical examinations.

Panel Physician Vaccination Price List

Dtap	$ 60.00 currently not available
Tdap	$ 60.00
Polio (IPV/Salk)	$ 50.00 currently not available
MMR (measles/mumps/rubella)	$ 40.00
Rotavirus	$ 75.00
Hib	$ 32.00 currently not available
Hepatitis A	$ 35.00
Hepatitis B	$ 30.00
Varicella	$ 60.00
Pneumococcal (adult)	$ 95.00
Influenza (seasonal)	$ 30.00
Pneumococcal (pediatric)	$ 95.00
Meningococcal	$125.00

Mexwide 202 SEP2018

APPENDIX 15
SAMPLE ADVISAL

PROVISIONAL WAIVER ADVISAL

Your application for a provisional waiver of the unlawful presence ground of inadmissibility has been approved. The approval of a provisional waiver application **does not** guarantee that the U.S. consulate will grant your immigrant visa. The consulate will determine whether you are inadmissible on any other ground. If the consulate decides you are inadmissible for any other ground in addition to unlawful presence, your provisional waiver approval will be revoked. You will then need to apply for a waiver of inadmissibility on Form I-601 and remain outside the United States until it is adjudicated.

If you depart and return to the United States without permission you may be subject to the permanent bar under INA § 212(a)(9)(C).

I understand and have been advised of the risks associated with consular processing after the approval of a provisional waiver.

_____

Name

_____

Signature

_____

Date

AVISO DE LA EXENCIÓN PROVISIONAL

Ha sido aprobada su solicitud para una exención provisional de causal de inadmisibilidad por la presencia ilegal. La aprobación de una exención provisional **no garantiza** que el consulado de los Estados Unidos le otorgará su visa de inmigrante. El consulado determinará si usted es inadmisible por cualquier otro criterio. Si el consulado determina que usted sí es inadmisible por cualquier otro criterio además de la presencia ilegal, la aprobación de su exención provisional se revocará. Entonces deberá solicitar una exención de inadmisibilidad con el Formulario I-601 y permanecer fuera de los Estados Unidos hasta que se procese este formulario.

Si usted sale y vuelve a entrar a los Estados Unidos sin permiso, podría ser sujeto a una prohibición permanente bajo la ley, INA § 212(a)(9)(C).

Comprendo y he sido informado de los riesgos asociados con el proceso consular después de la aprobación de una exención provisional.

_____

Nombre

_____

Firma

_____

Fecha